THE GLYNNS OF KILRUSH, CO. CLARE, 1811–1940

Family, business and politics

The Glynns of Kilrush, Co. Clare, 1811–1940

Family, business and politics

PAUL O'BRIEN

OPEN AIR

Typeset in 10.5pt on 12.5pt EhrhardtMtPro by
Carrigboy Typesetting Services for
OPEN AIR, an imprint of
FOUR COURTS PRESS LTD
7 Malpas Street, Dublin 8, Ireland
www.fourcourtspress.ie
and in North America for
FOUR COURTS PRESS
c/o IPG, 814 N Franklin St, Chicago, IL 60622

A catalogue record for this title is available
from the British Library.

ISBN 978-1-84682-776-1

Printed in England,
by CPI Antony Rowe, Chippenham, Wilts.

For Charles W. Glynn

Contents

Acknowledgments

THIS BOOK COULD NOT HAVE BEEN written without the cooperation of the Glynn family, who trusted me to piece together the story of their incredible history, and whose forebears possessed exceptional foresight in saving and assembling their papers. I wish to extend special thanks to Charlie, John, Jane, Edel and Bryan Glynn, who were unfailingly generous in sharing with me detailed insights into their family history. I also owe a debt of gratitude to Deirdre Glynn-Wirzburger and her late father, Michael Glynn. The enthusiasm and support of the Glynn family throughout the research process made the experience all the more enjoyable and productive. I am immensely grateful to Josephine Glynn for giving of her time on several occasions.

Dr Maura Cronin of the Department of History, Mary Immaculate College (MIC), University of Limerick, supervised my scholarly studies and I could not have asked for a better mentor, supporter and friend. Maura's insight, knowledge and advice went beyond what I could have expected, and I will forever be in her debt. I want to extend my sincere thanks to my internal examiner, Dr Deirdre McMahon, for generously sharing with me her knowledge of the political context in which the Glynn family lived. A note of thanks too, to my external examiner, Professor David Dickson of Trinity College Dublin. I would also like to thank my colleagues in the Department of History for their guidance, in particular Dr Liam Chambers, for offering his advice on the editorial process. Also, Dr Úna Ní Bhroiméil for her detailed advice on visuals. The research process greatly benefitted from the knowledge of the staff in the library at MIC – in particular, Elizabeth, Norma, Marian and Carmel – who sourced an endless supply of books from libraries the world over. Thanks to my colleagues in the Academic Learning Centre (MIC), Dr Geraldine Brosnan, Dr Brian Clancy and Dr James Binchy for their support, and to Dr Helene Bradley Davies of the Department of Geography (MIC). And thanks also to Dr Éamon Phoenix, Dr Matthew Potter and Dr John Logan.

I wish to acknowledge the assistance of the staff of the many other libraries and archives I consulted during the course of my research: the National Library of Ireland; the National Archives in Dublin; the UCD Archives, Belfield; the Clare County Archives; the Limerick County Archives; the Library of Clongowes Wood School, Kildare; the Library of the Reform Club, London; and the Public Record Office of Northern Ireland, Belfast. A special word of appreciation to Ken Bergin, Special Collections, University of Limerick, and to Brian O'Donnell of the

National Archives of Ireland for assisting me in navigating through a myriad of sources. I would like to acknowledge the financial support of Cllr Ian Lynch and Clare County Council. I am indebted to Dr Jackie Uí Chionna, NUI Galway, for her generous and kind advice in the early stages of the editorial process. A special word of thanks to Ciara Comerford, solicitor, Kilrush, for helping me navigate the many legal documents in the Glynn family archive. Many thanks to Julie Long of GBM Printing for her expert assistance and to Eric Shaw for bringing the 1940s postcard of Glynn's mills to my attention. Thanks are also due to my editor, Sam Tranum, and all at Four Courts Press for their professionalism and assistance with the editorial process.

I owe a great debt of gratitude to Dr Paddy Waldron for sharing with me his extraordinary knowledge of the history of west Clare and of families related to the Glynns. Also, Dr Ursula Callaghan for her expertise in newspaper research, kind words and good counsel. And my long-suffering friends Sinéad, Eoghan, Robert, Amy, Ciarán, Manus, Colin, Sean, Kieran, Dave, Richie M., Kay and Dave Loughnane – who graciously listened to my endless meanderings about the book.

I owe an enormous debt of gratitude to my wonderful parents, Seán and Bridie O'Brien, for their love and support throughout the research process. Also, my siblings Barbara, Helen, Fiona and Daithi for their encouragement and advice. And my late uncle Jimmy, for his support and friendship. Thanks also to Shay, Fiadh, Lily, Niamh, James, Ian and Rachel.

Finally, I would also like to thank the countless Kilrush and west Clare people who provided me with numerous stories about the Glynn family and business – these personal insights helped to shape this book.

Illustrations

Introduction

BARTHOLOMEW GLYNN's death in Kilrush in 1855 was reported widely, including in the *Limerick Chronicle*, which remembered him as a 'corn merchant and an old and respectable inhabitant of that town'.[1] This can be taken as the moment when a formerly obscure corn merchant was firmly placed in the category of gentleman, thus confirming his legacy and safeguarding the position of his family in local society. Glynn's extraordinary rise – from the son of a stonemason to a respectable man of means – illustrates the rise of the Catholic middle class in nineteenth-century Ireland. This book provides an in-depth account of his family's extraordinary ascent, from possessing one plot of land in the west of Ireland *c.*1800 to being presented at court *c.*1870.

Today the name Glynn has deep resonances in the town of Kilrush and throughout Co. Clare. From Bartholomew Glynn's first purchase of land in the town, through the eventual closure of the family's milling enterprise in 1984, the Glynn family has remained an integral part of the local business landscape in Kilrush for 208 years.[2] On the one hand, the family, despite its rising prosperity, remained resident in the town and played an active part in the community. On the other, they were viewed as apart from the town's population and described as 'being English until about the 1960s ... as they had fancy accents and they went away to school'.[3] This commonly held assumption of their being different was countered by the family's hands-on approach in the operation of their business, which mitigated much of their 'otherness' and helped them to be accepted as a part of the local community. The continuity of the Glynn business over a long period characterized by pervasive social and economic change firmly anchored the family in the identity of the town. Their 'fair, honest and decent reputation as employers' entered into local memory and continues to resonate to the present day in Kilrush.[4] One phrase, which has its origins in the nineteenth century, is still quoted in the town and is particularly revealing: it concerned the three categories of townspeople who stood far above the others in terms of prosperity, and to whom the people of Kilrush might be indebted – 'the Glynns, the Flynns, and the clergy'.[5]

1 *Limerick Chronicle*, 23 Aug. 1855; see also *Clare Journal*, 27 Aug. 1855. 2 While the milling, railway and shipping parts of the Glynn business are no longer extant, the family maintains a business presence in Kilrush through their investment in the Shannon Ferry Group and their company Glynn Marine Investments; John Glynn, email correspondence, 5 May 2015. 3 Interview with James O'Brien of Kilrush, Co. Clare (24 Oct. 2011). 4 Interview with Tommy Scully of Kilrush, Co. Clare (11 Mar. 2013). 5 The Glynns were the flour millers and the Flynns were the bakers.

The Glynn business grew from its origins in the early 1800s as a small-scale concern trading in oats to become a large firm that boasted railway investments, the ownership of shipping companies and large-scale milling enterprises. The symbiotic nature of business expansion and social progression from small tradesman, manufacturer and retailer to dynasty-building merchants typifies the rise of the middle class in the nineteenth century. The consistent reinvestment of profits by the Glynn family and business into the local economy helped to create and shape an identity that the local community recognized as respectable, deserving and trustworthy. In essence, this economic activity constructed an image of the family over many generations that enabled them emerge as the de facto leaders of the town.[6] Their patronage of local charities and their emphasis on the fair treatment of their workforce conferred a moral worthiness on the Glynn family and business in the eyes of their neighbours.

Geography and advancement went hand-in-hand, and the location of Kilrush, Co. Clare, on the river Shannon contributed to the town's development in the nineteenth century. Fifty miles west of Limerick city, Kilrush had an enviable position on a navigable river and served as a trading and commercial centre for much of the west of Ireland. In addition to the river facilitating trade, the deep waters around Scattery Island and located close to Kilrush pier – referred to as 'Scattery Roads' – serve as a natural harbour for ships sheltering from the often stormy conditions of the Atlantic. Continuous investment by both the local landed gentry and the merchant class meant Kilrush was equipped with modern municipal buildings, civic institutions, educational facilities and bustling markets and fairs, all of which encouraged the urbanization and socialization of the town and its wider environs. The development of modern harbour facilities such as a revenue pier in 1769 followed by a custom house in 1806 promoted growth in the trade of oats, corn, butter, cattle and pigs. Kilrush served as an entrepôt between the west of Ireland and Limerick's harbour. In his account of the improved transport facilities of the town in 1837, Lewis noted that 'this improvement is chiefly to be attributed to the facility of communication with Limerick, afforded by the steam navigation company; the quantity of agricultural produce which passed through the market in 1835, including pigs, amounted in value to £50,000'.[7] Kilrush's advantageous location at the mouth of the river Shannon was exploited and enhanced by an emergent middle class who sought to increase their wealth and in doing so created a particular trajectory of social and economic development that resulted in the emergence of modern Kilrush. The modernization of the town was greatly encouraged by aggressive investment and frequently commented upon by travel writers and government surveyors. However, developing trade in the town was not always deemed a priority and this, too, was commented on in official reports and surveys. One such survey, conducted in 1831 on behalf of the

6 The use of the term de facto is not reflective of a strict hegemony as exercised by the Glynn family rather more of a social leadership related to their dual role as large employers and supporters of local charities. 7 Samuel Lewis, *A topographical tour of Clare* (London, 1837), pp 204–6.

Commission for the Improvement of the Navigation of the Shannon, concluded that

> the extension of this pier would afford the means of the farmer having a more cheerful prospect of seeing his commodities get a speedy and safe conveyance to the markets; and since the establishment of the steam packet which now runs between Kilrush and Limerick, the extension of this pier becomes a matter of actual necessity, for at present all the cargo is obliged to be shipped by means of a boat, as the vessel cannot lie alongside for want of water.[8]

As the century progressed, the infrastructural development of Kilrush continued apace, and by 1859 the revenue pier at Cappagh, some 2 miles west of the town, was further extended by 85 feet, which brought it to a total length of 435 feet and greatly increased its berthing capabilities. An influx of merchants from Limerick attested to the growing importance of Kilrush and the profitable trade that characterized it in this period.[9] The Limerick-based milling family of J.N. Russell constructed a three-bay, six-storey grain store at Kilrush Creek in the 1830s and their competitors, the Spaight family of merchants, who operated a general-goods depot at the creek in the 1840s, followed a similar set-up. Both families carried out extensive trade in Limerick and its surrounding counties of Clare, Kerry, Tipperary and Galway throughout the nineteenth-century. Spaight generated substantial profits from a successful Atlantic trade and regularly held auctions of timber that he imported from Newfoundland.[10] Aside from his trade in raw materials, Spaight operated emigrant ships with regular sailings from Kilrush on 'British built first class vessels'.[11] In addition to local competitors who began to emerge from the 1860s onwards, the *Kilrush Herald and Kilkee Gazette* reported in 1871 that the Co. Kilkenny brewing firm of Smithwicks had established a store in the town.[12] However, the most important development in terms of modernization came in 1892 when the West Clare Railway linked Kilrush to the national network, the result of which increased commercial activity to and from the town. The coming of the railway increased the prosperity of traders and merchants, who previously relied solely on steamships to export or import their produce, especially perishable goods such as eggs and butter. The Glynns promoted and heavily invested in the railway and various members of the family served on the board of the West Clare Railway from its onset.[13] The Glynn flour-milling business established in 1811 was initially a local enterprise. Although it never moved from its original site at Frances Street in Kilrush, it expanded and

8 C.W. Williams, *Observations on the inland navigation of Ireland and the want of employment for its population, with a description of the river Shannon* (Liverpool, 1833), p. 86. 9 *Clare Journal*, 24 Sept. 1810. 10 *Limerick Reporter*, 20 Oct. 1840. 11 *Limerick and Clare Examiner*, 18 Apr. 1849; *Limerick Reporter*, 18 July 1851, 1 Apr. 1853. 12 *Kilrush Herald and Kilkee Gazette*, 16 June 1871. 13 While Michael Glynn promoted it (later discussion), his son, Henry Richard, acted as 'baronial director' for the West Clare Railway; Glynn archive, box 9 (1890–1900).

established offices and depots throughout the neighbouring counties of Kerry and Limerick. The firm, therefore, offers a window into how an early nineteenth-century milling business managed to survive and then thrive, despite its isolated location in the west of Ireland.

Business families such as the Glynns are often held in an unquestioning esteem, with no systematic study of their contribution to the economic, social and cultural development of Kilrush. Local memory and lore can often generate confused and inaccurate accounts of the history of a family and this was certainly the case with the Glynns. This book argues that entrepreneurial families such as the Glynns formed an essential part of the social, economic and cultural development of provincial Irish towns in the nineteenth-century, and that in-depth studies of such families can add to our understanding of such developments in the island-wide context.

Of course, an examination of the Glynn family and business could easily produce a narrow provincial study on the local impact and influence of one family without ever assessing their role in the wider socio-economic development of the town and its environs. In order to overcome this limitation, this book examines the extended social and business networks where the family members deliberately placed themselves. It is very much an examination of the urban as well as the rural spheres, which a small-town family and business inhabited and developed. The involvement of the Glynn family in local administration, magisterial commitments and charitable endeavours all reinforced their local standing while facilitating their journey towards gentrification. This study of the family and business therefore not only reveals the networks between family members and their local community, but also examines the marriage and inheritance practices of an aspirational provincial middle-class family. It reveals how the family became representative of the attitudes and identities of a burgeoning group of provincial merchants and how similar families acted as the energizer between provincial and urban elites.

CHAPTER ONE

The rise of a provincial Irish town

THE PORT OF KILRUSH, far from being an isolated coastal town on the western seaboard, experienced steady growth in the early years of the nineteenth century. Goods exported included flour, oats, pork and butter. For instance, the export of oats from Kilrush in the four-year period between 1811 and 1815 amounted to 9,675 barrels, with the main trading partners being Dublin, Liverpool and Glasgow.[1] In 1815, the *Limerick Chronicle* reported that 'eighty-nine tons of fried codfish', the production of which must have generated significant employment, were exported to St Andero on the north coast of Spain.[2] Kilrush merchants also imported Irish porter, rock salt and coal. The capacity of such businesses to generate economic prosperity offered a fast route to social success for aspiring Irish entrepreneurs in the early part of the nineteenth-century. The development of family firms gave rise to a confident and highly motivated provincial merchant class, many of whom were from a secure farming background.

Ireland's turbulent agrarian history, coupled with the fall-out from the Famine, had an adverse effect on the development of new manufacturing opportunities and processes. The difficult social and economic conditions that defined Ireland from the early to the mid-nineteenth century were unlikely to encourage wide-scale investment in Irish industry, particularly away from large urban centres. Lewis reported in 1837 that Kilrush was home to some minor-scale industry such as a soap manufactory, a salt-refining enterprise and a nail manufactory.[3] While there is no denying the effect of famine, emigration and social unrest on Kilrush, the provincial merchant class, as illustrated by the Glynn family, managed to establish a foothold, which placed them firmly between the landed and the middle class.

In 1839, the ever-entrepreneurial James Paterson, a former gun boat lieutenant, established a distilling business in Kilrush to supply 'real malt whiskey' to the town. However, it was not a success and within four years, the substantial investment had failed.[4] While there are no statistics available for the output of Paterson's distilling enterprise, his investment must have been considerable as the building that housed his still was solely erected for that purpose and was located, for ease of access no doubt, adjacent to two small quays at Kilrush Creek. Even during the calamitous years of the Famine, products including 'thirty tons of white

1 *Clare Journal*, 25 Apr. 1811; *Limerick Chronicle*, 30 June 1813. 2 *Limerick Chronicle*, 23–4 June 1815. St Andero is modern-day Santander. 3 Samuel Lewis, *A topographical dictionary of Ireland* (London, 1837), p. 204. 4 *Clare Journal*, 12 Dec. 1839.

salt, two boxes of soap and twenty-five empty caskets' were exported from Kilrush to Liverpool.[5] An examination of the development of enterprise in a town like Kilrush suggests that factors such as famine and social unrest, although damaging in the extreme, did not prevent a small number of hard-working and highly motivated individuals primarily from the secure farming and shop-keeping classes from establishing themselves as successful merchants of their towns.

'KILRUSH: THE PORTICO TO THE HIGHWAYS OF THE WESTERN WORLD'[6]

In order to facilitate growth and encourage trade in Kilrush, the lord lieutenant of Ireland, Philip Yorke (1757–1834), put into place several key personnel and encouraged structural improvements to advance the port. He directed that a pro-collector and pilot-surveyor 'be placed in Kilrush so that merchants may make entries and clear out their ships at Kilrush without being subject to delay by resorting to the Custom House in Limerick'.[7] In addition to the deployment of key revenue administrative personnel in the town, Yorke ordered the construction of additional infrastructure such as a revenue pier, boat slips and a boathouse to support the new measures. Revenue vessels such as barges and cruisers were permanently based in Kilrush. Additionally, a 'king's store' was erected owing to the 'very great supply of corn and provisions from that part of the county'.[8]

All of this investment enabled local businessmen to establish lucrative trade routes from 1816. The pier was originally a 200-foot structure built by the Commissioners of Customs in 1764 and extended by 186 feet in 1829 and again by 85 feet between 1835 and 1839. By 1837, it was in the ownership of the town's major landowner, John Ormsby Vandeleur, and it was described by Lewis as 'very commodious both for commercial and agricultural uses; it affords great facility for landing passengers from the steam-vessels which regularly ply between this place and Limerick'.[9] In 1835, *Saunders's Newsletter* reported that the City of Dublin Steam-Packet Company planned to send two large iron steamers to Kilrush, noting that the pier at Tarbert, on the Co. Kerry side of the estuary, 'is much wanting'.[10] This was followed in 1841 by a report in the *Dublin Morning Register* that noted that the 'Shannon Navigation Improvement Commissioners will take possession of Kilrush pier … and appoint a collector of quayage and dues'.[11] The inclusion of these articles in periodicals that were circulated throughout Ireland highlights the importance of trade in provincial towns like Kilrush to the national economy. It was

5 *Tipperary Vindicator*, 4 Feb. 1846. 6 Kilrush native Captain J.F. Studdert RN, in the *Belfast News-Letter*, 29 Oct. 1851. 7 *Clare Journal*, 2 Sept. 1805. A pilot boat accompanied ships in and out of Kilrush pier and was involved in rescue and salvage activities as early as 1816: 'a schooner bound for Lisbon … was towed four miles to Kilrush by the pilot-boat'; *Public Ledger & Daily Advertiser*, 19 Jan. 1816. 8 *Clare Journal*, 2 Sept. 1805. 9 Samuel Lewis, *A topographical dictionary of Ireland* (London, 1837), p. 205. 10 *Saunders's Newsletter*, 18 Mar. 1835. 11 *Dublin Morning Register*,

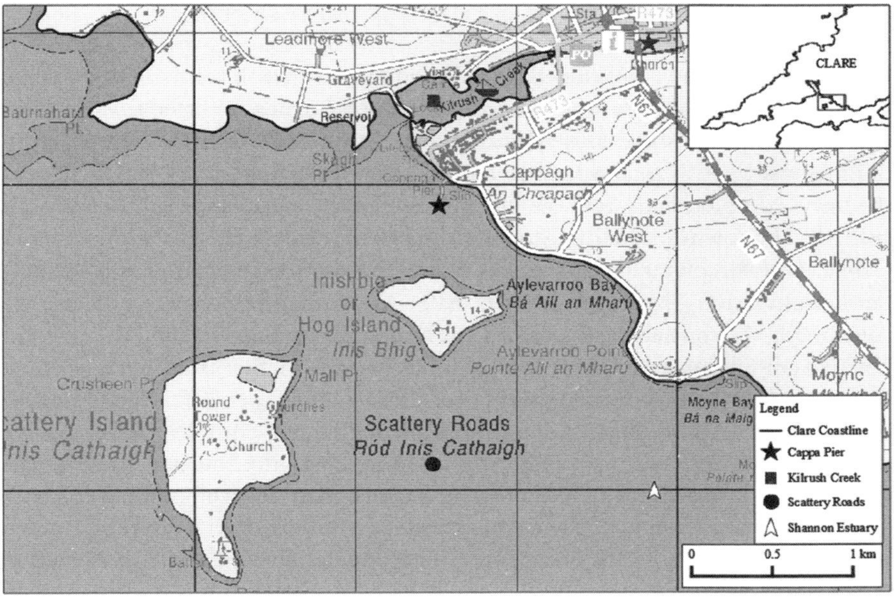

1. Location of Kilrush showing the estuary, creek, pier and Scattery Roads.[12]

in these vital trade routes that the Glynn family invested, in the form of steamships that plied between Kilrush and Limerick.

Certainly, by the mid-1840s, the increased passenger traffic was noted in contemporary trade directories, which reported on conveyancing arrangements to Limerick from Kilrush and Tarbert.[13] This point was referred to in the 1844 annual report of the Shannon Navigation, which stated that 'trading steam vessels ... and vessels of large tonnage are enabled to discharge cargoes without interfering with river craft ... the extension is deserving of every support'.[14] In 1842, the Board of Works constructed two additional smaller piers on the river at Querrin to the west and Cahircon to the east, some 10 miles and 16 miles, respectively, from Kilrush.[15] The harbour facilities were further strengthened by the addition of a pier constructed by the City of Dublin Steam-Packet Company at Tarbert across the estuary, some 8 miles from Kilrush.[16] Capital investment of this nature, in the infrastructure of regional towns and villages, illustrated the huge benefit and importance of the river to the economic viability of west Clare and parts of north Kerry and Limerick.

26 Mar. 1841. 12 Map constructed using multiple primary sources from the Glynn family archive. 13 *Slater's Directory*, 1846, listed entries for 'conveyance by water' that was provided by a steamship that made three weekly trips in the winter months which rose to daily trips during the summertime. 14 *Report of the commissioners for improving navigation of river Shannon 1844*, H.C. 1844 [178] 367 vol. 26. 15 *Limerick Chronicle*, 17 Dec. 1842. 16 *Limerick Reporter*, 24 Dec. 1842.

PROVINCIAL PROTO-INDUSTRIALIZATION

Kilrush experienced a prolonged period of intensive growth from *c.*1790 to 1840. As early as 1808, Hely Dutton, a noted landscape gardener, reported that the town was 'rising fast into some consequence'.[17] Just three years later, the fledging Glynn milling business was established. In Kilrush, the two major factors that facilitated the town's development were the introduction of the steamships and the railway. Initially, the town gradually developed westwards towards Kilrush Creek and Cappa (Kilrush) pier. However, as was typical for towns in the period, it ultimately fanned-out from the central town hall. Municipal buildings such as the courthouse, the constabulary barracks, the bridewell, the town hall and the customs house were all constructed in the opening decades of the nineteenth century. Elsewhere, the town's denominational needs were catered for with the construction of Church of Ireland, Presbyterian and Roman Catholic churches in 1813, 1815 and 1839, respectively. The emerging importance of the tourism trade to the economy of the town was reflected in the establishment of two hotels and an inn. The layout and planning of the town's streets was largely determined and funded by the Vandeleur family, the local landowners, and culminated in the construction of the impressive Georgian boulevard of Frances Street. The town developed concurrently with the increased wealth of this landed family and the prosperity of its emergent middle class. In 1835, Jonathan Binns, an assistant agricultural commissioner for Clare, observed that 'the annual rental income for the Vandeleur estate was stated to be £15,500'.[18] Another indication of the rising prosperity of Kilrush was made by Lewis in 1837, when he noted that there were 712 houses in the town.[19] Modernization continued apace throughout the mid-nineteenth century, and in 1856 the *Nenagh Guardian* reported that Vandeleur had commissioned gas lighting for the town. It described 'a lively scene which occurred at Kilrush last night in consequence that the town was to be lighted with gas'.[20] The steady rise of Kilrush prompted businessmen from outside the county to establish enterprises there. James Quin moved his young wife Mary Anne (née Scott) and family from Limerick to Kilrush in the early 1840s. Quin's business in Kilrush comprised a grocers and spirit dealers.[21] In 1867, he acquired the lease for a house in the fashionable Frances Street area of Kilrush.[22] Quin's business endeavours were clearly profitable as he left an estate of nearly £2,000 at his death in 1873.[23] Another Limerick-based businessman, Ambrose Hall, opened a branch of his enterprise in Kilrush in the late 1850s. Hall manufactured 'kitchen ranges for turf fires' and had a substantial showroom located in William Street, Limerick.

17 Hely Dutton, *Statistical survey of the county of Clare*, undertaken for the Royal Dublin Society (RDS). 18 Jonathan Binns, 'Miseries and beauties of Clare, 1835' in Brían Ó Dálaigh (ed.), *The strangers gaze: travels in County Clare, 1534–1950* (Ennis, 1998), p. 185. 19 Samuel Lewis, *A topographical dictionary of Ireland* (Dublin, 1837), p. 204. 20 *Nenagh Guardian*, 23 Jan. 1856. 21 *Slater's Directory*, 1846. 22 Garett Doherty to James Quin, lease, 18 Aug. 1867; Glynn archive, box 6 (1860–70). 23 John Quin, will, 5 Dec. 1873; Glynn archive, box 7 (1870–80).

By 1857, his advertising targeted 'country gentlemen and farmers' and his Kilrush branch boasted an array of typical goods including 'house furnishings, ironmongery and saddlery'; however, perhaps more indicative of an improvement in the affluence of some Kilrush inhabitants, Hall also offered 'Sheffield plated goods'.[24] In addition to an influx of provincial businessmen investing in commerce in Kilrush, local individuals also established prosperous operations in the town. For instance, in 1860, Charles McDonnell of Kilkee (some 8 miles north of Kilrush) announced the opening of his sawmill in Henry Street and the ready availability of superior quality brick (manufactured in Kilkee).[25]

FROM ISOLATED FISHING VILLAGE TO IMPORTANT PROVINCIAL TOWN

Overall, the development and commercialization of Kilrush in the nineteenth-century was broadly in line with similarly sized towns throughout Ireland and Britain. The role of the individual entrepreneur was fundamental in stimulating investment in provincial towns, and this was best illustrated in the case of Kilrush by James Paterson, who established a thriving milling business in the town in the early years of the nineteenth century. Hely Dutton noted Paterson as a 'very active and intelligent inhabitant, who has been of the utmost benefit to Kilrush, and the adjoining counties'.[26] The bridge between the landed and the emergent entrepreneurial classes was reinforced by mutually beneficial partnerships: John Ormsby Vandeleur supported Paterson. The Vandeleur family had a long pedigree. They were Dutch merchants, who had settled in Ireland by the early seventeenth century. John Ormsby Vandeleur played a major role in the development of the town of Kilrush in the early nineteenth century and built a mansion, Kilrush House, in 1808. Following Vandeleur's death in 1828, his son, Colonel Crofton Moore Vandeleur, continued to make his mark on the town, giving land for the building of the Catholic church, a convent, a fever hospital and the workhouse. However, this largesse was soon forgotten and he is principally associated with the large number of evictions that took place in the Kilrush Union during the Famine years.

In the first half of the nineteenth century, landlord benevolence coupled with steady though limited entrepreneurial investment had helped to transform Kilrush from a small backwater fishing village in the eighteenth century into a thriving market town and seaport, primarily engaged in the production and sale of oats. Mason reported that 'in 1802, when he [Paterson] commenced, the quantity of oats sold in Kilrush market amounted to 12,000 barrels, and cost £6,666. By 1812, it had grown to 34,000 barrels, and cost £33,681, which amounted to increase of nearly sixteen per cent. The overall increase in the production of oats from 1802 to 1812 was just under seventy-five per cent.'[27]

24 *Limerick Reporter*, 17 Apr. 1857. 25 *Clare Journal* and *Ennis Advertiser*, 7 May 1860. 26 Dutton, *Statistical survey of the county of Clare.* 27 *Mason's parochial survey* (Dublin, 1814–19).

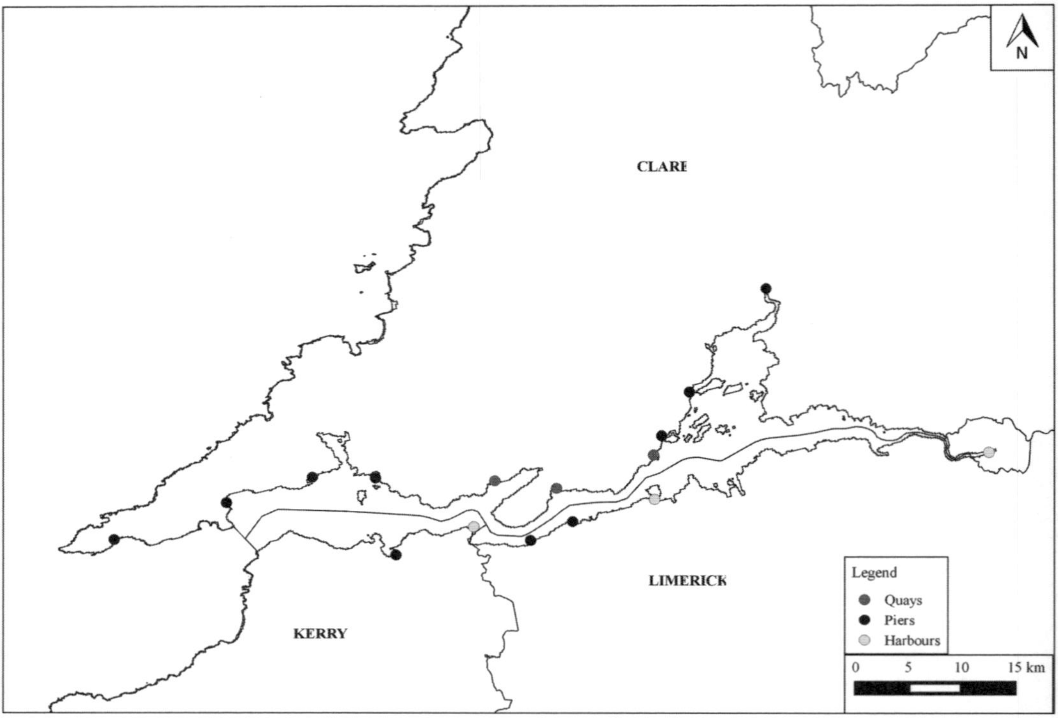

2. Location of piers, quays and harbours in Clare, Kerry and Limerick.

Enterprise of this nature was vital to the expansion of other coastal towns in Ireland, such as Tralee to the south and Waterford to the east, while maritime trade also accounted for the rapid expansion that these towns experienced in the nineteenth century.[28] Traditionally, sections of the coastal population had supplemented their income from both fishing and trading on the river, and the introduction of steam-powered vessels threatened their livelihoods. In Co. Clare, traditional vessels known as cots were generally operated by individuals rather than businesses and regularly visited coastal villages in the county and the adjoining counties of Kerry and Limerick with their cargoes of turf, fish and kelp. These vessels carried cargoes of turf to larger boats on the river which then transported it to Limerick city. On their return trip, the cots often carried limestone, which was used as fertilizer. These turf boats also helped to establish passenger traffic, though this method of transport was subsequently replaced by the steamship in 1816. By 1812, Paterson had developed his business to include a successful shipping company. By 1816, the first steamship passenger service was introduced and operated regularly between Limerick city and Kilrush.[29]

28 *Clonmel Herald*, 21 June 1834; *Waterford News*, 26 Feb. 1858. 29 Paterson's steamship, *Lady of the Shannon*, operated between 1816 and 1826.

Paterson's business model highlighted the importance of the river Shannon to the economic development of the town. There had always been a coastal trade in Kilrush but significant growth in goods traffic between Limerick city and the towns and villages along the river estuary resulted in sustained economic benefit for Kilrush. This was facilitated predominantly by the addition of new products and services and numerous mercantile enterprises that resulted in an intensification of commercial activity along the river. Initially, this service catered for individual travellers, but it proved so popular that it expanded to the establishment of a dedicated transport for tourists visiting the area. As early as 1822, the *Limerick Chronicle* reported that a hotel in Kilrush was expecting a surge in custom as 'several of the officers of the Garrison intend to proceed tomorrow in the Steam Packet to avail themselves of the expected gay scene'.[30] Similarly, in 1829 the *Clare Journal* described the beginning of the season in Kilkee when it noted that 'the steam packet, to ply between Limerick and Kilrush, during the summer months for the accommodation of sea bathers, will arrive in Limerick on the first of May'.[31]

The rise in numbers of passengers availing of travel by steamship led to the provision of tourist accommodation in the town and suggests that for some a modicum of disposable income and leisure time was available. Ever the shrewd and opportunistic entrepreneur, Paterson established the Kilrush Bathing Hotel (also known as the Kilrush Hotel and Tepid Baths) in 1817. A deed of 1 October 1817 described the location of Paterson's hotel as being in Cappa: 'Vandeleur demised to James Paterson … part of the lands of Cappagh lying between the revenue pier and the Creek of Kilrush … on which Paterson had then lately erected an Hotel.'[32] Writing in 1836, a visitor to west Clare, Mary Knott, noted that 'we got seated in a jaunting car … and passed a neat square of bathing lodges, with a hotel in the centre, situated near the revenue pier'.[33] When contemporary maps are consulted, it seems likely that Knott was describing Samuel Lomas' hotel, located in the square some 2 miles west of Kilrush and situated close to Kilrush pier. There is evidence he linked his steamship business with his hotel endeavour, as the *Dublin Evening Post* reported that '*The Lady of the Shannon* steam packet leaves the hotel for Limerick on Mondays, Wednesdays and Fridays'.[34] In addition to offering hotel accommodation, the Kilrush Bathing Hotel featured tepid baths that catered for the contemporary obsession with the health benefits associated with seawater. It also notified the public that 'the only bathing machines in Ireland are to be found at this establishment'.

Paterson's hotel was followed by the establishment of two further hotels in the 1830s.[35] For a town the size of Kilrush to have three hotels in the early nineteenth century was significant and cannot be ignored when looking at the economic development of the town. The development of the leisure business in tandem with

30 *Limerick Chronicle*, 21 Aug. 1822. 31 *Clare Journal*, 2 May 1829. 32 Registry of Deeds, 1841, book 2, no. 235. 'Latouche & ors.' to Fitzgerald, registered 27 Jan. 1841. 33 Mary Knott, *Two months at Kilkee* (Dublin, 1836), p. 30. 34 *Dublin Evening Post*, 13 June 1822. A bathing machine was a roofed and walled cart, usually on wheels, meant to protect an individual's modesty. It was usually rolled directly into the sea, where the occupant alighted. 35 Samuel Leigh, *Leigh's new pocket road-book of Ireland* (London, 1835), p. 386, recorded two hotels in the town: the Kilrush Hotel and the

the main entrepreneurial trade of the town brought with it added financial prosperity, and the extension of that prosperity beyond the boundaries of Kilrush itself.[36] In 1842, a notice about the opening of a fourth hotel in the town – Williams' hotel on Frances Street – informed the public that it was a 'new splendid hotel, which no hotel in Clare can compete with … a large sum of money having been expended on the establishment'.[37] Its proprietor, Michael Williams, recognised the economic value of the export trade from the town:

> The trade and commerce of Kilrush … was contrasted with the former obscurity of the town and the high position it now holds in the commercial world … its exports in bacon and other commodities were considered in England and Scotland as superior to those of Limerick.[38]

In spite of the Famine, commercial activity in Kilrush continued, and this suggests that the town continued to experience economic growth. A description of the Vandeleur Arms Hotel was included in an advertisement in the *Limerick Chronicle* in 1855 that offered the premises for lease.[39] It described the building as being 'in the rising town of Kilrush … and is a hotel and posting establishment containing twenty rooms with commodious out-offices'.[40] The *Kilrush Magazine and Monthly Journal* of May 1847 also carried an advertisement for the Vandeleur Arms Hotel, giving Frances Street as its location. Lomas, the proprietor, announced that 'he has fitted up the above establishment in a superior manner' and that it 'is beautifully situated on the water's edge as you enter Kilrush from the Steam-Boat Quay'.[41] By 1881, the robust tourist trade in Kilrush prompted a description of the town to be included in a guidebook aimed at American tourists.[42] This guidebook described the steamship journey to Kilrush in great detail: '[T]he passage steamer from Foynes [Co. Limerick] occupies about three hours … Kilrush … is a thriving town with 4,424 inhabitants and a hotel [the Vandeleur Arms] … [F]rom here an excursion to Kilkee might be arranged.'

As well as being a major artery, the estuary also supported a thriving fishing industry that provided seasonal employment and was a source of additional income for both the locals and the landed families whose shore-side properties often featured profitable salmon weirs. For instance, the *Clare Journal* reported in 1917 that 'a splendid salmon, weighing forty-eight and a half pounds was taken at the Kilmore Church Weir, Knock the other day. This fishery belongs to Mr F.W.G. Hickman' of Kilmore House, Knock.[43] Local lore has proven a valuable source for

Vandeleur Arms. **36** *Second report of the commissioners appointed to consider and recommend a general system of Railways for Ireland*, H.C. 1838 [145] 449, vol. 35. **37** *Limerick Chronicle*, 7 Sept. 1842. **38** *Clare Journal*, 11 Aug. 1842. **39** *Limerick Chronicle*, 11 May 1855. **40** Ibid. See also D. O'Dea, 'What it says in the papers or a hundred years ago on this day' in Noel Mulqueen (ed.), *Kilrush CBS centenary souvenir, 1874–1974* (Kilrush, 1974), pp 107–10; and Christian Brothers, *Souvenir of the golden jubilee of the Christian Brothers, Kilrush, 1874–1924* (Ennis, 1924). **41** *Kilrush Magazine and Monthly Journal*, May 1847. **42** W. Pembroke-Fetridge, *The American Travellers' Guides: handbooks for travellers in Europe* (London, 1881), p. 63. **43** *Clare Journal*, 22 Feb. 1917.

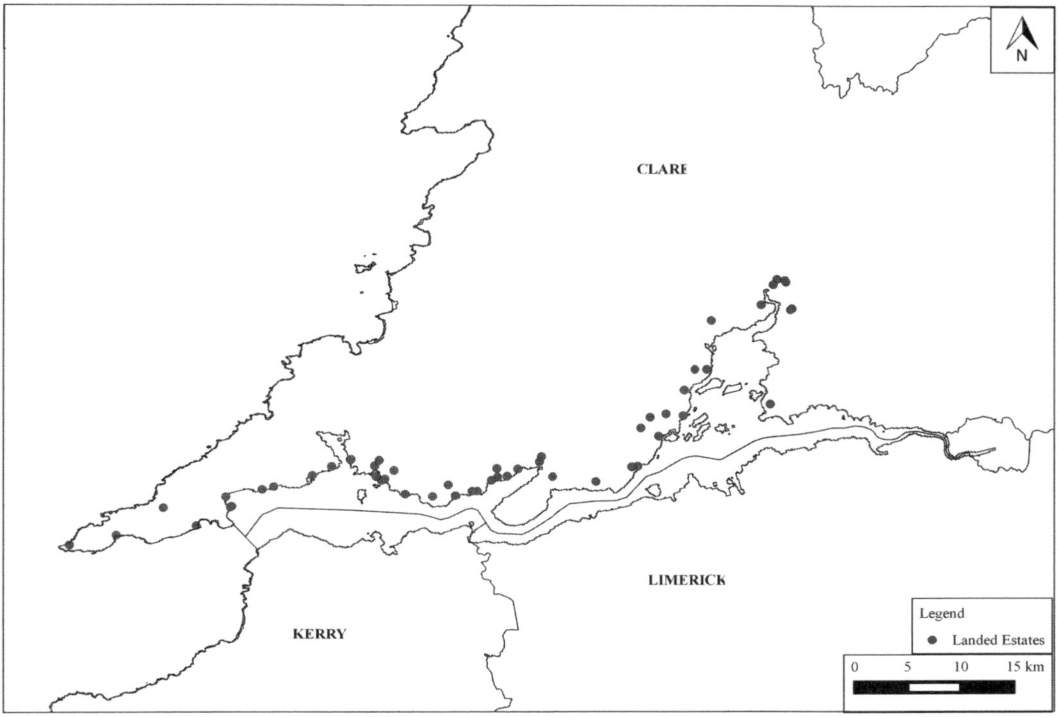

3. The 'Planter's Mile', showing the distribution of the houses of landed gentry along the Co. Clare side of the Shannon estuary.[44]

understanding the significance of Kilrush's position on the river estuary. The Shannon estuary has been described as being the old road to Limerick, and for a distance of about 1 mile towards Limerick city its shore was known as the 'Planter's Mile' (see fig. 3) as this area contained the best land and offered the easiest access to the river.

The commercial success of Kilrush pier was primarily due to the under-developed road network that existed in Clare. The public road network was largely inadequate and particularly prohibitive to further trade expansion. Published in 1783, George Taylor and Andrew Skinner's *Maps of the roads of Clare* included two routes leading to Kilrush. The map 'from Clarecastle to Kildysart' showed a portion of a road marked as 'intended road to Kilrush', whereas the 'Kilfenora to Kilrush' map clearly shows a defined route that originated in Kilfenora in north Clare and ran to Kilrush in west Clare. The maps were rudimentary though considered accurate by contemporaries. However, neither of the roads described followed a straight route from Kilrush towards the county town of Ennis, instead they meandered through bogland and countryside.[45] The planning of roads was

44 David Dickson, *Old world colony: Cork and south Munster, 1630–1830* (Cork, 2005), p. 175.
45 George Taylor and Andrew Skinner, *Maps of the roads of Clare* (2nd ed., Dublin, 1783).

still problematic in 1802, when Hely Dutton commented, 'I am convinced [that] until a National Board of Roads is established, we can never expect matters to mend.'[46] However, improvement was already apparent in the following decade and the *Clare Journal* reported in 1816 that 'a new line of road from Ennis to Kilrush is now open … [T]he line brings Ennis five miles nearer Kilrush.'[47] The establishment of the Board of Works in 1831 went some way to addressing the building of roads and it oversaw rapid improvement to the national road network and in particular in remote areas.

The growth of commerce facilitated continued investment in the harbour facilities of Kilrush. This was evident in the granting of £3,000 to improve the town's harbour.[48] Though Kilrush was ideally located at the mouth of the Shannon and this position was exploited by local merchants, such as Paterson who had established profitable trading routes, it still drew criticism from official commissions and reports. One such report, published by the Commission for the Improvement of the Navigation of the Shannon, appointed in October 1831, concluded that the Shannon was not being fully utilized for trade and navigation and the surveyor, Captain Mudge, reported that

> The place is frequented by a few vessels from 100 to 120 tons, which ship off cargoes of grain to England, but owing to the shallowness of the harbour they are generally detained a considerable time … I do not think from what I have seen that any capital could be expended on this harbour likely to be of general utility … this can be easily accomplished by the proprietors, who derive immediate benefit from the trade and have an interest in the harbour.[49]

Mudge's report was part of a larger survey undertaken to develop and implement strategies for the improvement of navigation on the river Shannon, both inland along the associated canal system and along the coast. Mudge was tasked with surveying the navigation of the river from Limerick city to the sea. A number of local merchants provided evidence that the construction of piers and ancillary works along the lower Shannon would increase trade and employment for the area. Commenting on the employment brought about by the construction of the pier, the government report stated that 'the average number of persons employed daily at Kilrush pier from January to December was forty'.[50] The introduction of steamships on the river drew particularly positive commentary in the report, 'since the voyage is [now] made in general with so much certainty from Limerick to Kilrush that jaunting cars and other public conveyances are ready to start

46 Hely Dutton, *Observations on survey of County Dublin* in David Broderick, *The first toll-roads: Ireland's turnpike roads, 1729–1858* (Cork, 2002), p. 182. 47 *Clare Journal*, 11 July 1816. 48 *Dublin Evening Post*, 11 May 1824. It is unclear which body awarded the grant. 49 *Commission for the improvement of the navigation of the Shannon*, report of Commander William Mudge RN, admiralty surveyor, Oct. 1831. Mudge was scathing in his reports on Kilrush merchants and traders and the manner in which he felt the town's natural harbour was not utilized by them to its full extent. 50 *Report of the commissioners for improving navigation of river Shannon 1831*, H.C. 1831 [731] 333, vol. 45.

immediately after the arrival of the steamer'.[51] Jaunting-car services were being advertised in the provincial press from about 1845 and the *Limerick Reporter* noted their availability in Kilkee: 'well-appointed jaunting cars to and from Steamboat Quay, Kilrush'.[52]

By 1846, it had become apparent that the pier at Kilrush was no longer fit for purpose. The gradual but consistent increase in traffic on the river led to a demand for improved harbour facilities as the steamers competed to use overcrowded berths.[53] The problem was finally resolved when Vandeleur invested from the late 1840s in a port less than 1 mile down river that complemented the harbour facilities at Kilrush pier. This development was Kilrush Creek and consisted of a quay built in 1846, which was further enhanced by the addition of a pier in 1848: Vandeleur expended more than £2,413 on the facilities.[54] Thus, over a period of some twenty years, Kilrush developed from a small fishing town to a port of considerable size, which boasted the most up-to-date harbour facilities capable of accommodating vessels of up to 700 tons.[55] The location of the Glynn milling business adjacent to the newly developed Kilrush Creek was the vital element that secured their dominant position as the most successful millers and ship owners in west Clare. The Glynn firm enjoyed almost exclusive access to the key piece of infrastructure that was to drive the economic development of business enterprise in Kilrush for the next one hundred years or so.

Kilrush town was home to a large number of traders, retailers and merchants. As early as 1837, Lewis noted that Kilrush manufactured 'friezes, flannels, stockings, strong sheetings [sail making] and narrow linen'.[56] The patronage of industry by the landed gentry is evidenced by Vandeleur's approach to the proprietor of Limerick Lace, Charles Walker, who he urged to establish a lace factory in Kilrush. In 1839, Vandeleur incentivized Walker by providing him with rent-free premises at Lower Moore Street. Thus, Walker established his lace factory aided by a cohort of his Nottingham and Coggeshall lace-making tutors and trainers. The typical population of a provincial Irish town included artisan-traders: tailors, boot-makers, dressmakers and so on. Though not providing a precise measure of growth, trade directories offer an indication of the development of products, services and occupations in Irish towns in the nineteenth century. The earliest available directory for the town is *Pigot's Directory* of 1824, which listed some twenty-three categories of occupation, including skilled trades such as wool combers and tanners.[57] Paterson was recorded as a merchant and not a miller, while Glynn, his direct competitor, was not featured at all in the directory. His omission

51 *Report of the commissioners for improving navigation of river Shannon 1834*, H.C. 1834 [532] 141, vol. 17. 52 *Limerick Reporter*, 27 June 1843; 15 July 1845. 53 *Dublin Mercantile Advertiser and Weekly Price Current*, 16 Mar. 1829. 54 *Clare Journal*, 30 Apr. 1900. See also 'Report on Kilrush Creek Improvement' prepared by James Price of the harbour engineer's office, 9–10 Lapps Quay, Cork for Kilrush Urban District Council, which described the creek as 'about three-quarters of a mile long and 400 feet wide', Mar. 1909. 55 *Irish Times*, 26 Nov. 1926. 56 Samuel Lewis, *County Clare: a history and topography* (London, 1837). 57 *Pigot's Directory*, 1824.

raises questions as to the directory's accuracy and the manner in which the data was collected, as leases and deeds contained within the Glynn archive confirm that by 1811 Glynn was recognized locally as a merchant.[58] Clearly, his business was profitable as by 1817 he was included in the rent rolls for the barony of Kilrush as a £20 freeholder.[59] While he wasn't included in the 1824 directory, by 1846 Glynn was recorded as a 'corn merchant' along with three other individuals.[60] Analysis of the directory shows that the number of occupations in the town had grown exponentially, and over eighty were listed. Additional occupations included distillers, bankers and auctioneers, the latter two reflecting the broader economic growth of the town. In terms of business longevity, Nenadic has noted that 'most businesses were small and short-lived, they were clustered in retail and services and they served a predominantly local market'.[61] This is certainly true in the case of Kilrush, as is evidenced from trade directories. In the case of bakers, for instance, the 1824 directory listed five individuals, while by 1846 *Slater's Directory* only included two of the original names. This pattern is broadly the same for the remaining categories of occupations in the town.[62] However, the Glynn dynasty clearly bucked this trend and continued to thrive throughout the nineteenth century.

Kilrush's economy was dominated by mixed agriculture, fishing and minor manufactories. Hely Dutton's optimistic account of trade in the town during this period appears to support Ó Gráda's argument that the Irish economy was dominated by agriculture rather than manufacture.[63] Ó Gráda noted that the 1821 census confirmed that 'over two-fifths of Irishmen and Irishwomen were chiefly employed in trades, manufactures and handicrafts'.[64] There is certainly evidence of artisan-traders operating in Kilrush in the 1830s.[65] The production of linen-related goods in Kilrush and their benefit to the local economy is evident in contemporary trade directories. For example, in 1846 *Slater* noted that 'linen, woollen drapers and haberdashers' provided employment for eighteen individuals while 'dress-makers, milliners and dyers' accounted for a further seven entries.[66] The same source recorded approximately 262 individuals employed across 68 occupations. Similarly, the Vandeleur leases for the period 1785 to 1928 show seven artisan occupations and included three blacksmiths, two coopers and seven carpenters.[67] However, not all the necessary trading conditions were in place to encourage the growth of commerce in Kilrush.

58 Lease between Crofton Moore Vandeleur and Bartholomew Glynn for a property located at Market Square Kilrush, 15 Apr. 1811; Glynn archive, box 1 (1811–20). 59 Clare County Library, 'List of freeholders: county of Clare, 1821', clarelibrary.ie/eolas/coclare/genealogy/freeholders_1821/list_of_freeholders_1821.htm, accessed 15 May 2011. 60 *Pigot's Directory*, 1824; *Slater's Directory*, 1846. 61 Stana Nenadic, 'The small family firm in Victorian Britain', *Business History* (1993), p. 89. 62 The two directories available for the period are *Pigot's Directory*, 1824, and *Slater's Directory*, 1846. 63 Cormac Ó Gráda, *Ireland: a new economic history, 1780–1939* (Oxford, 1994), p. 12. 64 Ibid., p. 12. 65 A lease between Bartholomew Glynn and Matthew Mulcahy confirmed that the occupation of the latter was weaver. Deed of assignment of tenement in Kilrush, Co. Clare between Matthew Mulcahy, weaver and Bartholomew Glynn, merchant, 1 June 1835; Glynn archive, box 1 (1811–20). The value of the tenement was given as £54. 66 *Slater's Directory*, 1846. 67 Vandeleur leases in

Though Vandeleur had supported Paterson in some of his business endeavours, his support did not prevent contemporary commentators from criticizing the landed gentry in Clare because of their restrictive approach to business practices. While a criticism of landlords investment practices is not easy to find, there is one provided by Edward Wakefield, who commented on the exorbitant cost of rent in Kilrush: 'Vandeleur charges six shillings per foot in front for building ground … this is the price in Bond Street [London].'[68] Wakefield blamed Vandeleur's approach for the obstruction of commerce to the town: '[T]he view of the landed proprietor seems to be directed more to immediate gain, than to future advantage, and confined rather to private gain.'[69]

It was in this environment, characterized by what appears to have been excessively high rents, archaic business practices on the part of the local landlord and a milling industry dominated by Paterson, that Bartholomew Glynn first appeared as a member of the emergent middle class.

National Archives, 1785–1928. Extracted from the National Archives, Dublin, private accessions, 1997–2002, catalogue no. 99/13, and from copy of accession no. 1074/2 1816–1929. **68** Edward Wakefield, *Ireland: statistical and political* (London, 1812), p. 630. **69** Ibid., p. 631.

CHAPTER TWO

The Glynn enterprise

TRADE, COMMERCE AND FINANCE

THE GLYNNS WERE A LOCAL Catholic family who first emerged in business in Kilrush in the early years of the nineteenth century. Over the course of one hundred years, the family built up a substantial multifaceted business empire whose interests included flour milling, distilling, woollen manufacture, shipping and railways. The firm benefitted from an unbroken inter-generational ownership that thrived on innovation and growth. The benefit of this type of ownership structure was twofold: it ensured future careers for sons and marriage settlements for daughters, while at the same time family relationships guaranteed a source of management for the business. Family firms were also heavily reliant on family connections for advice and finance.[1] Moreover, as Rose has noted, 'with respect to the choice of partners … networks of trust, based on family or shared values, provided reservoirs of managerial talent which could be tapped, sometimes on a meritocratic basis'.[2] However, when a family member died, the company experienced a loss of expertise, collective knowledge and shared experience.

Bartholomew Glynn was born in *c.*1775 and established his corn mill in Kilrush in 1811. The available documentary evidence suggests that Glynn's maternal lineage came from Ballyartney, a townland some 10 miles south-east of Kilrush, and family tradition suggests that his paternal lineage came from Kilmacduane, a townland some 5 miles to the north of the town.[3] Bartholomew Glynn's uncle Darby and his brother William were active in Kilrush enterprise from the late eighteenth century. William was described as a mason in his will of 1831.[4] As noted by Lewis in 1837, the town contained over 712 houses and there can be little doubt that the skills of a mason were much in demand for the construction of these buildings.[5] Therefore, it is suggested that the later Glynn enterprise benefited in some way from William Glynn's occupation as a mason, which must have been profitable as suggested by a deed from 1827, which described a house he erected in

1 Graeme J. Milne, *Trades and traders in mid-Victorian Liverpool* (Liverpool, 2000), p. 124. 2 Mary B. Rose, 'Beyond Buddenbrooks: the family firm and the management of succession in nineteenth-century Britain' in Jonathan Brown (ed.), *Entrepreneurship, networks, and modern business* (Manchester, 1993), pp 127–43. 3 Henry Glynn noted in his diary 17 Feb. 1889 how 'B. Glynn, my grandfather, his mother's name was Crowe, one of six sisters from Ballyartney. Mrs Shannon, Dysart is to find out the name of my great grandfather … and if father was a son of another of the Miss Crowes'; Glynn archive, box 9 (1890–1900). 4 National Library of Ireland, will of William Glynn of Kilrush, Co. Clare, 1 Dec. 1831, D.26, 739. 5 Lewis, *A topographical dictionary of Ireland.*

the market square, a prominent location in the town.[6] In his will, he left £28 to his sister Margaret and £15 to his sister Mary.[7] Both the deed and the will confirm that the Glynn family were involved in local business before they emerged as millers in 1811. As Ballyartney contained no known industry and consisted mainly of small farms, it is therefore reasonable to assume that the maternal side of Bartholomew Glynn's family were of the smallholding or cottier class in an area where the big house and relatively good land dominated the landscape.[8] These rural origins are important, suggesting that individuals from a secure farming background were able to cross the social divide in respect of advancement of status and position.

A typed two-page account, dating from 1934 and tracing the origin of the firm, claimed that 'Bartholomew Glynn started in the grain business about 1803 … having earlier built on a plot of land in the Market Square in 1798.'[9] Glynn's first property transaction is recorded in an 1811 lease for a house in the Market Square, Kilrush.[10] He became a prosperous miller and married locally. The available sources give no indication as to how he raised the capital to start his milling endeavour. Between *c.*1850 and 1860, the Glynn family purchased a number of mill buildings for the considerable sum of £940, which provides some insight into the start-up capital needed for mills in the mid-nineteenth century. There is a suggestion in the family tradition that Glynn's wife's marriage settlement may have been substantial enough to allow him to set up in business.[11] A lease noted that 'in 1811, he married Miss McInerney from Cooraclare'. This is also the date that Bartholomew Glynn started his milling business. Glynn's first concern was a small mill centrally located in the Market Square where he also purchased the lease on the house in 1811. In the following forty years, at precisely the same time as Kilrush was experiencing steady growth, he rapidly expanded his business and aggressively acquired an extensive building complex of mills, stores, kilns and bakeries.[12]

At various stages throughout its history, the firm used turf sourced and purchased locally to power the mill. This was mainly due to the irregular supply of coal. However, this turf trade was also an important contribution to the agricultural economy and no doubt won favour with local farmers.[13] The success of Glynn's commercial endeavours allowed him to become a man of considerable means. The extensive milling complex, located at the western end of the town and at the entrance to Kilrush Creek, offered unrivalled access for the loading and discharging of cargo from his ships. By 1855, in addition to the mill complex,

6 National Library of Ireland, leases and assignment of plot of ground adjoining market house in Kilrush, Co. Clare: principal parties Frances Russell of Limerick, William Glynn and Thomas Studdert, 1827–32. D. 26,736–8. 7 National Library of Ireland, will of William Glynn of Kilrush Co. Clare, Dec. 1, 1831, D.26, 739. 8 Griffith's Valuation, 1855, Co. Clare, parish of Killofin, townland of Ballyartney, p. 43. 9 C.E. Glynn, typed two-page account of the origin of 'Glynn Kilrush', 13 Jan. 1934; Glynn archive, box 13 (1930–40). 10 Lease, John O. Vandeleur esq. to Bartholomew Glynn, merchant for lease of house situated in Kilrush, Co. Clare, 28 Dec. 1811; Glynn archive, box 1 (1811–20). 11 Ibid. 12 *Limerick & Clare Examiner*, 7 Oct. 1848. 13 *Irish Times*, 2 Nov. 1926.

Bartholomew Glynn had acquired a further six properties in the town of Kilrush, all which were tenanted and for private use.[14]

Glynn's acquisition of property was indicative of the importance placed on the ownership of land and property, which was often viewed as a measure of an individual's position in society. Glynn held all of his properties from the landlord, Crofton Moore Vandeleur, and they were all tenanted, making him a landlord too. According to Griffith's Valuation, recorded in the same year of his death, Bartholomew Glynn held six properties with a total rateable annual value of £42.[15] Conversely, various members of the Glynn family were also recorded as Bartholomew's tenants in 1855.

In essence, Glynn's milling venture proved to be so successful that he owned and controlled an entire street – Frances Street Lower, conveniently located beside Merchant's Quay at the western side of the town. Positioned at the entrance to Kilrush Creek, Merchant's Quay afforded Glynn unhindered access to load and unload his produce into boats. Though Bartholomew Glynn experienced rapid advancement in terms of both his business and his position in society, his wealth did not propel him into the ranks of the landed classes. For instance, in the 1830s, during the establishment of the Kilrush Fever Hospital, the *Clare Journal* noted that 'the following subscribers are requested to meet in the court house to enter into the necessary arrangements'.[16] The newspaper then listed members of the landed gentry, professionals, the clergy and merchants as among those who had contributed to the appeal. However, Glynn, who had been established as a merchant since 1811, did not appear on the list. The desire of aspiring merchants to own a small estate has been well-documented, and Wilson has shown that English merchants in the late eighteenth century tended to invest their fortunes in land as a means to gaining social acceptance among the landed class.[17] Later generations of the Glynn family certainly purchased large local houses (Pella House and Leadmore House) and their adjoining farms.[18] Griffith's Valuation of 1855 described the tenanted Pella House and offices as having a rateable annual valuation of £13, as being comprised of four separate plots of land and as totalling 49 acres, 2 roods and 18 perches. Leadmore House was described as a house and offices with a rateable annual valuation of £7 10*s*. on 73 acres and 7 perches. Both houses were located in the townland of Leadmore East and were rented from Col. Crofton Moore Vandeleur.[19]

The elevation of the Glynns' position over the course of the nineteenth century from that of ordinary corn millers to prominent and affluent members of local

14 See Glynn leases in family papers. For example: Lease, 28 Dec. 1811 between John Ormsby Vandeleur esq. and Bartholomew Glynn, merchant. Glynn archive. 15 Griffith's Valuation, 1855, Co. Clare, parish of Kilrush, townland of Drimna, pp 126, 133, 137, 139. 16 *Clare Journal*, 30 Aug. 1838. 17 R.G. Wilson, *Gentlemen merchants: the merchant community in Leeds, 1700–1830* (Manchester, 1971), p. 3. 18 William Joynt-Glynn purchased Pella House in *c.*1895 from the landed Studdert family. His brother, Henry Richard Glynn, purchased Leadmore House from the Brew family in the 1890s. 19 Griffith's Valuation, 1855, Co. Clare, parish of Kilrush, townland of

society highlights the importance of upward mobility to the emergent middle class in a provincial town. The route to their enhanced position in society was opened by the entrepreneurship of Bartholomew Glynn. When he died in Kilrush in 1855, it was reported not only in Clare but also in Limerick.[20] The success he had enjoyed was largely similar to the fictitious Honest John in Kate O'Brien's novel *Without my cloak*, which focused on a nineteenth-century family's rise in terms of both business and social position. O'Brien's description of Honest John's emergence as a merchant could be that of Bartholomew Glynn: '[O]n his twentieth birthday he opened a small store, he prospered ... [H]e had himself a tireless capacity for work and an inclination to take risks ... [H]is trade expanded and he was accepted as an important citizen with a sufficiency for local patriotism.'[21] The purchase of property was the initial expansion of both Glynn's and Honest John's business interests, commonly accepted as the safest and most practical investment of one's fortune.

Unlike Denis Behan, a merchant and rival of Glynn's operation in Kilrush, Glynn did not court controversy or scandals and was not the subject of court proceedings or bankruptcy charges. Bankruptcy law was particularly harsh and demanded personal repayment and often incarceration.[22] It is unclear how Behan's business venture collapsed, but his bankruptcy notice in 1848 in the *Limerick and Clare Examiner* described him as a 'shopkeeper, dealer and chapman'.[23] It was alleged that in the previous year, Denis Behan and his son Patrick 'had removed to new shops in Kilrush and Ennistymon all the valuable goods from the shop of their father in an alleged attempt to protect them from his creditors'.[24] Behan's extensive range of stock was sold off and the auctioneer noted that 'several houses, stores and two farms will be sold at a future day'.[25] The buildings were purchased by Mrs Jones of Douglas House in Co. Cork in 1850, who subsequently offered them for sale in 1856.[26] The *Limerick Reporter* described the extensive concerns, which included 'one five-storey grain store, kiln, two four-storey grain stores, shop, dwelling house, stores, bakehouse, apartments and a spacious house lately occupied as a hotel'.[27] Glynn acquired Jones' Kilrush property and Behan's life insurance policy formed part of the sale too.[28] The three Behan stores had been the last remaining buildings in the milling complex not yet in Glynn's ownership.

Leadmore-East, p. 144. **20** *Limerick Chronicle*, 23 Aug. 1855. **21** Kate O'Brien, *Without my cloak* (London, 1984), pp 14–15. **22** Leonore Davidoff and Catherine Hall, *Family fortunes: men and women of the English middle class, 1780–1850* (Oxford, 2002), p. 201. **23** *Limerick & Clare Examiner*, 19 Apr. 1848. **24** *Clare Journal and Ennis Advertiser*, 9 July 1849. **25** *Limerick Reporter*, 2 May 1848. **26** Assignment of Vandeleur to Behan 1840 lease to Jones, 3 July 1850; Glynn archive, box 4 (1840–50); *Limerick Reporter*, 28 Oct. 1856. It is unclear as to how Jones came to acquire the buildings, although there is a possibility that her late husband was a creditor of Behans. Coincidentally, Jones also became bankrupt according to the *Cork Examiner*, 30 July 1855, which meant Glynn was the beneficiary of two bankruptcies. **27** *Limerick Reporter*, 28 Oct. 1856. **28** Denis Behan to B. Glynn, life insurance policy, 26 July 1842; Glynn archive, box 4 (1840–50). See the *Clare Freeman* of 9 July 1849 and the *Limerick & Clare Examiner* of 11 July 1849, which reported that 'Denis Beehan [*sic*] had become a bankrupt in the previous year'.

Ultimately, the collapse of Behan's business facilitated the continued expansion of the Glynn enterprise.

Behan's downfall illustrates that Kilrush was home to businesses comparable to the Glynn enterprise, and that by 1858 Glynn was sufficiently financially robust to expend £940 to acquire Behan's stores.[29] In 1860, a writer to the *Tipperary Vindicator* reported on the progress of Kilrush and noted that 'the Square contains several well-stocked shops, a market place and a fine market hall … and it is within living memory that it was a "mere fishing village" but its progress has been unusually rapid'.[30] The prosperity experienced in the town led to new mills being founded from the mid- to late nineteenth century and Glynn faced ongoing competition from other emergent middle-class entrepreneurs. The firm's main local rivals were Andrew Ryan & Sons, who set up business in 1869 and Garett O'Doherty & Sons who emerged in 1890. The former was a corn and flour miller and wholesaler and traded successfully until the mid-twentieth century. The latter began as a retailer and diversified into saw milling, and is still in operation at the time of writing, though no longer in the ownership of the O'Doherty family. The rise of the Glynns was impeded in some ways, and local rivalries coupled with protracted legal disputes with the local gentry hampered their ascent.

Where the Glynn enterprise differed from that of local rivals was in its ability to diversify its product range and embrace innovation in communication and technology, which was in turn put to good use in terms of expansion of the business. The river Shannon provided the Glynn business with such opportunities for diversification and the family established a significant presence on the river from the 1850s in order to facilitate its trade and export its corn beyond its main trading centre at Limerick city. Between the 1850s and 1900, the Glynns had up to eight vessels plying on the river and this must have prompted Henry Glynn to establish the Shannon Steamship Company in 1903. The utilization of the river was often a necessary component in nineteenth-century business expansion, and was evident in advertisements for provincial business premises, in centres other than Kilrush. For instance, the sale of an extensive milling concern in New Ross, Co. Wexford in 1831, noted that it was 'on the banks of the river Barrow, navigable above the shores for five-hundred tonnes'.[31] Similarly, in Galway in 1855 a large brewery was offered for sale, the advertisement noting that it 'contains many local advantages and is located at Nun's Island … and enjoys the benefit of a good water supply'.[32]

Modern developments in shipping technology had facilitated the commercial reach of the Glynn enterprise, which had a number of steamships at its disposal. While there is some confusion as to the exact date of the establishment of the Shannon Steamship Company, it appears that the Glynns had an extensive presence on the river from the mid-nineteenth century; however, their interest was

29 Registry of Deeds, 11 Feb. 1858, B. 4. 300 (contemporary reference); Glynn archive, box 5 (1850–60). 30 *Tipperary Vindicator*, 30 Apr. 1861. 31 *Dublin Mercantile Advertiser and Weekly Price Current*, 16 May 1831. 32 *General Advertiser for Dublin and All Ireland*, 18 Aug. 1855.

not consolidated into a limited company until 1903. A surviving company minute book from 1919 described the process of establishing the business: '[T]he Company is a Private Company within the meaning of Section 121 of the Companies (Consolidation) Act, 1908.'[33] This expansion granted access to previously untapped cross-Channel markets, particularly the important ports of Liverpool and Glasgow. Glynn capitalized on the growth in the tonnage of shipping leaving Ireland, which grew rapidly from the late eighteenth century until the mid-1870s.[34] This fits the picture drawn by Graeme Milne, who has examined the factors that affected trade in Liverpool in the 1850s. In the context of trade with Ireland, he noted that 'Irish corn traders ... found themselves central players in the famine crisis, as old patterns of emigration and food supply across the Irish Sea had to be urgently merged with a much wider overseas trading environment.'[35]

The range and diversity of products and commodities traded between Kilrush and Limerick and then exported to the British markets provides further insight into the importance of the Shannon to the economic development of the west of Ireland. Added to this was the multiplicity of associated occupations that were required in the production of commodities; sectors providing much employment in Kilrush included agriculture, fishing and food processing, while the primary exports from the port included, but were not restricted to, corn, pigs, butter and turf.[36] In 1885 it was reported that '[A]t Kilrush there were 496 vessels, the inward tonnage being 8,026 and the outward 1,820; the traffic inwards was principally coal, wheat and flour ... the outward traffic was chiefly pigs and cattle.'[37]

While official figures of the exact tonnage of cargo landed by the Glynns at Kilrush are not available, a note recorded by Henry Richard Glynn in 1910 provides an alternative source and gives hints of the competition faced by the Kilrush enterprise. Glynn stated that '[W]e are now bringing cargo [on] cross-channel steamers of 7/800 tons to Cappa Quay (Kilrush pier), Kilrush and then sailing it fifty miles inland, the other quays of the county only take steamers half this size.'[38] Several Irish steamship companies were in operation from the 1830s and although their headquarters were based in other locations, most of these served the Shannon estuary. Companies such as the City of Dublin Steam-Packet Steamship Company (1823), Waterford Steamship Company (1836) and Limerick Steamship Company (1896) all competed with Glynn's shipping business for lucrative contracts on the river. Competition from Kilrush-based firms was also

33 Minute book of the Shannon Steamship Company, 5 June 1903 to 8 Aug. 1934; Glynn family archive, box 11 (1910–20). 34 Peter M. Solar, 'Shipping and economic development in nineteenth-century Ireland', *Economic History Review*, n.s., 59:4 (2006), pp 717–42. 35 Milne, *Trade and traders in mid-Victorian Liverpool*, p. 52. 36 Poster, the Shannon Act, 1885, 'Quayage and wharfage, payable at Kilrush pier'. The notice contains the cost of importing or exporting a range of products, including: pigs, sheep, horses, cattle, corn, meal, flour, ballast and coal; Glynn archive, box 8 (1880–90). 37 *Shannon navigation bill: report from the select committee together with the proceedings of the committee, minutes of evidence and appendix*, H.C. 1885 [183] 1, vol. 12. 38 Carbon copy of telegram, 12 Feb. 1910; Glynn archive, box 11 (1910–20). 39 Postcard advertising the sailing of a Ford Line ship from the City Quay, Dublin to Kilrush on 22 July 1910; Glynn archive, box 11 (1910–20).

inevitable, and the rival firm Ryans held a shipping agency for the Ford Line, which operated vessels between Dublin and Kilrush from about 1870 to 1910.[39]

Michael Glynn cast some light on this competition when giving evidence before the House of Commons select committee on the Shannon navigation bill in 1885, the purpose of which was to 'deal with the piers on the river Shannon and to transfer control of piers to a local authority'. The first witness to be examined was Charles Frederick Green, the assistant engineer to the Board of Works and who described works done to Kilrush pier in 1869: '[A] new storehouse was built along with a waiting room and a toll collector's office, estimates were heard for extending the pier at a cost of £8,000.'[40] Michael Glynn was described as a 'miller, woollen manufacturer and merchant' and was examined by the chairman, who suggested that 'he had the monopoly of 150 feet on the best part of the pier'.[41] Glynn agreed with this statement and explained his position as 'one steamer pays two shillings for a double run, while another pays three shillings for a double run … the cargo they carry is then charged at 1.5 pence per ton'.[42]

This increased competition on the river led to the emergence of bitter rivalries between the various steamship companies, and Glynn seems to have been embroiled in a constant legal battle with the Waterford Steamship Company (W.S. Co.). A detailed account of the latter's business was recorded by Glynn as evidence in a dispute in 1911. Glynn noted that

> In 1894, the W.S. Co. began a coasting steamer service from Dublin to the south west of Ireland including Tralee, Kilrush and Tarbert … [T]he W.S. Co. also owned the service between Waterford, Liverpool and Bristol so that all traffic from the Shannon Estuary was sent via Waterford. The company also owned the Limerick S.S. Co., which traded principally between Limerick and Liverpool, by direct steamer.[43]

From the beginning, Glynn's capacity to publicize his shipping enterprise was obvious, as he actively advertised his steamship company in the provincial press and numerous notices informed the public of specific cargoes, sailing times and special excursions. During a court case in 1860, in which Michael Glynn was a co-defendant, he stated that he had previously advertised in the *Clare Journal* but owing to existing circumstances he was withdrawing his custom from that paper.[44] However, by 1870, Glynn began to advertise in the provincial press once more.

By diversifying their range of business interests, the Glynns positioned their firm as the 'largest employer in the district' and this continued to be the case for the ensuing one hundred years, the milling section of their enterprise employing upwards of 130 men. An examination of newspaper advertisements for similar west

40 *Shannon navigation bill: report from the select committee together with the proceedings of the committee, minutes of evidence and appendix*, H.C. 1885 [183] 1, vol. 12. 41 Ibid. 42 Ibid. 43 Six-page, typed copy of evidence submitted on behalf of M. Glynn & Sons to unknown party, 25 Jan. 1911; Glynn archive, box 11 (1910–20). 44 *Limerick Reporter*, 23 Oct. 1860.

Clare firms that were dependent on the river confirms that the Shannon artery remained a vital conduit for the transport of cargo and passengers. What is remarkable is that even after the advent of the West Clare Railway in 1892, individual traders and larger firms such as the Glynns continued to invest in shipping to service their business needs. A useful illustration of minor-scale investment in local shipping is provided by L. McAuliffe, a farmer and fisherman from Knock, a small fishing village some 12 miles south-west from Kilrush, who put a steamship in operation on the river in 1889 for the conveyance of fish to Limerick.[45] The subsequent fate of McAuliffe's investment is not clear: it may well have been surpassed by the railway, although there is no evidence to support this theory. However, the success of Glynn's shipping enterprise was noted in 1904 by F.M. Fitt, who remarked to Glynn that '[Y]our route by steamer from Limerick to Kilrush is one of the main routes to Clare and the principal route to South Clare.' This success was also boosted by a solid base of family control: the company minute book in 1903 listed Henry, William, Charles, Jane and Florence Glynn as the shareholders, in addition to Herbert Wright, John C. Ryan and William de Courcy – all of whom were in-laws.[46] Glynn's investment in river transport continued to grow throughout the early part of the twentieth century and by 1907, the steamship company was valued at the considerable sum of £40,000.[47] Lucrative cargo contracts with companies such as Guinness of Dublin, the bacon firm Mattersons in Limerick and Dwyers' fuels of Cork all boosted the profits of the Shannon Steamship Company, and ultimately of the Glynn enterprise. For example, from 6–8 August 1918, Glynn signed contracts worth £83 11*s.* per week to the company.[48]

During the First World War (1914–18), Glynn's Shannon Steamship Company took over the Steam Packet Service to Kildysart, a town located some 30 miles south-west of Kilrush. In 1917, the firm purchased a steamer, the *Turk*, from J. Bianconi JP and the proprietor of the Kildysart Steam Packet Service, for £1,500.[49] In addition to his steam-packet service, Bianconi was recorded as a 'farmer, miller and merchant' in the census of 1911. The continuing capital investment indicated both the importance of the river and the entrepreneurial spirit in the ongoing success of the firm.[50] The Shannon Steamship Company's fleet of eight ships on the Shannon represented a major investment in terms of both capital and employment. In addition, the company acquired the 'interest of some public carriers on the river, and employed the captains and owners of the smacks ... to become public carriers'.[51] The costs of such expansion were not small: the average

45 *Clare Journal*, 27 May 1889. 46 F.M. Fitt, solicitor to Henry Richard Glynn, Shannon Steamship Ltd, minute book (1903–34); Glynn archive, box 10 (1900–10). 47 Henry Richard Glynn, typed note, 1907; Glynn archive, box 10 (1900–10). 48 Shannon Steamship Company Ltd, invoices for carriage of goods, 6–8 Aug. 1918; Glynn archive, box 11 (1910–20). 49 Shannon Steamship Company Ltd, minute book, 20 June 1917; Glynn archive, box no. 11 (1910–20). 50 *Clare Journal*, 27 Jan. 1917. 51 Six-page typed copy of evidence submitted on behalf of M. Glynn & Sons to unknown party, 25 Jan. 1911, the vessels were the SS *Start*, SS *Leven, Bella, Mary Anne, John Thomas*

cost of a second-hand steamer (six of the Glynn ships were second-hand) was approximately £2,000 by the late nineteenth century. However, such investments meant increased local employment. While the numbers of men employed on each steamer varied, the available evidence suggests an average of ten men per ship. Goggin has noted that based on some passing references to the crew of the *Garryowen* operated by the City of Dublin Steam-Packet Company,

> there must have had at least a captain, engineer and helmsman. The captain could give hand signals to the helmsman, but not to the engineer, and could not be heard by the engineer … therefore that information was carried to the engineer by a messenger boy or man, also on board was a least one stoker or engine-room hand, a musician (probably self-employed), a mate and deckhands to manage the sails, mooring and so on, giving a total of approximately ten crew.[52]

The Ordnance Survey maps of *c.*1840 and *c.*1890 provide the best means to trace the development of Glynn's mill complex itself. The 1840s map shows that the complex comprised just four large granaries, and a few smaller structures. It was located at the end of the town beside the river and did not include any noticeable infrastructure. However, by the time the town was surveyed in the 1890s, a massive expansion and development of the site had been undertaken. The mill complex had been extended considerably to include over thirty structures. The railway siding and station are visible and the area was now clearly marked 'Merchant's Quay'. The previously under-utilized river had also been dredged so that boats could tie up alongside the mills and grain stores.[53] A mill race, which supplied water that powered the steam mill, was also installed.

Similarly, when the town is examined for the same fifty year period, the rate of development is staggering. This is broadly in line with the experience of other provincial Irish towns, such as Wexford, which witnessed the building of shops, timber yards, grain stores and warehouses in the mid-nineteenth century, and Castlerea in Co. Roscommon.[54] By 1846, the latter boasted a well-established professional class comprised of attorneys, architects and doctors. In addition, the town was home to distillers, millers and coach builders.[55] Entrepreneurial middle-class merchants were firmly established in Irish provincial towns by the mid-

and *Rose*. Glynn archive, box 11 (1910–20). **52** The Dublin Steam-Packet Company launched the *Garryowen* in 1835; *Saunders's Newsletter*, 15 June 1835. The author is grateful to Irish waterways historian Brian J. Goggin for making me aware of the information regarding the crews of the steamers. See Glynn workmen's wage books, which include entries for two of their ships from 1915: the *Corona* had a crew of eight, while the *Bella* had just one crew member; NLI, Business Records Survey (Glynn & Shannon Steamship Company Collection, Code CL4). **53** *Freeman's Journal*, 20 Aug. 1897; *Irish Times*, 29 Jan. 1898. **54** Kevin Whelan, 'Wexford' in Anngret Simms and J.H. Andrews (eds) *More Irish country towns* (Cork, 1995), p. 201. See also the *Dublin Mercantile Advertiser and Weekly Price Current*, which advertised the sale of an 'extensive brewery, malt house and corn store' in New Ross, Co. Wexford, 16 May 1831. **55** *Slater's Directory*, 1846.

nineteenth century. For instance, by 1846 Bandon in Co. Cork boasted ten corn millers and two cotton spinners; Dungarvan in Co. Waterford counted butter merchants, coal dealers and corn merchants among its commercially minded inhabitants.[56] The entrepreneurial endeavour of the middle class was also evident in Ballinalsoe, Co. Galway, and by 1862, the *Penny Despatch and Irish Weekly Newspaper* noted that 'one of the leading millers at Ballinalsoe had shipped considerable oaten meal to Liverpool'.[57]

Glynn was typical of this entrepreneurial class. Foreman-Peck, Boccaletti and Nicholas have argued that

> However we define the entrepreneur, risk and innovation are involved. An entrepreneur is someone who takes advantage of opportunities not perceived by others, or makes use of information more quickly. In an economy with well-defined and well-enforced property rights, such business acumen will improve resource allocation and raise productivity.[58]

The activities of the firm during the period of the Great Famine (1845–51) remain unclear, as there is gap in the Glynn family archive from the period, though whether that gap is due to accident or to the deliberate removal of material as a way of guarding the family's reputation remains unclear.[59] In the absence of archival material, newspapers remain the only source as to the economic activities of the Glynn family during the 1840s, and these random references indicate that business continued to thrive. For instance, in 1846, the *Limerick and Clare Examiner* noted that 'Bartholomew Glynn exported 100 firkins of butter and 1,032 quarts of oats for the London market.'[60] In 1850, Glynn was also recorded as purchasing, along with three other Kilrush merchants, 'upwards of six hundred firkins of butter from forty to forty-two shillings each at the Butter Market in Milltown [*sic*] Malbay, Co. Clare'.[61] In 1846, the abolition of the Corn Laws, despite causing damage to the economics of Glynn's enterprise, did not undermine its success.

In terms of charitable activities during the years of the Famine, there is no evidence available to suggest that Glynn was involved in or contributed to local relief committees. Kilrush was serviced by a workhouse, which had opened on 9 July 1842. This was complemented by the creation of up to eight auxiliary workhouses during the Famine years. The composition of the Kilrush Poor Law Board was typical – it was an amalgam of landed proprietors and local merchants. In 1847, Crofton Moore Vandeleur acted as chairman; he was assisted by William

56 Ibid. 57 *Penny Despatch & Irish Weekly Newspaper*, 31 May 1862. 58 James Foreman-Peck, Elisa Boccaletti and Tom Nicholas, 'Entrepreneurs and business performance in nineteenth-century France', *European Review of Economic History*, 2 (1998), pp 235–62. 59 That there is an obvious gap in the records for the period of the Great Famine suggests that papers were removed. 60 *Limerick & Clare Examiner*, 21 Oct. 1846. Glynn was not the only Kilrush merchant to export during the crisis years of the Famine. Contained in the same report is the following information: William Blair exported 1,302 quarts of oats; both Joseph Moody and John Walsh exported 100 firkins of butter; and Michael McMahon dispatched 63 firkins of butter. 61 *Limerick & Clare Examiner*, 18 Sept. 1850. Glynn was

Foley, a doctor; Francis Keane, a land agent; Jeremiah Dowling, a pawnbroker; and Denis Hynes, a grocer and spirit merchant.[62] No member of the Glynn family served as a poor law guardian during the Famine years, and this is puzzling as their peers both in business and in status acted as members of the local poor law board. The available documentary evidence does not indicate why the Glynn family were excluded from its membership. Neither is there an explanation provided as to why Glynn did not tender for lucrative contracts to supply the workhouse with some of his products. Regular notices appeared in local newspapers of successful tenders to supply everything from flour, oatmeal and barley to moleskin, calico and cotton, but Glynn was not mentioned in these.[63] By the late 1840s, Glynn was certainly in a position to supply the former to the workhouse and as noted earlier, he was active in business during the years of the Famine. Supplementary evidence confirms that the business continued to be profitable during the period – as suggested by a number of leases in the Glynn family collection.[64] The leases generated for this period also suggest that despite the effects of the Famine, the town of Kilrush remained an attractive option not only to tourists, as discussed elsewhere, but also to outside investors and speculators. When Glynn purchased the mill buildings from Mrs Jones, also mentioned in the transaction were other businessmen from Dublin and Cork and a bank manager from Tipperary.[65] The appearance of investors and speculators from outside Kilrush confirms Lewis' description of the town as being 'convenient for export trade to which it owes its present importance' was justified.[66] In addition to property speculators, new business initiatives were established during the early 1850s. For instance, the *Cork Examiner* noted that 'a powerful steam boat belonging to the Cork Steam Packet Company arrived in Kilrush yesterday, and commences to ply between Limerick and Kilrush'.[67] Similarly, the *Irish Industrial Journal* reported on the activities of the Messrs Franklin, enterprising operators of thirteen mines throughout Britain. In 1850, it established a commercial venture in Kilrush and its quarry 'produces large and valuable flags of excellent quality … , the Messrs Franklin have chartered a vessel to take the Kilrush flags to New York'.[68] In addition to local investment in Kilrush, the *Dublin Evening Packet and Correspondent* described the town as 'a large and improving town on the Clare side of the Shannon. From which an extensive and increasing export trade is carried on.'[69] Such descriptions of enterprise and

not listed as a butter merchant in any available trade directory. **62** *Clare Journal and Ennis Advertiser*, 27 Sept. 1847; *Slater's Directory*, 1846. **63** For a selection of advertisements relating to the supply of foodstuffs and related items to the Kilrush Union Workhouse, see *Limerick & Clare Examiner*, 3 May 1849, 7 July 1849 and 2 Nov. 1850. **64** There are a number of leases in the family papers for the period (1845–52): copy of lease between Crofton Moore Vandeleur esq. and Bartholomew Glynn, merchant for houses and premises in Henry Street in the town of Kilrush from 25 Mar. 1846, yearly rent of £3 4*s*.; assignment of dwelling houses and premises in the town of Kilrush and county of Clare, 3 July 1850. **65** Lease, Jones to Glynn, 3 July 1850; Glynn family archive, box 5 (1850–60). **66** Lewis, *A topographical dictionary of Ireland*, p. 204. **67** *Cork Examiner*, 2 Sept. 1850. **68** *The Advocate; or, Irish Industrial Journal*, 6 Feb. 1850. **69** *Dublin Evening Packet and Correspondent*, 11 Nov. 1851.

development of the local economy challenge the assumption that the economic experience of Kilrush during the Famine years was one of stagnation and austerity.

Undoubtedly, it was James Paterson's early business model – his twin investments in milling and shipping – that provided the template worked upon by Bartholomew Glynn and his descendants. But Paterson's family enterprise did not last as long. In 1846, Paterson was recorded as a miller in a trade directory. However, in the same year, the *Clare Journal* noted his death: '[A]t Kilrush, James Paterson, Esq. This estimable gentleman, who was a native of Argyllshire, in 1798, commanded one of the gunboats then protecting the Irish coast from a foreign foe.'[70] Paterson's descendant, Angus Campbell, has speculated that 'the determining factor for the dispersal of the family was down to their chosen careers of the sons or the marriages of the daughters. Another significant factor has been the deaths of all the male heirs in the male line.'[71] Some of the Paterson sons cultivated careers in the military and the merchant navy, and the daughters married into landed families such as the Burtons of Carrigaholt Castle, Co. Clare and the Spaights of Derry Castle, Nenagh, Co. Tipperary. Several of the family ended up living in Scotland:

> Irwin was the best bet to continue the family presence in Kilrush as he was running the business but he seemed to be in conflict with his brother-in-law, Francis Spaight. He died in Scotland in 1872, pre-deceased by his son, Crawford in 1851. Sarah married Anthony Pierce Pack and she died in Scotland at Duncan's estate. Francis Spaight seemed to have been mercenary in his business dealings and most of the family assets seemed to end up with him [in Limerick].[72]

A further potential explanation for the decline of Paterson's myriad of enterprises in Kilrush was that the business was stretched too far in terms of diversification. For example, the distilling business opened in 1839 and ceased trading in 1845. This was in stark contrast to the Glynn family who maintained a presence in the town for over two hundred years. It may be that this success was due to the Glynn family's settlement patterns, which suggest that even though some family members, particularly the women, married out of the town from the 1880s, the male line continued to make Kilrush their main base for raising their families and – most importantly – operating their businesses. The family business provided employment for sons, whereas the daughters were generally guaranteed a generous marriage settlement, or if they remained single were cared for by brothers.[73]

70 *Clare Journal*, 3 Aug. 1846. Despite an exhaustive search, the location of the Paterson family grave has not been discovered. 71 Email correspondence with Angus Campbell, who is James Paterson's direct descendant and is writing a history of the family. 72 Ibid. 73 This contradicts the memory of Josephine Glynn, who commented that when her parents were married in 1918 and took up residence in Kilrush House, the two old unmarried aunts living in the house were 'shipped out' to Dublin. Interview with Josephine Glynn of Kilrush, Co. Clare (5 May 2011).

The documentary evidence does not suggest that family control of the business was diluted in any way: certainly, the business relationship that had existed between Paterson and Vandeleur was not in any way replicated between Glynn and Vandeleur. Aside from the latter's name being on each lease or deed, there is no evidence in the archive to suggest that he entered into or conducted business with Glynn. The two families – landlord and merchant – were not, however, natural enemies. An examination of contemporary local newspapers shows that the Vandeleurs and Glynns maintained an amicable though distant relationship both in terms of business dealings and social engagements. Ultimately, though, the two families ended up in the courts and the House of Lords after a lengthy legal battle.[74]

Secure and supportive family networks were the best way of raising capital and keeping costs such as labour to a minimum. This is where the Glynn business differed from that of Paterson who had courted financial support from Vandeleur. While there is no documentary evidence available to confirm that Vandeleur directly funded Paterson in his business investments, Mason reported in 1814 that 'Paterson met with the attention and encouragement from Mr Vandeleur, which he merited.' Inter-generational success of family businesses in the nineteenth century has been well-documented.[75] In her research into the structure of sibling partnerships in small Victorian firms, Nenadic has noted that 'male sibling partnerships were more usual than father and son partnerships, but rates of business survival were similarly poor, and it was not unusual for one brother to emerge dominant and in possession of the firm, whilst the second faded from the scene.'[76]

Glynn's will of 1854, although largely formulaic, offers an insight into inheritance trends in a propertied self-made family such as the Glynns. It attested to the wealth he had accumulated in a relatively short period of time in business and it was reflective of the broader aspirations and achievements of the provincial middle class in their business endeavours. Glynn was a far-sighted businessman and he left substantial property and money to his children. His sons John and Michael each inherited several houses and the milling concerns as well as a sum of money. His daughters Ann and Bridget inherited their houses and his son-in-law Andrew Madigan also received some property. Interestingly, there is no mention of a dowry payment for his unmarried daughter Bridget.[77] The distance maintained by Glynn in respect of the clergy was also evidenced in the meagre

74 This involved a court case taken against M. Glynn & Sons, millers, by Hector Stewart Vandeleur, landlord. The dispute concerned the Glynns' withholding of quayage, wharfage and tolls in response to Vandeleur's allegedly negligent upkeep of Kilrush Creek and the harbour. The case lasted 1886–1907, ultimately being referred to the House of Lords in 1907, which ruled in favour of Vandeleur; Glynn court documents; Glynn archive, box 8 (1880–90); 9 (1890–1900); 10 (1900–10). 75 For a discussion of the history of family businesses see Andrea Colli, *The history of family business, 1850–2000* (Cambridge, 2003), while the topic of succession is examined by Ivan Lansberg, *Succeeding generations: realizing the dream of families in business* (Boston, 1995). 76 Nenadic, 'The small family firm in Victorian Britain', pp 86–114. 77 Last will and testament of Bartholomew Glynn, 26 July 1854; Glynn archive, box 5 (1850–60). As the will was made before 1858, it was not required to include

amount of money he left to the church: '[U]nto my parish clergyman, the Reverend Timothy Kelly for his spiritual attendance I leave the sum of three pounds sterling and also the sum of one pound sterling to each of his curates.' Although Bartholomew Glynn was primarily focused on establishing and securing his business interests, it was through such provision that the family members, collectively and individually, ultimately became the de facto leaders of Kilrush.[78]

The difference between the family-centeredness of the Glynns' approach to sourcing credit and investment is therefore contrasted with the reliance on outsiders by Paterson. There is no evidence of any external or non-family investment in the Glynn enterprise. The first generation to run the business was that of Bartholomew Glynn (1775–1855) and he did this on his own. The second generation initially operated the business as a partnership, but this was dissolved by mutual agreement and Michael Glynn purchased his brother John's share of the company for £450. Thereafter, the firm became known as 'M. Glynn & Sons'.[79] In 1855, the *London Gazette* listed John Glynn as a 'flour dealer', which suggests that he established his own milling business in the town. However, there is no information contained in the family papers regarding his business venture. The extensive family pedigree recorded his marriage but in respect of the family firm, his involvement disappeared from the company records from the date of the dissolution of the partnership in 1857. However, though his will reflects little of his personal entrepreneurship or of his family's rapid advancement, Bartholomew Glynn's resources were substantial enough for his two sons to continue (separately) in business and become successful merchants in their own right. The dissolution of their partnership arrangement seems unusual for a family-operated firm as 'family networks were usually critical in terms of capital investment'.[80] Dynasty building was fundamental to the way in which provincial mills operated. However, there does seem to have been some provision made for the arrangement in the will of their father, Bartholomew – a further indication of his business acumen and foresight:

> Should my sons at any time hereafter think it advisable to divide the said corn store … they may enter into an amicable arrangement by casting tolls and the person favoured by these tolls … shall pay onto the other the sum of four hundred pounds sterling which shall be deemed a sufficient discharge to any claim to said corn store …[81]

a list of debts or provide an overall figure for the value of his estate. This practice was changed in 1858 with the Probate Act. **78** Ibid. **79** C.E. Glynn, typed two-page account of the origin of 'Glynn Kilrush' (13 Jan. 1934); Glynn archive, box 13 (1930–40). See also the *London Gazette*, 28 Feb. 1855. **80** Andy Bielenberg (ed.), *Irish flour milling: a history, 600–2000* (Dublin, 2003), p. 98. **81** Last will and testament of Bartholomew Glynn, 26 July 1854; Glynn archive, box 5 (1850–60). The meaning of the phrase 'casting tolls' remains elusive. The solicitor Ciara Comerford suggested the following: 'I've never heard the expression but from how it reads I would guess that it might be the equivalent of casting lots/drawing straws.'

4. Postcard showing the milling concerns of the Glynns, *c*.1940s.

The ensuing expansion and success of the firm was largely due to the efforts of Michael Glynn (1818–89), who oversaw the development of the Shannon Steamship Company and ensured its contribution to the consolidation and monopolization of trade on the Shannon in favour of the firm. An insight into Michael Glynn's comfortable financial position was provided by a remark he made to his brother-in-law William Lane-Joynt. Commenting in 1860 on his application for a £3,000 loan from a provincial bank, Glynn confidentially noted that 'I don't care much about their potentially refusing me as I can just enter the National [Bank] and draw as I did last season to the tune of £3,000.'[82] Glynn's comment confirms that merchants of his status and position had ready access to established sources of credit by the mid-nineteenth century. The National Bank, co-founded by Daniel O'Connell in 1835, seemed tailor-made for the Glynns' needs since it aimed 'both to provide capital for Irish economic development and to serve the needs of small traders and tenant farmers, as well as those of the gentry'.[83] The loan application required Glynn to furnish the details of all property both tenanted and untenanted in his ownership and to include the rateable value and rental income that they realized. The total number of properties stood at eight, all of which were tenanted.[84] It seems reasonable to assume that the loan was used as the outlay to

82 Copy of letter to William Lane-Joynt from Michael Glynn, 19 Oct. 1860; Glynn archive, box 5 (1850–60). 83 Royal Bank of Scotland, 'National Bank Ltd', heritagearchives.rbs.com/companies/list/the-national-bank-ltd.html, accessed 12 Jan. 2015. 84 Instructions for the loan of £3,000 from the National Bank to Michael Glynn esq., merchant of Kilrush, including a list of property in the town of Kilrush in the barony of Moyarta, Co. Clare, 22 Sept. 1860. The document described eight

purchase the lease for the remaining mill premises – Kelly's Store to the west – in early 1861.[85] This store was the third of the three large five-storey grain stores that had been built by previous merchants, some of whom failed in their enterprises and some of whom sold their interest to Glynn. The tall corn store towards the left was originally Foley's Store, and the tall building towards the right was originally Behan's Store. These buildings date from the late 1830s, per leases and insurance maps in the Glynn archive. These stores are visible in fig. 4.

Not content with their regional expansion into Limerick milling, Glynn moved into wool production, founding extensive carding mills by the late 1870s.[86] This was followed by the establishment of the Kilrush Woollen Factory in 1879, which offered an extensive product range:

> Tweeds, serges, friezes, flannels and blankets which are made from pure wool and the finish and durability of which cannot be excelled. Any quantity of the above can be had at their factory at exceedingly low prices for cash or in exchange for wool. All colours and shades in dyeing done on the premises together with carding scouring finishing.[87]

The firms' investment in the woollen industry occurred at a time when factory-produced wool was enjoying a resurgence following a long decline in the industry. While the Glynns appeared confident to invest in the woollen industry, locally the enterprise had resulted in failure for another individual. In 1872, the *Clare Journal* carried a notice informing the public of the winding up of Charles Copeland's Kilrush Woollen Factory.[88] Andy Bielenberg has shown that in the case of Cork significant growth occurred in the industry in the second half of the nineteenth century, and that 'the number of mills in the county had risen to twenty-three by 1904 … the number of hands employed ranged between two and three thousand people'.[89] Employment figures for the Glynns' operation in Kilrush are unavailable, although the woollen factory was still in production in 1920, when the building was surveyed for the installation of electricity.[90] The woollen factory tendered for a number of contracts in Limerick and the *Clare Journal* noted in 1886 that 'the Limerick Lunatic Asylum accepted the tender of M. Glynn & Sons for the supply of frieze and tweed'.[91] Also in 1886, the Kilrush Woollen Mills was

properties that realized a total net value of £179 10*s*. 1*d*.; Glynn archive, box 6 (1860–70). **85** John Kelly, merchant to Michael Glynn esq., lease dated 24 Jan. 1861; Glynn archive, box 6 (1860–70). **86** The date that the carding mill was founded is unclear but the term 'extensive carding mill' was added to the firm's letterhead in the late 1870s; Glynn archive, box 6 (1860–70). **87** *Kilrush Herald and Kilkee Gazette*, 25 May 1889. See also *Cork Examiner*, 1 Aug. 1885, Glynns advertised for a 'woollen factory blue and fancy dyer'. **88** *Clare Journal*, 1 July 1872. **89** Andy Bielenberg, *Cork's industrial revolution, 1780–1880: development or decline?* (Cork, 1991), p. 38. **90** Schedule of charges prepared by Ferguson and Bruty, Dublin for the installation of electrical power to M. Glynn & Sons, Kilrush, 9 Jan. 1920. A description of the woollen factory is as follows: card fitting shop, card fitting entrance, carding mill, first, second and third floors, loft; Glynn archive, box 12 (1920–30). **91** *Clare Journal*, 23 Dec. 1886.

represented at the Viceregal Garden Party in Dublin, which had as its theme 'Irish-made dress material'. This event was designed to promote 'Irish manufacture to suit the varied tastes of Irish ladies'.[92] The party featured women and boys dressed in clothes made of everything from tweeds to poplin silk. The report in the *Freeman's Journal* noted that '[T]he Kilrush Woollen Factory of Messrs Glynn & Sons sends white, black, blue, brown and green hand and tucked flannels, heavy serges and a variety of suit tweeds.'[93] Careful accounting and monitoring of production, coupled with stringent stock control prevented the woollen factory from incurring serious debt, a point noted by the company auditor, who also cautioned that: 'Your audit informs us that the books are well kept … your stock at the present time is £2,402 … and your sales for the year only amounted to £2,255 … [Y]our sales should be increased or your stock reduced.'[94] However, sales must have increased as the following year in 1891, the firm placed an advertisement in the national press for 'power loom weavers'.[95]

The growing tourist industry of the 1840s offered a further opportunity for the Glynn firm to expand its interests. As noted earlier, Michael Glynn diversified his business interests to include railway investments. First proposed in 1840, the railway scheme connecting Kilrush to the national network took fifty-two years to be realized, and the Dublin Steam-Packet Company in the meantime considered building a railway between Kilrush and Kilkee to facilitate the thriving passenger service on the Shannon.[96] In the expanding tourist industry, Kilkee was a pivotal element. Located some 8 miles north of Kilrush, Kilkee was developed as a Victorian beach resort from the mid-1840s. In 1859, the *Irish Times* reported that 'there are two conveyances to Kilkee, one by boat from the quay of Limerick, the other is by rail to Foynes, and thence by the *Kelpic* steamer to Kilrush'.[97] The remainder of the journey was made on horse-drawn jaunting cars from Kilrush pier.[98] Travel by steamer was lucrative for the operators and after the railway to Foynes opened in 1858 the *Kelpic* ran mainly from Foynes to Kilrush. In her first four months, she carried 14,000 passengers with takings of £80 per week.[99] It was suggested that the steamship operators should place 'two-horse drawn vehicles on the road for the conveyance of passengers only by the steam packet, as a protection against the private car-drivers who have raised the charge to 1*s*. 6*d*. a head'.[100] Though the burden of providing these vehicles was to be absorbed by the travelling

92 *Freeman's Journal*, 8 Apr. 1886. 93 Ibid. Other companies who contributed to the party included the Athlone Woollen Mills, Blarney Tweed Mills and the Simpson Vale Mills, Bailieboro, Co. Cavan. 94 Gardner & Co. Auditors and Accountants to Messrs Glynn & Sons, Woollen Manufacturers, 30 Sept. 1890; Glynn archive, box 9 (1890–1900). 95 *Freeman's Journal*, 25 July 1891. 96 Ignatius Murphy, *Before the Famine struck: life in west Clare, 1834–1845* (Dublin, 1990), p. 19. 97 *Irish Times*, 12 July 1859; *Nenagh Guardian*, 18 Aug. 1858. 98 Ignatius Murphy, 'The Kilrush-Kilkee Railway and the reclamation of Poulnasherry Bay', *The Other Clare*, 6 (1982), p. 16. 99 Senan Scanlan, 'Passenger services on the lower Shannon', Clare County Library, clarelibrary.ie/eolas/coclare/history/kilrush_notes_1760_1960/passenger_services.htm, accessed 7 Mar. 2013. 100 *Clare Journal*, 20 Aug. 1840.

public, the issue highlighted the lengths to which the steamship operators were willing to go in order to protect their businesses.

In any event, the 1840s railway project did not materialize and it was not until ten years later that a second proposal was announced. This second attempt in the 1850s attracted the support of the influential and pioneering railway contractor William Dargan, who confidently stated that he would 'undertake the building of the line and also build a monster hotel in Kilkee'.[101] Even though the local railway committee courted Dargan, nothing came of this plan until construction work finally began in 1863.[102] The Kilrush and Kilkee Railway and Poulnasherry Bay Reclamation Company placed advertisements in the Clare and Limerick newspapers stating that application forms for shares were now available.[103] The proposed reclamation of Poulnasherry Bay occupied the House of Commons in London for much of the late nineteenth century.[104] Ultimately, this early attempt at establishing the railway was abandoned in 1883 following the destruction of reclaimed slobland during a severe storm. The *Munster News* reported that 'the embankment ... was washed away ... the company could find the money to start the line but not to reconstruct the embankment'.[105]

This early attempt to connect Kilrush to the rapidly expanding national rail network was reflective of the modernization of communication and travel facilities in Ireland. During the 1840s the railway network experienced a massive expansion, from only 31.25 miles of track in 1847 to 1,700 miles in 1857.[106] Lee has noted that the railway 'increased the range of small, personal wants by distributing imports and Dublin goods throughout the countryside'.[107] Interestingly, the Glynn family were not involved at this stage in railway investment and while there is no documentary evidence to explain this, it may simply be that their funds were tied up in the recently established Shannon Steamship Company and their continued attempt to purchase the remaining buildings in the mill complex in Frances Street, Kilrush. The chief investors in the railways were the landed class and middle-class entrepreneurs, the former benefitting from the sale of the land through which the railways passed, the latter experiencing growth in sales as a result of the wider distribution of their products.[108] The committee of the Kilrush and Kilkee Railway and Poulnasherry Bay Reclamation Company in 1855 comprised individuals from the largest landowning families of west Clare. Of the eighteen member committee, 50 per cent had west Clare addresses, with the remainder spread from Ennis to

101 *Limerick Chronicle*, 20 Aug. 1856; *Freeman's Journal*, 11 Sept. 1856. **102** It is unclear why the second attempt at establishing the railway did not materialize but it was likely related to the slow process of passing bills and acts through parliament, which delayed its construction. **103** Ibid. See *Limerick Reporter*, 26 May 1840. **104** Kilrush and Kilkee Railway and Poulnasherry Reclamation Act 1860 (23 & 24 Vict.), c. clv; Kilrush and Kilkee Railway and Poulnasherry Reclamation Amendment Act 1861 (24 & 25 Vict.), c. xxix; Kilrush and Kilkee Railway and Poulnasherry Reclamation Act 1872 (35 & 36 Vict.), c. xc; Poulnasherry Reclamation Act 1884 (47 & 48 Vict.), c. ccxliii. **105** *Munster News*, 25 Aug. 1883. **106** Joseph Lee, 'The provision of capital for early Irish railways 1830–53', *Historical Studies*, 16:61 (Mar. 1968), p. 35. **107** Joseph Lee, *The modernisation of Irish society, 1848–1918* (Dublin, 1973), p. 13. **108** Murphy, 'The Kilrush-Kilkee railway', p. 16.

Limerick to Dublin. Seven were local magistrates, one was a hotel proprietor, one was a naval officer and three held landed estates in Co. Limerick – in fact, all members of the committee with the exception of two individuals held landed estates.[109]

By the 1880s, developments in railway expansion had resulted in the establishment of numerous companies, including the Dublin-based Great Southern and Western Railway, whose main line ran from the capital to Cork but also serviced provincial locations such as Carlow and Limerick.[110] In 1886, thirty years after the unsuccessful Dargan-backed initiative, Michael Glynn funded the mapping and surveying of the extension in the rail line to connect Kilrush and west Clare to the national network.[111] The firm had become heavily involved in railway investment from the early 1880s. As one of the largest rate-payers in the district, Glynn had been involved in the second railway committee from the outset. He understood the potential for the expansion in his trade and the commercial opportunities offered by railway freight. Glynn contracted an independent engineer to undertake a survey to estimate the costs involved in bringing the railway to Kilrush and west Clare. A surviving report documented the project. Glynn disputed the official costing for the project, which stood at £140,000, and an engineer he contracted countered with a costing of £120,000. Glynn offered to carry the entire cost of the project himself.[112] The official costing was reduced to match his revised estimate, and the project proceeded without Glynn having to put up the capital, but his readiness to do so clearly illustrates the man's entrepreneurial character, willingness to grasp every opportunity and eye to the future – all this despite the ill-health he suffered for most of his final years. The advent of the railway in Kilrush introduced several new product lines to Glynn's business interests, perhaps the most profitable of all being a contract to supply Guinness to the public houses and inns of west Clare. In 1892, the letterhead of the business changed to include an embellished illustration of its headquarters in Kilrush, showing the Great Southern and Western Railway passing by the front of their concern. This was in addition to a representation of steamships tied up alongside the slipway at the same location. Further county-wide expansion resulted in the establishment of offices at Ennistymon and Carrigaholt, 27 miles north and 14 miles west of Kilrush, respectively.

The meticulous and innovative business practices of Henry Glynn are evident in notes contained in his diaries. One such note concerned the large-scale milling firm of Bannatyne & Sons in Limerick city. Henry sought the advice of his father, Michael, who pointed out that business was based on personal contacts and said that 'Bannatyne brings the customer to him and that's how he turns a profit all the

109 *Limerick Reporter*, 25 Sept. 1855. Two of the committee members were also directors of the Foynes (Co. Limerick) Railway Company. **110** *Cork Examiner*, 16 Nov. 1846. **111** Henry Glynn diary entry, 3 Oct. 1895; Glynn archive, box 9 (1890–1900). **112** F.M. Fitt, 'Some plain statements about the South Clare Railway Company Limited made by F.M. Fitt, solicitor … the company was registered on 6 June 1884', p. 2; Glynn archive, box 8 (1880–90).

5. Updated letterhead of M. Glynn & Sons.[113]

time.'[114] Not content merely to follow the advice offered by his father, Henry also investigated the possibility of installing up-to-date technology in his mill in 1888 and undertook an assiduous research tour to this end. The first part of this tour was to Britain, where he familiarized himself with the latest 'roller-mill' innovations.[115] This technology was already available in other mills in Ireland and involved a considerable investment in new plant. An insight into Henry's personality and fastidious nature is gained from examining his extensive drawings and meticulous note-taking. He calculated the cost of each constituent part of the roller mill and was supplied with detailed quotes for equipment. He visited several engineering firms and interviewed engineers and proprietors. The firms spanned the length of England and included Robinsons of Rochdale, Carters of London and Donaldsons of Liverpool. The second part of his research tour involved drawing on his extensive Irish business network, including conversations with flour millers in Cork who had invested in the 'new technology'. An entry in his diary described how the process of networking occurred:

> I called to James O'Brien's office … he got me a letter of introduction to Hallinan's, Middleton from Mr Horgan, solicitor, Cork and to the O'Brien Brothers at St Patrick's Mills, Cork … who was among the first to erect a complete roller mill in Ireland … and whose opinion would I think be very valuable to us.[116]

Though he was engaged in researching flour-milling technology, Glynn seized the opportunity to inspect innovative practices within the broader field of Irish

113 Glynn archive, box 9 (1890–1900). **114** Henry Richard Glynn, diary entry, 14 Apr. 1888; Glynn archive, box 8 (1880–90). **115** Diary and notebook of Henry Richard Glynn, May to July 1888, box 8 (1880–90). **116** Ibid., p. 47.

manufacture. As part of his research, Glynn had free access to the workings of St Patrick's Woollen Mills in Cork, a company in competition with his own. He toured the Cork plant and was impressed by O'Brien's three nephews whom he described as 'three steady fellows who understand the business thoroughly, as two of them spent three years in factories in Scotland and the third [nephew] spent a year in a factory in Ireland'.[117] Glynn described the output and production methods of the factory: '[T]hey have 300 hands working the place and have £30,000 to £40,000 invested in the whole thing, they have forty double looms working and they intend extending everything in a very large scale.'[118] Jones has commented on technological advancements and noted that 'by the mid-1880s it was recognised that gradual reduction roller milling was replacing traditional flour-milling practice in the Britain, and this movement was clearly represented in Ireland'.[119] However, O'Brien had traded successfully since 1882, and he exported throughout Britain and the USA. That Glynn had such unhindered access to what were essentially rival firms illustrated the close-knit world of Irish industrialists in the late nineteenth century and further underlines the importance of business networking to the development of enterprise. On examining the relationships between these different milling enterprises, the ledgers, minute books and wage books provide a clear picture of the inter-connectivity and inter-dependency of Irish millers and suggests the existence of a shared knowledge and a professional understanding that promoted the interests of the industry.[120] Ultimately, Glynn hired the market-leading firm of Henry Simon Ltd of Manchester. The entire cost of the project, which included the 'machinery, plant and installation', stood at £3,400, a considerable investment in capital for the firm.[121] Following the installation of the roller milling technology, Glynn's became the most modern mill in Co. Clare.

CLIMBING THE LADDER

However, it was not just in capital and innovation that the firm invested and concentrated their energies. Simultaneously, Michael Glynn continued to improve the family's status and considerable influence beyond the sphere of industry. Bielenberg has noted that '[T]he increasingly grand houses of the elite, in both rural and suburban contexts, provide another manifestation of their improved position in the social landscape.'[122] Glynn followed this path, in 1886 purchasing

117 Diary and notebook of Henry Richard Glynn, May to July 1888; Glynn archive, box 8 (1880–90). **118** Henry R. Glynn, diary entry, 13 Jan. 1888; Glynn archive, box 8 (1880–90). See also Bielenberg, *Cork's industrial revolution*, p. 39. **119** Jones, 'The introduction and establishment of roller milling in Ireland' in Bielenberg (ed.), *Irish flour milling*, p. 106. **120** National Library of Ireland, Business Records Survey (Glynn & Shannon Steamship Company Collection, Code CL4). **121** Henry R. Glynn, diary entry, 13 Jan. 1888; Glynn archive, box 8 (1880–90). Glynn hired Henry Simon Ltd for the installation of the roller flour mills. However, his rivals had costed the project at considerably less, for instance, Donaldson's quoted £1,329, Carter's quoted £2,468 10*s*. while Robinson's final price was £2,749; Glynn archive, box 8 (1880–90). **122** Bielenberg, 'The industrial elite in Ireland' in Lane

6. Henry Richard Glynn. Photograph © the Glynn family.

the large house that adjoined his mill and overlooked Merchant's Quay. Glynn was appointed as a local magistrate in 1874. His son Henry Richard became a member of Kilrush Town Council and chairman of Clare County Council and of its finance committee. Henry Richard's brother and two cousins were both members of the magistracy and one of them was several times a member of the Clare Grand Jury. Additional influence and status was derived from association with Henry Richard's uncle, William Lane-Joynt, a former lord mayor of Dublin and mayor of Limerick, crown and treasury solicitor for the country, keeper of the hanaper and district lieutenant for Co. Clare.

Michael Glynn died in 1889 and his death notice was printed in both the national and the provincial press. However, it was a Clare newspaper, the *Clare Advertiser*, which printed an extensive obituary, stressing his entrepreneurial spirit rather than his public life:

> His powerful advocacy for every useful project to benefit the trade and commerce of Kilrush … His efforts to have Cappa Pier extended, as well as every other local project … and the construction of his Steam Flour Mills was the first outlet to give encouragement to the unemployed … Grain-laden ships have come again and again to the port consigned to him, thereby conferring great advantages on the labouring classes.[123]

Even in death, Michael Glynn continued to mirror customs more usually associated with the landed gentry. He was interred in Old Shanakyle graveyard, in the large family mausoleum he had commissioned some months before his death. While not as elaborate as the mausoleum of the Vandeleur family in Kilrush churchyard, it was nevertheless the largest and most prominent structure in Old Shanakyle. Glynn had clearly taken the decision to move the family burial ground from Kilrush churchyard (where his parents and several members of his family were interred) to Old Shanakyle, the Catholic graveyard located 1 mile from Kilrush town.

INHERITANCE AND REFINED NETWORKING, 1870–1920

It was Michael's third son, Henry Richard (1865–1916), who ultimately propelled the firm into the major social and commercial success that it enjoyed at the zenith of its existence.[124] Henry Richard was educated by the Jesuits at the prestigious boarding school Clongowes Wood College, in Co. Kildare. He was described as a 'hard working, diligent young man' who was highly motivated and ambitious – not only in his business dealings, but also socially in the circles in which he mixed,

(ed.), *Politics, society and the middle class*, p. 167. **123** *Clare Advertiser*, 18 May 1889; for country-wide coverage see the *Cork Examiner*, 23 May 1889, *Freeman's Journal*, 22 May 1889 and the *Limerick Chronicle*, 21 May 1889. **124** I have estimated the zenith of the firm to be from 1880–1930. This was calculated in terms of the expansion of the business, increased access to elite education and successful marriage contracts which led to advancement in terms of rank and position.

which included the elite Reform Club in London.[125] Gentlemen's clubs emerged in the early decades of the nineteenth century and though initially dominated by politicians, they rapidly transformed and became exclusive meeting places for aristocrats and men at the top of the business, professional and military worlds.[126] Membership of the Reform Club offered Henry Richard, an Irish entrepreneur, access to the leading industrialists of Britain.[127] In fact, it is reasonable to assume that it was in that club that Glynn became acquainted with Lord Pirrie, the chairman of the extensive Belfast ship-building firm of Harland & Wolff.[128] Henry Richard died after a short illness in November 1916. The *Limerick Chronicle* printed an extensive obituary in which he was described as a 'prominent industrialist', and it was noted that his funeral was attended by representatives from the legal, political, military, civic and industrial spheres.[129] The *Freeman's Journal*, a national newspaper, also dedicated an entire column to Glynn's death, recording that 'he was a magistrate, a member of Clare Co. Council and he had strove for over thirty years for the advancement of his native town and the deepening of the creek ... he was instrumental in getting a railway extension to Kilrush'.[130] All this illustrated the importance of the Glynn family – and by extension the middle class – to the development of the provincial economy.

Over the course of the nineteenth century the Glynn business, which began as a modest corn-milling concern, grew to achieve economic dominance over Kilrush and much of Co. Clare. The Glynns' success was partly attributable to their entrepreneurial spirit and perhaps more importantly to the location of Kilrush at the mouth of the estuary. The successive generations of Glynns exhibited a forward-looking attitude and a willingness to take risks that complemented their knowledge of local trade. Moreover, this enterprise was fuelled by diversification and the ability to reinvest in the town of Kilrush. Family solidarity was a further key factor that contributed to increased commercial success. This, in turn, confirmed the family's position and reputation as respected members of the local community to such an extent that the Glynn name became synonymous with local prosperity.

125 During numerous interviews with family members all agreed it was Henry Richard (known as Harry within the family) who was the most aspirational and business-minded member of the family to have taken over the business. 'When he died suddenly in 1916, the firm never really recovered, he was a workaholic'; email correspondence, Bryan Glynn, 17 Apr. 2014. **126** For general information about gentlemen's clubs see Amy Milne-Smith, 'Clubland: masculinity, status, and community in the gentlemen's clubs of London, *c.*1880–1914' (PhD, University of Toronto, 2006). **127** Henry Richard Glynn became a member of the Reform Club on 29 Nov. 1900. He was proposed by John Eustace Jameson, MP (Irish Parliamentary Party) for west Clare. Jameson was of the famous distilling family. **128** William James Pirrie (1847–1924) was chairman of Harland & Wolff, the largest shipbuilding company of that time. His politics were that of a Liberal and he supported home rule. For Pirrie's obituary see *The Times*, 9 June 1924. See also Herbert Jefferson, *Viscount Pirrie of Belfast* (Belfast, 1948), which is a useful biography of Pirrie, though limited in scope. **129** *Limerick Chronicle*, 23 Nov. 1916. Glynn's obituary occupied two full-page columns and included two public tributes, one from Kilrush Petty Sessions and the other from Kilrush Urban District Council; Glynn had served on both. **130** *Freeman's Journal*, 23 Nov. 1916.

CHAPTER THREE

'Rule breakers and rule makers': education, marriage and sociability

THE TWIN THEMES OF NETWORKING and social mobility are closely intertwined in the experience of middle-class education in the nineteenth century. The emergent middle class emphasized competition, thrift, prudence, self-reliance and personal achievement, as opposed to the privilege and inheritance that was largely associated with the landed class. Following a sharp rise in their self-made fortunes and a newly achieved confidence in their place in society, the provincial Irish middle classes enrolled their children in elite schools run by religious orders from about the 1830s. Previously, education of this nature had been the preserve of the landed class. However, lines between the aspirational middle class and the established landed class were now becoming blurred. Access to elite education played no small part in this change. O'Neill has recently argued for 'a more nuanced treatment of the whole spectrum of Irish Catholic wealth and a reappraisal of the role played by them in Irish society in the period'.[1] In the case of the provincial middle class, their rise was as a measure of the economic and social hegemony that they exercised in their respective towns. Their improved position and increased wealth was based on their entrepreneurial approach to work, which facilitated their rise from humble origins as small traders and farmers. Their rise was measured and strategic and it was on the basis of this newly found confidence that families such as the Glynns had emerged.

An examination of the swift rise of the Glynn family provides an insight into the private world occupied by provincial Catholic families and sheds light on how that realm was strategically cultivated. A carefully chosen exclusive education offered networking advancements for the Glynn family, which likely informed their decision to have their sons and daughters educated at elite boarding schools such as Clongowes Wood College in Co. Kildare and Loreto convent in Dublin's St Stephen's Green.[2] Their engagement with the elite stratum of Irish society meant that for a considerable number of the Catholic middle class, their experience was

1 Ciarán O'Neill, 'Power, wealth and Catholic identity in Ireland, 1850–1900' in O. Rafferty (ed.), *Irish Catholic identities* (Manchester, 2013), p. 259. 2 An entry in Henry Richard Glynn's diary for Apr. 1888 mentioned a 'Sister Calista in Convent, La Union Sacre Coeur, Paris'; Glynn archive, box 8 (1880–90). This was a well-known finishing school for middle-class girls in France. While there is no evidence to confirm that the Glynn girls attended the school, the comment suggests that there was possibly some contact with a staff member.

more identifiable with that of the landed class. Their ambitious and unashamedly aspirational attitude included furthering their sons' (and in an ad hoc fashion, their daughters') status through elite education, which ensured that their own position within 'polite' society was secured and strengthened. However, it is worth noting that 'education beyond the first level was constrained by gender and class, and particularly the latter'.[3]

The expense of such an elite education was justified by alliances that were formed with those from a similar professional and entrepreneurial background and the long-term benefit derived from these friendships had the potential to inform future business dealings.[4] In addition to networking benefits offered by private boarding schools, Pašeta has shown that 'respectability and social status were intrinsically linked with the character of the educated Catholic middle class'.[5] Though the personal experiences of the Glynn children's days in boarding school are not documented in any precise manner in the family papers, there is enough supplementary evidence to construct an accurate picture of their schooling. Deliberately placed in an environment with others from a similar background, the outcome was more or less guaranteed – future access to an 'old-boys' network' and satisfactory marriage opportunities for the girls. Such networks created links within the leading non-landed Irish provincial families that generally lasted a lifetime. There is evidence contained in Henry Glynn's later diaries that confirms he maintained friendships that were formed at his alma mater and he kept up to date with the careers of former classmates. In one such entry, from 1906, he noted that 'Matt Byrne from Clongowes was now at the firm of O'Neill and Byrne of 4, Nassau St., Dublin'.[6] Luddy has shown that a shift away from a sole focus on marriage to the need for an education for women began in the late nineteenth century. In the case of the Glynn women, it is clear that being educated in a private school opened doors that hitherto would have been closed to them. Writing about the educational theories of the pioneering activist Isabella Tod, Luddy noted that 'while marriage was the most desirable outcome for parents to aspire to, women should not rule out the advantages of a good education and the role of the same in their future lives'.[7]

FORMAL EDUCATION IN KILRUSH

Within the context of Kilrush, formal education was available from the early years of the nineteenth century within seventeen primary schools that catered for all

3 Margaret Ó hÓgartaigh, 'A quiet revolution: women and second-level education in Ireland, 1878–1930', *New Hibernia Review*, 13 (2009), pp 36–51. 4 When the Glynn boys attended Clongowes in the 1880s, the fees per individual student amounted to forty guineas per year. 5 Senia Pašeta, *Before the revolution: nationalism, social change and Ireland's Catholic elite, 1879–1922* (Cork, 1999), p. 5. 6 Henry Richard Glynn, diary entry, 3 Mar. 1906; Glynn archive, box 10 (1900–10). Henry Glynn had graduated from Clongowes twenty-six years earlier. 7 Maria Luddy, *Women in Ireland, 1800–1918: a documentary history* (Cork, 1995), pp 108–9.

classes in the town and the two main denominations. In the 1820s, the first generation of Glynn sons most likely attended one or more of the local Catholic fee-paying schools.[8] The earliest mention of education in the Glynn papers is an article from the *Limerick Chronicle* in 1875 reporting that 'Bartholomew Glynn signed a testimonial to James McCarthy, principal of the fee-paying Kilrush Academy in 1845.'[9] Such an endorsement suggests that for their primary education, his sons most likely attended the Kilrush Academy, which the Trinity College-educated McCarthy had established in 1838.[10] A network of such academies, usually patronized by the upper sections of the middle class, had emerged in the 1820s throughout Co. Clare.[11] The curriculum of the Kilrush Academy was largely based on the classics, with instruction through English. No evidence is available of extra-curricular activities offered at the school, or of fees paid. The results of summer examinations held at the academy confirm that it was the sons of bankers, shopkeepers and merchants who patronized the school.[12] Advertisements reveal that it offered a 'sound English education' coupled with moral and intellectual improvement.[13] McCarthy tailored his advertisements to suit the sons of local gentlemen who desired a career in the 'learned professions or in mercantile pursuits'.[14]

The third generation of the Glynn sons received their primary education at the Christian Brothers school in Kilrush. In addition to this, there is a family tradition that the Glynn sons were provided with private instruction in Kilrush.[15] In the late nineteenth century, formal educational opportunities for the lower classes in Kilrush were provided for the most part by the Christian Brothers, who had established a school in the town in 1874. For the greater part of the nineteenth century, the Christian Brothers had sought to 'instruct male children, especially the poor, in the principles of religion and Christian piety.'[16] However, by 1924 and its golden jubilee celebrations in Kilrush, the local Christian Brothers school was swelled by the ranks of the middle class of Kilrush.[17] Coldrey has argued that the shift away from the education of the poor by the Christian Brothers can be explained by a number of factors, including the excellent education offered and the relatively inexpensive cost to the middle-class parents.[18] An examination of a locally produced publication to mark the centenary of the Christian Brothers school in Kilrush confirms Coldrey's national findings. The middle class occupied 85 per

8 Kilrush Schools: Clare Library, clarelibrary.ie/eolas/coclare/history/teachers/ kilrush.htm, accessed 19 Sept. 2012. 9 *Limerick Chronicle*, 12 May 1845. 10 Lucey Bowen, 'James M'Carthy: teacher, publisher and politician', *Old Limerick Journal*, 46 (2012), pp 39–45. 11 '[A]s early as 1807, Mr Cole's English and French Academy under the patronage of the bishop of Killaloe opened at Arthur's Row, Ennis.' Joe Power, 'Education in Clare', Clare Library, clarelibrary.ie/eolas/ coclare/history/education2.htm, accessed 15 Jan. 2013. 12 *Limerick Reporter*, 29 July 1842. 13 Ibid., 25 July 1843. 14 Ibid., 7 Apr. 1843; *Limerick Reporter and Tipperary Vindicator*, 7 July 1850. 15 Interview with Josephine Glynn, Kilrush, Co. Clare (10 May 2011). 16 J. Blundell, *Rules and constitutions of the Society of Religious Brothers* (Dublin, 1832), p. 1. 17 Christian Brothers, *Souvenir of the golden jubilee*, p. 29. 18 Barry Coldrey, 'The social classes attending Christian Brothers schools in the nineteenth century', *British Journal for Educational Studies*, 38:1 (1990), p. 64.

cent of the publication and it proudly listed the achievements of some of its 'distinguished past pupils', which included the five Glynn and nine Counihan boys, all of whom subsequently attended Clongowes for their secondary schooling. Of the remaining 102 Kilrush Christian Brothers pupils profiled, more than half seem to have entered university, with the highest concentration pursuing careers in religious life, the civil service and the medical profession. The Glynn boys are described as 'among the earliest attendees … the success of their firm is a sufficient testimony to their business capabilities'.[19] For those who did not attend university, a career in the family firm was realized and this was the case for about 15 per cent of those who sat the Intermediate Examination. While there appears to have been bias towards the achievements of the middle-class students, recognition is also given to boys from less well-off Kilrush families. The Intermediate class members were described as 'looking very clever, working very hard and with big books, who learn French and all sorts of *queer* things'.[20] Some of the pupils mentioned later enjoyed careers in education and medicine.[21] In terms of scholarly achievement, extensive coverage is given to 'recent successes', which recorded the results of the University and Intermediate Examinations. In addition to the recording of national grades, a number of school prizes sponsored by local businesses and families are also mentioned. Business rivalries wormed their way into educational matters as prizes for best middle and junior grades in the Intermediate Examination were awarded by the firms of O'Doherty and Ryan, Glynn's main competitors, which was counterbalanced by the Glynn family also sponsoring a prize for best pupil at senior grade.[22] Sponsoring the prize meant that even though Glynn transferred his sons' further education out of the town, to the more select milieu of Clongowes, he still maintained his profile and presence within lower middle-class educational circles in Kilrush. These three families – Glynn, O'Doherty and Ryan – provide a good insight into the importance of social position within a provincial context: all three were millers, all three educated their sons locally at primary level, then at an elite boarding school at secondary level, and all three sponsored academic prizes of more or less the same value at the local Christian Brothers school.[23] What is certain though is that with the exception of the first, all the Glynn boys took the Intermediate Examination in Clongowes Wood.[24] The sponsoring of academic prizes may have increased a family's reputation and standing in the town but there was also a practical element involved in the donation of financial awards. Writing about his experience of the Christian Brothers school in Kerry, O'Connor noted that 'the Christian Brothers schools were absolutely independent of government

19 Christian Brothers, *Souvenir of the golden jubilee*, pp 37–43. 20 Ibid., p. 29. 21 Ibid., p. 31. 22 Ibid., p. 34. The prize sponsored by the Glynns was the 'Messrs Glynn Prize, five pounds for the highest aggregate marks in the senior grade'. 23 Timothy Corcoran, *The Clongowes Record: 1814–1932* (Dublin, 1932). O'Doherty first sent a son to Clongowes in 1871; Glynn first sent a son in 1876; and Ryan followed in 1927. 24 Clongowes Wood College, Intermediate Examination results, 1878–93. The first Glynn boy to attend the school graduated before the introduction of the examination.

control. They received no financial support from public funds and depended for their support on voluntary local subscriptions and annual concerts.'[25] This was reflected in Kilrush by fundraising efforts to aid the local Christian Brothers schools.[26] While there is no record of the Glynns having patronized these events, there is evidence that the sons of the firm's employees all attended the local CBS, a query in the annual company accounts from 1919 stating that 'except for £5 paid to the Christian Brothers School, where most of our workmen's boys attend school, no other charitable gifts were charged [to the business].'[27]

Prior to the introduction of the national school system in 1831, there was limited provision for the education of boys and girls. Luddy has noted that 'for those with money, education was provided privately either by a tutor or a governess'.[28] The Glynn girls' attended a preparatory school in Kilrush run by Miss Chambers, who taught them 'good manners and etiquette'.[29] Chambers aimed her school at the local middle class, and in 1851 an advertisement in the provincial press informed the public that 'Mr and Mrs Chambers Boarding and Day School at Frances Street, Kilrush' was open for enrolments.[30] It is clear that the Glynn girls were deliberately placed in an educational setting with individuals of a similar social rank, which prevented them from mixing with girls of a lower status. Preparatory schools provided the rudiments of knowledge as well as moral instruction by introducing them to skills that prepared the middle classes for the regularity of working life.[31] In the case of the Glynn boys, the upward mobility is evident in terms of educational provision, since with the exception of the first Glynn boy, all subsequent Glynn males took the Intermediate Examination in the socially exclusive context of Clongowes Wood.[32]

SCHOOLED OUT

It is clear that Michael Glynn deliberately placed his sons in an educational setting with individuals of a similar social rank, who included sons of merchants, booksellers, grocers and spirit dealers, those associated with trade and commerce and with whom Glynn identified closely.[33] This strategy was typical of the aspirational attitude of the burgeoning provincial middle class in the mid-nineteenth century. But while wealthy and aspirant Catholic families increasingly viewed education as an acceptable way of improving social mobility, education alone did not confer status: it was only one of a number of factors that facilitated

25 Joseph O'Connor, *Hostage to fortune* (Dublin, 1983), p. 54. 26 *Clare Journal*, 12 July 1883. 27 H.B. Brandon, accountant and Charles E. Glynn, letter regarding annual company accounts, 26 Mar. 1919; Glynn archive, box 11 (1910–20). 28 Luddy, *Women in Ireland*, p. 89. 29 Interview with Josephine Glynn, Kilrush, Co. Clare (10 May 2011). See also General Thomas Kelly-Kenny's 1911 unpublished memoir. He spoke of his distaste for Chambers' school: 'The first school I went to was to a Miss Chambers, called Dolly Chambers, a vile tempered, cruel, little pedagogue.' 30 *Limerick and Clare Examiner*, 4 Jan. 1851. 31 Davidoff, and Hall, *Family fortunes*, pp 234–5. 32 Clongowes Wood College, Intermediate Examination results, 1878–93. 33 *Slater's Directory*, 1846.

entry into the ranks of middle-class respectability. Additional factors included income and occupational background. In the case of the Glynn family, neither of these factors were in any doubt and their flour mill, shipping company and landed property had catapulted them into the upper ranks of society as large employers, magistrates and individuals who graced social gatherings.

The education offered by elite schools nearly always guaranteed later employment in the professions and the civil service, and it was this factor that convinced the middle classes to send their children to boarding school. However, such an education was unattainable for many and this was illustrated by the small proportion of children from Kilrush who were sent to elite schools. For instance, the population of Kilrush was approximately 4,600 in 1875–6 and less than 1 per cent of middle-class families from the town were in a position to send their children to boarding schools.[34] Clongowes was established in 1814 by the Jesuits to provide a 'distinctly Catholic, national education to upper-middle-class boys'.[35] In the early years of the school, the boys attending came mostly from Dublin and the surrounding counties. However, by the 1870s when the Glynn boys first attended, an increasing number came from beyond the immediate hinterland – from as far afield as Kerry, Limerick and Clare – while a number of the boys' addresses are given as Liverpool, London and the USA.[36]

The curriculum was based on the traditional Jesuit method known as the *Ratio*, which comprised of classical subjects such as history, Latin and French.[37] Following the amalgamation in 1886 with its sister school, Tullabeg College in Co. Offaly, the focus of learning shifted from the traditional Jesuit approach to allow for the development of skills required for entering the expanding civil service. Tullabeg had cultivated this approach as early as 1865 and 'adapted its studies to preparation for the universities, competitive examinations, and commercial pursuits'.[38] Aside from an excellent academic reputation, Tullabeg brought its sporting prowess to Clongowes, which secured its position as the country's leading Catholic boarding school of the day. Following the amalgamation, Clongowes resembled an English public school, the sports, games, blazers and coat of arms being adapted to such an extent that the school more closely resembled Eton or Harrow than its Irish counterparts, such as Blackrock College in Dublin or Rockwell in Tipperary. The opportunity to access an education similar to that offered by elite schools in England was something to which only a relatively small number of middle-class Irish families could aspire, as schools like Clongowes charged 'prohibitive fees and deliberately targeted the wealthiest Irish Catholic families'.[39]

34 *Bassett's Directory of Clare* (Limerick, 1875). 35 Aline Courtois, 'Becoming elite: exclusion, excellence, and collective identity in Ireland's top fee-paying schools' in Jon Abbink and Tijo Salverda (eds), *The anthropology of elites: power, culture, and the complexities of distinction* (New York, 2013), p. 166. 36 Corcoran, *The Clongowes Record, 1814–1932*, pp 165–221. 37 Paul Andrews, 'The Jesuits and education', *Studies: An Irish Quarterly Review*, 80:317 (1991), pp 22–30. 38 Peter Costello, *Clongowes Wood: a history of Clongowes Wood College, 1814–1989* (Dublin, 1989), p. 51. 39 Ciaran O'Neill, 'Education, imperial careers and the Irish Catholic elite in the nineteenth century' in David

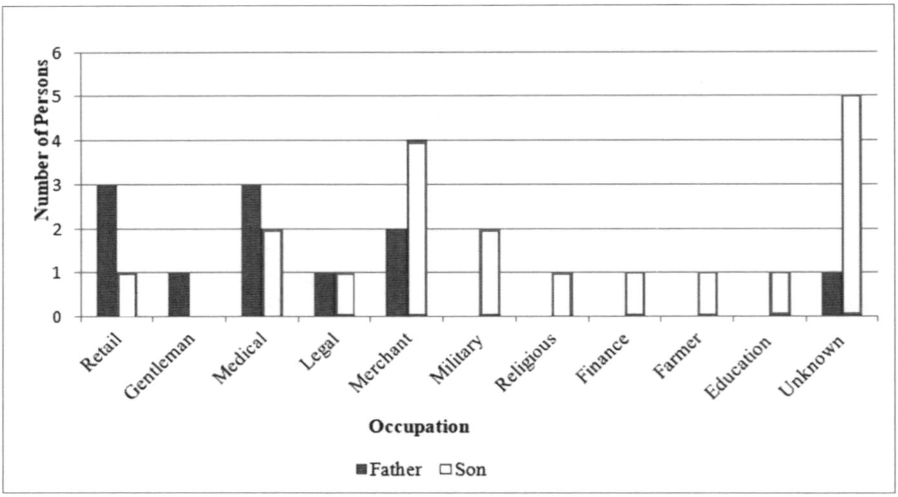

7. Parental occupations of Kilrush Clongowes students, 1860–1900.[40]

The desire to place their sons (for the most part) in schools like Clongowes indicates that 'Irish parents seem to have envied the opportunity for forming great connections that were to be gained from an education in England.'[41] By the time the Glynn boys attended the school from 1877 to 1893 the family were placed in the category of merchants. The occupational background of the other Kilrush families whose sons attended Clongowes is immediately recognizable: the list represents the sons of merchants, manufacturers, doctors and solicitors.[42]

One example is provided by Michael O'Doherty, who attended Clongowes from 1871 to 1873, three years before Mitchel Glynn. At that time, O'Doherty's father's occupation was given as 'timber merchant', yet by the time he began his own career in 1885 he had qualified as a solicitor. Inter-generational continuity in terms of occupation is best illustrated by brothers Randal and Francis Counihan (1889–92), both of whom qualified as doctors, and ultimately inherited their father's practice in Kilrush. Most striking, however, is the case of Matthew Devitt (1865–9), who served as rector of Clongowes for two terms and whose father was a draper. Of the twenty Kilrush boys who attended Clongowes between 1862 and 1900, nearly half entered the professions and qualified as solicitors and doctors, and the remainder subsequently spread throughout family businesses, religious life and banking.[43]

Kilrush was not the only provincial Clare town to be represented in the Clongowes registers. In all, between 1860 and 1900, no less than sixty-one boys

Dickson, Justyna Pyz and Christopher Shepard (eds), *Irish classrooms and British empire: imperial contexts in the origins of modern education* (Dublin, 2012), p. 101. **40** To establish the occupations of the fathers, the Clongowes College register was cross-checked with census data from 1901. **41** Costello, *Clongowes Wood*, p. 87. **42** Ibid., pp 165–221. **43** See also Corcoran, *The Clongowes Record, 1814–1932*, pp 165–221.

from throughout the county attended the school. Of this number, just seven families were from west Clare, while the majority resided in Ennis and the east of the county.[44] Clongowes clearly catered for the sons of the leading provincial legal, medical and retail families from the west of Ireland. For example, John MacClancy from Miltown Malbay attended the school from 1897 to 1901; his father was a farmer and rate collector, and he became a doctor. Landed proprietors also featured in the school's register, and the most notable Clare landowner was Cornelius Creagh, of Tulla, who attended Clongowes from 1862 to 1864. In 1876, Creagh inherited his father's estates, which amounted to over 6,000 acres.[45]

When the geographical scope is extended to include the neighbouring counties of Limerick and Kerry, between 1862 and 1899 it is clear that for the provincial middle classes, the education and guidance that Clongowes Wood offered was very attractive. In this thirty-four-year period, just over 102 boys from prominent Limerick city and county families were educated at Clongowes Wood.[46] The Glynn boys rubbed shoulders with some of Limerick's leading retail and professional families.[47] Take, for example, Robert Clery and his four brothers, whose father first established Cannocks department store in Limerick and then developed Clerys & Co. in Dublin; he attended Clongowes in the 1880s,[48] the same period when both Henry and William Glynn attended. Clery's four brothers were also educated at Clongowes. Another prominent Limerick pupil was Ralph Barry-Brereton (1871–3), who became a senior barrister and resided in Dublin city.[49] When Kerry families are examined, the figures more or less match those of Limerick: just over 111 boys from the county attended Clongowes between 1860 and 1900. The most notable of the Kerry pupils was Michael J. Rahilly (1890–3), from Ballylongford, the son of a businessman, shopkeeper and entrepreneur. Rahilly, who became a man of 'independent means', was better known as 'The O'Rahilly', co-founder of the Irish Volunteers, who was killed during the 1916 Rising.[50]

It is clear that the Glynn boys were educated with those of the same rank, position and class. Moreover, it is worth noting that the established provincial elite boarding schools in the centre and west of the country, such as Rockwell College, Co. Tipperary (1864) and the later Mungret College, Co. Limerick (1882), appear in the case of the Glynn family to have been leapfrogged in favour of Clongowes Wood. Both Rockwell and Mungret seem to have been more popular with large farmers and shopkeepers than with the professional and merchant class.

44 Clongowes Wood College, school registers (1860–1900). 45 *Landowners in Ireland: Return of owners of land of one acre and upwards in the several counties of cities and counties of towns in Ireland* (Dublin, 1876). 46 Corcoran, *The Clongowes Record, 1814–1932*, pp 165–221. 47 Mary Wilcox, 'The development of retailing in Ireland, 1900–2010' in Edmund O'Callaghan and Don O'Riordan (eds), *Retailing in Ireland* (Dublin, 2012), p. 5. 48 Ibid., p. 5. 49 Census of Ireland, 1901, city of Dublin, DED South Dublin, townland of Mount Street Upper. 50 Marcus Bourke, *The O'Rahilly* (Tralee, 1967), p. 117. Charles E. Glynn attended school with O'Rahilly, and the Glynn family also owned land and property in Ballylongford, Co. Kerry.

SECONDARY SCHOOLING

The new orientation towards British-type Catholic education was also evidenced by the decision to send later generations of Glynn boys to the prestigious Benedictine Ampleforth College in Yorkshire, England.[51] In Ireland, in addition to Clongowes, the boys were sent to Blackrock College in Dublin, which was operated by the Holy Ghost Fathers. A clear pattern emerges of the Glynn sons being sent to the most exclusive schools, operated by the most select religious orders. It is possible to argue that religion had little to do with this tradition, and that it was wealth and status that informed their decision. Indeed, the noticeable lack of religious material in the family papers, coupled with the absence of family memorials in the local church (unlike other Kilrush business families) goes a long way to suggest that it was the wish for social advancement that informed succeeding generations' decision to educate their sons at elite boarding schools.[52]

But this lack of emphasis on involvement with the church does not imply a lack of religious fervour, something that comes across obliquely in a number of records in the family's archive. Henry Glynn's later diaries disclose issues about faith and conscience and are peppered throughout with oblique scriptural references – practically all from Proverbs – such as 'and thy barns shall be filled with abundance, and thy presses shall run over with wine'.[53] And 'like vinegar to the teeth and smoke to the eyes, so is the sluggard to those who send him'.[54] Proverbs of this nature are more usually associated with the Protestant faith, their inclusion in his private diaries suggest that his mother may have engendered a strong religious sense in him, though it is not necessarily devotionally bounded. His education by the Jesuits, who were considered to be among the more open-minded and liberal orders of the time, may have quietly accommodated the religious influences from his mother, a staunch Church of Ireland member all of her life. Charles Glynn, Henry's brother, writing in 1932 noted that '[O]ur mother instilled in her children the principles of truth, honesty and sobriety, unity and loyalty to each other.'[55] While pious in their own way, the Jesuits were not overly concerned with instilling a deep and pervasive form of Catholicism into their students.

Eclectic religious reading featured in Henry's library, and in 1889 he purchased a number of religious texts including *Imitation of Christ* by Thomas à Kempis, and *Christian perfection*, perhaps by John Wesley.[56] These two religious texts both

51 The second generation attended Clongowes Wood from the 1870s to the 1890s; the third generation attended Ampleforth College from the 1890s to the 1920s; and the fourth generation attended Blackrock College from the 1920s to the 1950s. Anselm Cramer OSB, archivist at Ampleforth abbey, stated that 'George Glynn attended from 1920–1921'; email correspondence, 3 Oct. 2013. 52 Paul Gleeson, *St Senan's Roman Catholic church Kilrush: 150 years, 1839–1989* (Kilrush, 1989), pp 3–4. 53 Henry Richard Glynn, diary entry, 8 Feb. 1888, Proverbs 3:10; Glynn archive, box 8 (1880–90). 54 Ibid., 26 Oct. 1888, Proverbs 10:26; Glynn archive, box 8 (1880–90). 55 Charles E. Glynn to James McInerney, 19 Jan. 1932; Glynn archive, box 13 (1930–40). 56 Henry Richard Glynn, diary entry, 26 Oct. 1889; Thomas à Kempis, *Imitation of Christ* (London, 1889); author unknown, *Christian Perfection* may be the religious text by John Wesley founder of the Methodists. Glynn archive, box 8

address issues of Christian devotionalism, however à Kempis is more readily associated with the Jesuits, whereas *Christian perfection* (if penned by Wesley) represents the Methodist faith. When the Baptist preacher Charles Spurgeon is added to the mix – it becomes clear that Henry had a diverse interest in religion and appeared to be well-read on the topic. Perhaps, an event in his flour mill had informed his decision to purchase the books. Noted on the same page as the book titles is a diary entry that suggests that his employees came from a variety of denominations.[57] Henry reminded himself to 'write up each man's name, what his duties are and my own work to end the religious controversy'.[58] The controversy to which he was referring to remains unknown.

State regulation and the democratization of education appeared in 1878 with the introduction of the Intermediate Examination Act, which provided state aid to secondary schooling in Ireland. Prizes were awarded to both boys and girls for the best answers in the annual examinations. These prizes took the form of small payments to both the successful pupil and the school that he or she attended. Participation in the Intermediate Examination was not mandatory, and it met with some opposition at Clongowes, a private college in which some of the staff were 'wedded to the older tradition of classical and literary studies, as the basis of scientific and professional training'.[59] However, the college did enter its students every year and the amalgamation with Tullabeg in 1886 had an immediate effect on the academic standing of Clongowes as it emerged as the leading Irish school in respect of Intermediate results. For the students, good marks resulted in employment in the 'Home and Indian Civil Service, in the banks and commerce and in the army and traditional professions.'[60] These results also helped to increase the numbers enrolling at the school.[61] It is interesting to note that the two Glynn boys who attended Clongowes following the amalgamation with Tullabeg became the most successful members of the family in terms of careers and social advancement. George, who attended from 1888 to 1891, qualified as a surgeon and physician in the Royal Navy, and Charles, who attended from 1890 to 1893, successfully took over the family business and became a noted industrialist. The family tradition of attending Clongowes did not, however, last beyond one generation, with the sons of Charles E. Glynn attending St Gerard's non-denominational school in Bray, Co. Wicklow. Josephine Glynn, Charles' daughter, explained why her father broke with the family tradition of sending his sons to Clongowes. She remarked that: 'My father didn't like Clongowes and he wouldn't have the boys go there and he was a very tolerant man but … what he didn't like

(1880–90). **57** Kilrush had a Protestant population of just over 400 out of a total population of 7,000, so it seems unlikely that many Protestants were within Glynn's workforce. Census of Ireland, 1881, province of Munster, county of Clare. table XXX, 'Religious professions and education'. **58** Henry Richard Glynn, diary entry, dated 26 Oct. 1889. Religious worship in Kilrush catered for Catholics, Protestants and Methodists, and there is evidence available that a Baptist mission operated in the town in the 1830s. See Revd Mr Thomas to the secretaries of Kilrush, *Baptist Magazine*, 19 July 1832. **59** Corcoran, *The Clongowes Record, 1814–1932*, p. 143. **60** Costello, *Clongowes Wood*, p. 61. **61** Ibid., p. 61.

was the clever boys sat at a special table and they had special food but they [the Jesuits] discriminated against the other boys … he didn't like Clongowes at all.'[62]

MOVING OUT: GEORGE GLYNN

As the middle classes expanded their influence in the nineteenth century, the well-educated and ambitious sons of this self-motivated class considered professions outside of the confines of the traditional family business. Many chose to enter the legal, financial and medical professions. This change was evident in the decision of the Clongowes educated George Glynn (1873–1906) who entered Trinity College Dublin on 4 February 1892 and graduated with a degree in medicine in 1898.[63] The other brothers entered the family milling and shipping business and settled in Kilrush, so George was the only family member who achieved a university education and forfeited his share of the Glynn enterprise. The contentious debate surrounding the establishment of a Catholic university in Ireland was of long standing. There was a choice of three institutions: the Catholic University, the Queen's Colleges and Trinity College. Michael Glynn had supported calls from the Catholic church and laity for the establishment of the Catholic University in Ireland as early as 1870. He had been joined by members of the Kilrush professional and merchant classes with their 'demand for a change in the system of collegiate and university education'.[64] However, when it came to it, it was to Trinity that George was sent.[65] Pašeta has noted that 'the Catholics who chose Trinity College over the Catholic and Royal Universities undoubtedly did so for both professional and social reasons … [I]t attracted the sons of Ireland's leading families, both Catholic and Protestant; the cultivation of useful connections and networks was one of the benefits of attending the prestigious institution.'[66] Nearly 8 per cent of students admitted to Trinity College in 1892 were from George Glynn's alma mater, Clongowes Wood. When the occupational background of each student's father is considered, the figures reveal that just under 16 per cent of the admissions were from a landed background, nearly 15 per cent gave their father's profession as clergy, and just under 9 per cent came from a mercantile background.[67] Surprisingly, the data revealed a number of working-class occupations in the college register, including flax spinner, labourer and postman. It is unclear if these students were the recipients of scholarships. Compared to

62 Interview with Josephine Glynn, Kilrush of Co. Clare (10 May 2013). **63** George Glynn, bachelor of medicine, Dublin University, 26 Feb. 1898; Glynn archive, box 8 (1880–90). **64** *Freeman's Journal*, 5 Apr. 1870. **65** Justice O'Hagan, 'The Irish Catholic University Question', *Irish Monthly*, 26:297 (Mar. 1898), pp 113–22. **66** Senia Pašeta, 'Trinity College Dublin, and the education of Irish Catholics, 1873–1908', *Studia Hibernica*, 30 (1998/9), pp 7–20. **67** The data is based on the total number of 210 admissions to Trinity College for the year 1892. The categories under which the percentages were calculated are included at Trinity College Dublin, digitalcollections.tcd.ie/home/index.php?DRIS_ID=MUN-V-23-6_001&utm_expid=68026435-1.utkesif9QkKGoMll18G2NQ.0, accessed 10 June 2015.

8. George Glynn, surgeon. Photograph © the Glynn family.

1892, in data on admissions from 1853, the background of each student is more easily identified with the traditional category of the 'gentleman of private means'. The inclusion of such a large number of sons of the middle class in the 1890s was reflective of the growing prosperity of that class and the advancement of their position in contemporary Irish society. However, though the numbers attending university had grown, Coolahan noted that a higher education was 'not a highly valued commodity among the majority of the Irish middle class … it was mainly people who could afford such a long education for their children'.[68]

Kehoe has noted that '[F]or many of these ambitious young professionals, medical training was a way out of Ireland, but as front-line surgeons working in dangerous environments, they did much to change perceptions of those traditionally perceived as socially and religiously peripheral.'[69] Ultimately, George Glynn sat the entrance exam for the Royal Navy and accepted a commission as a ship's surgeon in 1898, the *Clare Journal* noting that 'Surgeon George E. Glynn, M.B., Royal Navy … has been appointed to her majesty's first class armoured cruiser "Goliath". Mr Glynn had a brilliant course at Trinity College.'[70]

The Glynn family appears to have been proud of George's success and he seems to have spent a considerable amount of his leisure time with family members. Photograph albums record him in his uniform, playing tennis at his brother Henry's home, Leadmore House, and horse riding at the home of his sister Rose, Erindale House in Co. Carlow.[71] In 1898, he wrote to Rose describing his typical day at the Royal Hospital at Gosport, noting that 'we have lectures from 8.30 until 12.30 after which we either go sailing, play tennis or go for a bicycle ride, we dine together in the evening and I stand around a piano and sing choruses until 11pm.'[72] In a March 1906 letter, George thanked Rose for 'the shamrocks' and noted that 'Mother sent me *Irish Society* with yourself figuring in it'.[73]

Thereafter, George Glynn's nine-year career in the navy seems to have been typical. He served on board many of the navy's flagships and visited places such as India and Australia.[74] However, he suffered from chronic ill-health and retired from his commission at an early age, with the intention of forming a partnership in a general practice.[75] That business venture was to be funded by his retirement gratuity of £1,000, but he died almost immediately after leaving his post and thus

68 John Coolahan, *Irish education: history and structure* (Dublin, 2012), p. 109. 69 S.J. Kehoe, 'Accessing empire: Irish surgeons and the Royal Navy, 1840–1880', *Social History of Medicine*, 26 (2013), pp 204–22. 70 *Clare Journal*, 10 Nov. 1898. 71 Rose Ryan, photograph albums, 1901–5; Glynn archive, box 10 (1900–10). 72 George Glynn to Rose Glynn, Royal Hospital, Haslar, Gosport, 24 June 1898; Glynn archive, box 9 (1890–1900). These two siblings seem to have maintained a close relationship and their correspondence survives in the family archive. 73 George Glynn to Rose Ryan, letter, 17 Mar. 1906; Glynn archive, box 10 (1900–10). 74 George Glynn, series of letters from HMS *Albion* to Charles E. Glynn, 6 July–12 Sept. 1904; Glynn archive, box 10 (1900–10). 75 Charles E. Glynn, undated, typed three-page account of his brother George's retirement plans in which he planned to become a partner in the medical practice of Dr Ryan of Devonport, Plymouth (Ryan's brother, Charles, was married to Glynn's sister, Rose); Glynn archive, box 10 (1900–10).

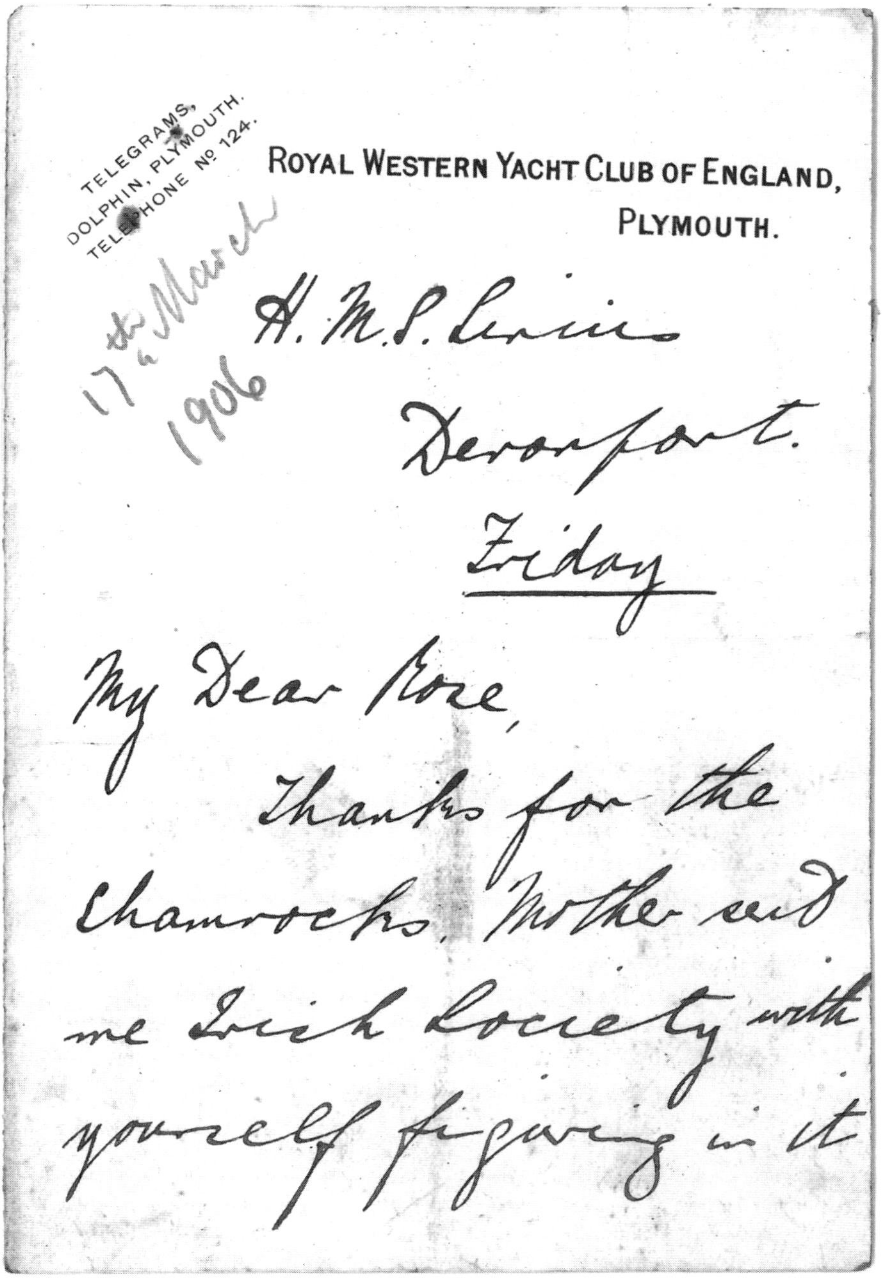
TELEGRAMS, DOLPHIN, PLYMOUTH.
TELEPHONE No 124.

ROYAL WESTERN YACHT CLUB OF ENGLAND,
PLYMOUTH.

17th March 1906

H.M.S. Sirius
Devonport.
Friday

My Dear Rose,
Thanks for the Shamrocks. Mother sent me Irish Society with yourself figuring in it

9. Letter (excerpt) from George Glynn to Rose Ryan (née Glynn), 17 March 1906.[76]

76 Glynn archive, box 10 (1900–10).

did not claim the payment. As George was unmarried his brothers acted as his next-of-kin and they began a lengthy process to claim the gratuity. Therefore, running concurrently with their long drawn-out and high-profile legal action against Vandeleur in relation to foreshore rights and exploitative charges and tolls, the Glynn family attempted to secure the pension of their late brother from the British Admiralty. Their rationale was logical: George had served his time and the family were claiming what was rightfully his; it was not in any way intended to be anti-establishment.[77] Ultimately, their attempt to secure George's gratuity failed, the British admiralty refusing to accept their arguments.

INFORMAL EDUCATION

Aside from academic study, Clongowes offered a wide range of extra-curricular activities. Both indoor and outdoor pursuits were available, at an additional charge. Indoor activities included fencing, gymnastics, dancing, music and the more dubious (and most popular) pastime of card-playing, in some of which the Glynn boys participated.[78] Tuition in fencing cost nearly £4 for six months, while access to the card table cost a mere 8*s*. for the same period. Fencing and dancing always occupied a special place in the college accounts; they were almost always taken together.[79] Activities such as these were aimed at the development of social refinement. Analysis of the Glynn family's Clongowes account reveals that all five of the sons availed of music, drawing and dance classes, which added a considerable amount to their school fees. On average it cost £60 per year to send each Glynn son to Clongowes, meaning that this type of secondary education was unattainable for most Catholic families from the lower middle classes.[80] Pašeta has described Clongowes Wood as 'the Eton of Ireland', the school that prepared its students on correct class lines.[81] Pupils were encouraged to engage in as many sporting activities as they could manage, especially outdoor activities such as tennis, cricket and rugby, the latter two games being seen as essentially British and represented as fostering in participants 'character' or 'manliness'.[82] The pursuit of manliness in elite boarding schools tended to emphasize physical ability. Even in the twenty-first century the school boasts 'ten rugby pitches and an all-weather cricket crease' whereas the more the traditionally identifiable 'Irish' sports are listed in a separate category as 'other sports available'.[83]

77 The family's papers include approximately 1,500 documents in manuscript form relating to their appeal; Glynn archive, box 10 (1900–10). 78 First prospectus of Clongowes Wood (June 1814), reprinted in William A. Menton, *The Clongowes Wood centenary chronicle* (Clane, 1997), p. 26. It is not clear from the records if the Glynn boys took fencing lessons. 79 Corcoran, *The Clongowes Record, 1814–1932*, p. 117. 80 Music, drawing and dance lessons cost on average £4 4*s*. each, per child and were paid on a half yearly rate of just over £13. Clongowes Wood College, Accounts, Sept. 1876. 81 Pašeta, *Before the revolution*, p. 36. 82 Ibid., p. 133. 83 Clongowes Wood College, clongowes.net/wordpress/?page_id=316, accessed 21 Jan. 2014.

Their attendance at an elite school like Clongowes was an indicator of the Glynns' share in the growing confidence of the middle classes in Ireland. The Glynn boys rubbed shoulders with those sons whose fathers held civic and administrative titles such as justice of the peace (JP), district lieutenant (DL) and honourable (Hon.).[84] In funding an elite education for his sons and daughters, Michael Glynn had successfully elevated his family's social position, and had guaranteed their future access to an 'old-boys' network'. The Glynn boys therefore shared a set of social and cultural references between the sons of upper middle-class families in both Ireland and Britain. Schools such as Clongowes, with their emphasis on social exclusivity, bestowed manners, manliness and practicality on their students.

WOMEN, EDUCATION AND ADVANCEMENT

The gendered attitudes to education, particularly in middle-class society, are very much to be seen in the experience of the women of the Glynn family.[85] An insight into the links between mid-nineteenth-century female education and social advancement is offered firstly by the experience of Jane Lane-Joynt (1834–1909), who married Michael Glynn in 1859 and was mother of twelve children.

Jane Lane-Joynt's father, William, ran a pawnbroker and chandlery business in Brunswick Street, Limerick city. Jane's lineage included minor landed gentry, high sheriffs, solicitors and magistrates, and her brother became mayor of Limerick and subsequently lord mayor of Dublin.[86] Though information on Jane's early life is scant, it is likely that she was educated either by her mother or a governess and she may have attended a fee-paying day school in Limerick city afterwards, this being reflective of the experience of other girls of her class from Limerick.[87] Jane also attended a local Sunday school in St Mary's cathedral in the 1850s.[88] A brief analysis of some of the books from Jane's personal library reveals that she read pious titles that reflected her Protestant upbringing. The books covered wide-ranging and popular contemporary topics and included prayer books and collections of sermons, ecclesiastical histories and moral instruction guides. The library also had books containing devotional addresses and testimonials, and one

84 Clongowes Wood College, school registers (1876–93). 85 See Catherine Hall, *White, male and middle class* (New York, 1992) and Luddy, *Women in Ireland*. 86 Family questionnaire 'as to Joynt family', undated, Glynn archive, box 2. Jane was related to the landed Persses of Roxborough, Co. Galway. Roxborough was the childhood home of Lady Augusta Gregory (née Persse), 1852–1932; Glynn archive, box 10 (1900–10). 87 Sarah McNamara, 'Making the middle-class mind: middle-class culture in Limerick, 1830–1840' (PhD, Mary Immaculate College, University of Limerick, 2010), p. 141. 88 A handwritten inscription on the inside cover of another book, entitled *A history of the Vaudois church from its origin and of the Vaudois of Piedmont to the present day*, reads: 'St Mary's Sunday School, Limerick. This premium being the first in the first class (upper school) was awarded by the Very Revd the Dean to Jane Joynt for satisfactorily answering at an examination held on Wednesday 19 July 1850 and for general punctuality and attention.' Glynn archive, box 5 (1850–60).

10. Jane Lane-Joynt and Michael Glynn. Photographs © the Glynn family.

volume provided 'practical insight' into understanding the revelation of St John.[89] Some of the books were prizes from her days at Sunday school, some she purchased herself, others she received as gifts from her brother William, her son Henry and a cousin who was a rector in a parish in Bristol, England.[90] Jane's interest in religious texts may have encouraged her son Henry to develop an enthusiasm for similar material. Several of the books feature dated inscriptions and offer an insight into her religious beliefs, which confirms that she had a strong attachment to her Protestant faith and that it remained constant throughout her life. Following her early education, it is reasonable to assume that Jane Lane-Joynt attended one the few prestigious fee-paying day schools in Limerick that – with yearly charges of £8–£30 – catered for the middle and upper classes. For instance, Mrs Willis' female boarding and day school advised that 'education to be worthy of the name, must embrace or rather consist of a moral training, grounding of the mind in Religious principle, to be acquired by a course of instruction in the facts and doctrines of Christianity'.[91]

From 1845, Jane's widowed mother operated the pawnbroker business, which had relocated to Sir Harry's Mall.[92] Indeed, the profession of pawnbroker seems to have been an inter-generational occupation associated with the Joynt family in

89 A sample of Jane Glynn's religious texts include Charles Spurgeon, *Metropolitan tabernacle pulpit* (London, 1861), and John Watson, *The mind of the master* (London, 1897). **90** Other titles from Jane's collection include *Metropolitan tabernacle pulpit* (London, 1861); *The mind of the master* (London, 1897); *Instructions on the revelation of St John the Divine* (London, 1899); *Messages from the Old Testament* (London, 1905); *Candle of the Lord and other sermons* (London, 1906). See *The nineteenth report of the Sunday School Society for Ireland*, 8 Apr. 1829. **91** *Limerick Standard*, 8 Jan. 1839. **92** *Limerick Reporter*, 7 Jan. 1845; see also *Hansard's parliamentary debates*, H.C. Debate, 3 Aug. 1838, vol. 29, c730, House of Commons, Select Committee on Pawnbroking in Ireland.

Limerick. Family memory of the Lane-Joynts' occupation remained in the Glynn lore and Josephine Glynn recalled that there was always a family tradition that 'the Joynts were moneylenders or pawnbrokers of some kind or another'.[93] During her upbringing, Jane seems to have been exposed to basic bookkeeping and business management – hardly surprising in view of her widowed mother's management of the business – which subsequently informed her household management in later years. Between 1838 and 1856, no less than six separate pawnshops are listed in trade directories for individual Joynt family members.[94] Even though Limerick seemed to have been saturated with pawnbrokers, it was a profitable business. The average Dublin pawnbrokers' annual profits were calculated at £950 in the 1830s. Between 1840 and 1850 this figure rose to £1,795.[95] Although no comparable figures are available for Limerick, profits such as these would have allowed for a very comfortable upbringing.

Jane's daughters had quite a different experience. It would appear that they were not in any way involved in the family business and by the time they reached their adolescent years they were 'schooled out'. All four sisters – Arabella Lane (1866–1936), Jane Alice (1869–1950), Florence Elizabeth (1870–1940) and Rose Anna (1878–1950) – attended boarding school in Dublin. Between 1878 and 1900, they attended the elite convent boarding school operated by the Loreto Sisters in St Stephen's Green. The Institute of the Blessed Virgin Mary (IBVM) had established Loreto Abbey, a school for middle-class girls, in Rathfarnham in 1821. In 1833, the order opened a second school at St Stephen's Green. These congregations responded to the rise of Catholic middle-class females like the Glynns and by the latter part of the nineteenth century established day, boarding and high schools that educated girls for university examinations.[96] Moreover, the growth in educational opportunities for middle-class girls received support from the Catholic hierarchy and in 1862, Cardinal Cullen commented on 'a graver and more urgent' need of Catholic education for them than even the poor. It was hoped that a solid religious grounding would act as a deterrent to the moral dangers of the social milieu.[97] The founding of a number of notable establishments bolstered the position of middle-class girls' education. Clear has found that 'the most significant developments in female secondary education were the founding of the Ladies' Collegiate School in Belfast in 1859, the Queen's Institute in Dublin in 1861 and Alexandra College in Dublin in 1866. Both Dublin schools sought to give middle-class women the same education as their brothers and both participated in the fight for higher education in the 1890s and 1900s.'[98]

93 Interview with Josephine Glynn, Kilrush, Co. Clare (10 May 2014). 94 *Limerick General Advertiser*, 25 Aug. 1818, which reported on the offering of (stolen) items to Joynt's Pawnshop. 95 James R. Raymond, 'Pawnbrokers and pawnbroking in Dublin: 1830–1870', *Dublin Historical Record*, 32:1 (1978), pp 15–26. 96 Barbara Walsh, *Roman Catholic nuns in England and Wales, 1800–1937: a social history* (Dublin, 2002), p. 37 and Jean McDermid, *The schooling of girls in Britain and Ireland, 1800–1900* (New York, 2012), p. 75. 97 Catríona Clear, *Nuns in nineteenth-century Ireland* (Dublin, 1988), p. 104. 98 Jean McDermid, *The schooling of girls in Britain and Ireland, 1800–1900* (New York, 2012), p. 27.

The curriculum at Loreto convent schools was practical and prioritized subjects such as such as science (first examined in 1893), recitation, arithmetic, Latin, languages, needlework, ladylike deportment, Christian doctrine, art and music. They ensured that their girls were well-educated so that there would be jobs for them in the civil service and teaching, places for them at university and good marriages ahead. The change in the importance hitherto placed on subjects such as accomplishments and deportment was reflected in the career paths of students. O'Connor has shown that by the early years of the twentieth century 'a permanent pensionable career was becoming an acceptable role for a Catholic woman'.[99] Careers in the expanding civil service offered substantial work opportunities for young women and for the most part their parents encouraged them to sit the relevant examinations. Writing about the experience of a young Cork woman in 1912, Luddy noted that Siobhán Lankford successfully passed an exam and was offered a position in the Post Office.[100]

Not every student did every subject, but most of them were assessed in the first five from the outset. Physical education for girls in Loreto convents remained an integral part of the school curriculum. Much emphasis was placed on physical agility and appearance, fitting 'our children for the battle of life with a well-developed, symmetrical, physically educated body'.[101] Schools were equipped with up-to-date facilities and often had large grounds that surrounded their buildings, so it was not surprising that tennis, the great facilitator of social mixing, was a firm favourite of the Loreto schools. It also acted as a link between the generations and there is a strong tradition of the game in the Glynn family. The Glynn girls' house featured a tennis court and their family helped to found the Kilrush Lawn Tennis Club in 1926. Michael Glynn, born in 1933, recalled playing 'doubles with my mother at various tennis competitions across the county'.[102] Similarly, Rose Ryan (née Glynn), along with her husband Jack, hosted tennis matches at their large country home in Co. Carlow.[103] On the occasion of the diamond jubilee celebration of the Loreto convent at Rathfarnham in Dublin, a report in the *Irish Times* described the sporting facilities available to the young ladies as 'hockey, tennis and a wide variety of other games … a gymnasium fitted with all appliances requisite for a young lady's training'.[104]

Preparation for university was included in many of the advertisements for fee-paying convent schools. An advertisement for the Loreto convent in St Stephen's Green noted that the school prepared pupils 'for the Intermediate and Royal University Examinations, and also for the South Kensington Science and Art and the Royal Academy of Music, London'.[105] An *Irish Times* report also praised the

99 Anne V. O'Connor, 'Influences affecting girls' secondary education in Ireland, 1860–1910', *Archivium Hibernicum*, 41 (1986), p. 96. **100** Luddy, *Women in Ireland*, p. 118. **101** *Irish Times*, 2 Aug. 1902. **102** Interview with Michael Glynn of Boston, MA (2 Dec. 2014). **103** Rose Ryan, photograph albums, 1901–5; Glynn archive, box 10 (1900–10). **104** *Irish Times*, 5 Nov. 1897; see Jennifer A. Hargreaves, 'Playing like gentlemen while behaving like ladies: contradictory features of the formative years of women's sport', *British Journal of Sports History*, 2:2 (1985), pp 40–52. **105** *Irish Times*, 16 Sept. 1896.

large number of Loreto prize winners on the Intermediate and Royal University lists.[106] From 1909, there was an increase in the number taking Latin or Greek simply because one or the other met the matriculation requirements in the National University of Ireland.

Even into the early twentieth century, the topic of female education within the Glynn family led Josephine Glynn to claim that '[T]he education that the Glynn girls received was comparable to their brothers' education, but the difference was that the girls' education was treated as a stepping stone to marriage, whereas the boys were being trained to take over the family business.' She further commented: '[I]t did not matter if we were good at maths or music; we knew that there was not really a place in the family firm for the girls.'[107] Formal education was to prepare girls for the practicalities of household management, rather than to train them in the social graces to make them attractive marital prospects and companionable wives.[108] Socially acceptable marriages adhered to strict conventions and ideals. Considerations of the social status and reputation of the family of the prospective son- or daughter-in-law played an important role in assessing his or her suitability.[109] Financial transactions and inheritance issues often underpinned middle-class marriages and provision for dowries is evidenced in Glynn family wills, especially in that of Michael Glynn in 1889.

The role of religion in shaping any family's outlook is difficult to pinpoint. While the Glynns were a Catholic family (though certainly not openly devotional), two marriages that took place during the period covered by this book were mixed or inter-faith. The first example was in 1859. Jane Lane-Joynt, who married Michael Glynn, belonged to the Church of Ireland, and although their children were all raised as Catholics, Jane remained a devout Protestant and attended service in the local church once a week.[110] There is no mention in the family papers of this mixed marriage being viewed as a source of concern. The family archives suggest that what was important in the making of this marriage was that the two families shared a common social circle. Michael Glynn was a member of the Limerick Country Club and carried out extensive business in the city and both families attended the races, Henry Glynn noting in his personal papers that '[F]ather first saw mother at the old race course near Look-Out Hill in Kilkee and it was six or seven years afterwards that they married in Limerick.'[111]

Economic considerations must have played a part in their union although there is no record of a dowry being paid by Jane Lane-Joynt's family. But when their occupational background is considered it was probably substantial as she married Michael, a man of considerable substance and one of the second generation of the

106 Ibid., 5 Nov. 1897. **107** Interview with Josephine Glynn, Kilrush, Co. Clare (10 May 2011). **108** McDemid, *The schooling of girls in Britain and Ireland, 1800–1900*, p. 69. **109** Richard Breen, 'Dowry payments and the Irish case', *Comparative Studies in Society and History*, 26:2 (1984), pp 280–96. **110** Census of Ireland, 1901. Jane Glynn's granddaughter recalled that Jane's prayer book was recovered from the local Church of Ireland chapel during renovation work in the 1930s. **111** Henry Richard Glynn, handwritten note, 26 Nov. 1909; Glynn archive, box 11 (1910–20).

Glynn family, established corn merchants and millers. Jane Glynn took up residence in Kilrush in 1859 and gave birth to twelve children, three of whom died in infancy.[112] There is some evidence to suggest that Jane's family – initially at least – visited her in Kilrush. In 1860, her husband Michael noted that 'Jane and her aunt arrived here safely and are quite well.'[113] She seems to have taken a prominent role in the house and was responsible for the education of her children. As it is possible she received a private education herself, this may have informed the decision to have her children 'schooled out' of Kilrush, and when her husband Michael died in 1889, the three children still in boarding schools in Kildare and Dublin continued with their education.[114] Family memory of Jane suggests she was an industrious and formidable woman with a head for business. She managed various properties in Kilrush and in Castleconnell in Co. Limerick, some 60 miles away.[115] This situation must have been familiar to Jane Glynn, whose mother when widowed had successfully taken over the family pawnbroking business. Even after Jane's sons Henry, Charlie, William and to a lesser extent Mitchel assumed direct control of the business in the late 1880s, she continued to play a large part in how it operated. M. Glynn & Sons' account books attest to Jane's ongoing involvement in the business. Recorded in the annual company schedule of accounts for 1893 are various entries for transactions well beyond the domestic sphere. Jane was paying out wages, hiring tradesmen, paying for building and agricultural materials and covering travel expenses to Dublin and Limerick.[116] She is portrayed as an active co-manager of the firm, rather than a silent partner confined to the role of homemaker. Material improvement was itself an indicator of family success, but also of the continuing managerial role of Jane Glynn. She oversaw the refurbishment of the family home in 1893, with the addition of a large bay window and canopy, coupled with decorative architrave on the window frames. Jane Glynn noted the improvements and the cost of each item is recorded in her accounts. A photograph shows Glynn family members at Leadmore House, Kilrush, as well as members of the extended family: the de Courcys of Limerick, the Wrights of Dublin and the Ryans of Tipperary. Jane Glynn is in the centre of the photograph (fig. 11). The photograph album of the family provides a vital insight into the social attitudes and aspirations of the Glynns. While primarily documenting leisure time, the photographs also provide a snapshot of their social engagements. Occasions

112 See appendix for a list of Jane and Michael Glynn's children. **113** Copy of letter between Michael Glynn and unknown recipient, 19 July 1860; Glynn archive, box 8 (1850–60). **114** Clongowes Wood College, school accounts (1876–93). Jane paid the annual school fee and signed the yearly account book. **115** Rental agreement between Mrs Edmonds, Brookville, Castleconnell, Co. Limerick and Jane Glynn, Kilrush House, Co. Clare for thirty-one years from 1899, Glynn archive, box 6. See also Jane Glynn, last will and testament and documents related to probate including a registered letter from her solicitors to her executors 7 Mar. 1917. **116** Jane Glynn in account with Henry Richard Glynn, Feb. 1893 to Feb. 1894, various amounts paid out: Mar. 1, wages (19*s.* and 8*d.*); May 1, carpenters (£1 15*s.* 9*d.*) and timber (£1 14*s.* 6*d.*). The set of accounts include management of the household, collection of rent, support of family members, collection of taxes including the poor rate, property tax and cess tax; Glynn archive, box 9 (1890–1900).

11. Family group at Leadmore House, Kilrush, *c.*1904.[117]

such as formal family gatherings appear sombre when contrasted with scenes of celebration and sporting activities. The family seemed to enjoy pastimes such as costume parties and outings to the seaside resorts of Co. Clare. Contemporary gender-based differences were also recorded. Many of the images show the women grooming and tending to their pets (especially dogs), taking walks in the gardens of their houses and reading books, whereas the men are pictured tinkering with cars, shooting rifles and playing golf.[118]

In addition to the photographic archive, the existence of cine-films from the early twentieth century attest to the family's interest in recording and documenting the activities of their business enterprise. For instance, one roll of film documented the daily workings of the flour mill. The film captured the operation of a mechanized and crane-controlled bucket for transferring grain from the granary

117 Rose Ryan album; Glynn archive, box 11 (1900–10). 118 Rose Ryan album; Glynn archive, box 11 (1900–10). Later generations (from the 1920s onwards) of the Glynn women were captured driving sports cars and sailing yachts.

to the mill, surrounded by male workers who manually levelled off the bucket's contents prior to transfer. Moving images such as those captured by the Glynn family are particularly rare and provide an insight into the working conditions in an industry that was typical of similar industries in other provincial Irish towns in the period.[119]

'MIXED MARRIAGES', ARABELLA GLYNN

The union of the merchant and professional classes characterized the social progression and continued upward mobility of both groups at the beginning of the twentieth century. The merchant class had expanded greatly throughout the nineteenth century and was now at the zenith of its self-made prosperity and success. Marriages between the two classes were common. However, the apparently relaxed attitude towards denominationally mixed marriages was changing as the century passed. In 1859, Michael Glynn and Jane Lane-Joynt's mixed marriage does not appear to have raised any moral concerns. When their daughter Arabella married Herbert Montgomery Wright in 1889, Michael Glynn commented that 'there was no concern when I married your mother, so there should be no concern now'.[120] Michael, however, turned out to be somewhat out of step with the times.

Arabella, the eldest of four daughters, was educated in Loreto, Stephen's Green in the 1870s and married Herbert, a stock broker and member of the Dublin Stock Exchange, on 24 April 1889. Though there is no documentary evidence to confirm how they first met, Josephine Glynn, Arabella's niece, recalled that 'we had a cousin called Hannah Lane-Joynt in Dublin. The Lane-Joynts would have been mixing more in the party scene in Dublin and there is a good chance that Hannah, who was a Protestant, introduced Arabella to Herbert Wright.'[121] The Wrights subsequently lived in the exclusive middle-class suburbs of Clyde Road and St James' Terrace at Clonskeagh, Dublin. The newer, more suspicious outlook towards mixed marriages was clear in the sardonic retrospective remark by Arabella's niece, Josephine: 'Arabella was a "baddie", do you know what she did? She fell in love with Mr Wright, a Protestant, and Herb Wright was not very enthusiastic about having his children brought up as Catholics and Arabella went off and joined the Protestants.'[122]

In several diary entries on the matter, Arabella's brother Henry Richard Glynn documented the marriage episode, offering a rare insight into how one late nineteenth-century Catholic merchant family dealt with what was then the dilemma of a mixed marriage. They were concerned that Wright was a stranger –

119 Restored cine-film, date unclear; Glynn archive, box 12 (*c*.1910–20). **120** Michael Glynn to Henry Richard Glynn, diary entry in Henry R. Glynn's diary, 1 Apr. 1889; Glynn archive, box 8 (1880–90). **121** Interview with Josephine Glynn of Kilrush, Co. Clare (10 Aug. 2014). **122** Ibid., see Jesse Buck, 'The role of *Ne Temere* in the decline of an Irish custom regarding the religious affiliation of the children of mixed marriages', *Australian Journal of Irish Studies*, 11 (2011), pp 28–43, who stated that 'in the nineteenth century the custom in mixed marriages was that the sons followed the religion of their fathers and the daughters that of their mothers'.

12. Arabella Lane Glynn Wright. Photograph © the Glynn family.

he was not in their circle and was unknown to the family. This clearly caused a level of consternation and it was explicitly recorded by Henry in his diary; he noted that

> We never heard of him before that but Harry Joynt recommended him in the highest terms speaking most favourably of him. Father told me about Wright's letter and to give his consent, which I did … Wright, having mentioned that he and Bella were engaged three or four days.[123]

The engagement highlighted contemporary social and moral issues, as permission was required from her father, and her brother was also involved in the decision. Although her father had set aside £1,000 as a marriage settlement for his daughter, Henry was clearly concerned about Wright's prospects and questioned his ability to support Arabella:

> He would have about £350 a year income … he had about £2,000 of his own money but his father was entitled to interest in this until he, Herbert, got married. He said of course he expected to succeed his father and he thought their business was a good one.[124]

123 Henry Richard Glynn, diary entry, 1 Apr. 1889; Glynn archive, box 8 (1880–90). The letter referred to here has not appeared in the family papers. **124** Ibid., 26 Mar. 1889, note that the phrase

Not content with just relying on family opinion on the matter, Arabella's father sought clerical guidance. Whereas the priest had a moral concern regarding the marriage, the Glynn family had a much more pragmatic interest. The parish priest, Fr Dinan, was incensed by the prospect of Arabella marrying a Protestant and implied that her mother, Jane, must have exerted some 'undue influence' on her to marry Wright. Dinan threatened to excommunicate Jane Glynn from the altar.[125] Describing the reaction and advice of Dinan, Henry wrote in his diary that

> Father told Fr Dinan about the whole affair and how they had engaged themselves without his consent and told him that he would leave the whole matter in his hands. Father Dinan said they could take his oath and could not be married unless Wright signed documents so that the children would be brought up in the Catholic religion. It would then be forwarded to Rome and may or may not be granted, but he thought it would.[126]

Catholic family though they were, they challenged the idea of a church-ridden Irish middle class, their sanguine attitude to Arabella's match displaying a more practical reaction which averted a potential scandal for the family. The concern expressed by an overzealous local priest in relation to mixed marriages appeared far less problematic for Arabella's parents. The issue of religion seems to have been downplayed by the family. The diary entries appear to suggest that the family were more vexed by Arabella's flouting of the conventions – she had agreed to marry Wright without her father's consent – than about any religious or moral fallout. The family's primary concern was to ensure that Herbert had prospects and that he could provide for their daughter. Arabella's full marriage settlement does not form part of the family papers as, on her death, her brother Charles sent the documentation to her husband, Herbert Wright. He did, however, list the contents of the settlement as 'marriage settlement, copy of life assurance Caledonian and conveyance of houses at Newry'.

In attempting to encourage Wright to bring up the children as Catholics, Michael Glynn told him 'how he brought all of us up as Catholics although he had great opposition to it', Henry R. Glynn recorded in his diary.[127] This comment is not further explained, but it can safely be deduced that Glynn was inferring that the Lane-Joynt family likely took issue with the children being raised as Catholics. According to Fernihough, Ó Gráda and Walsh, 'the proportion of mixed marriages

'was a good one' was repeatedly underlined in the diary; see also Michael Glynn's will, in which he directed that 'my son Henry pay my daughters Alice, Florence and Rose legacies of £1,000 each on their attaining the age of twenty-eight or on their marriage', 17 May 1889. **125** As Jane Glynn remained a member of the Church of Ireland, it is clear that the threat of excommunication from the pulpit did not apply to her. The inclusion of the threat by Henry in his diary may have been a misinterpretation on his part. **126** Ibid., 1 Apr. 1889, the Synod of Thurles (1850) required that the children of interfaith couples would be raised as Catholics and a written undertaking was part of this requirement. **127** Michael Glynn to Herbert Wright, diary entry in Henry R. Glynn's diary, 1 Apr. 1889; Glynn archive, box 8 (1880–90).

as a proportion of all marriages was lowest in areas that were overwhelmingly Catholic. It is striking that in nearly three-quarters of mixed marriages (2,761 of 3,834) the wife was Catholic and the husband OD.'[128] There is no doubt that by the 1890s the Catholic church was concerned about the religious upbringing of children and moved to tighten the rules of interfaith marriages.[129] The *Ne Temere* decree of April 1907 addressed these concerns and stipulated that a mixed marriage had to be witnessed by a parish priest. However, there does not seem to have been any long-term animosity shown towards the Wrights and subsequently Herbert Wright was named as a witness to William Joynt Glynn's will in 1932, was listed as a shareholder in the Glynn's Shannon Steamship Company in 1934 and he and his family frequently featured at family events as recorded in Rose Ryan's photograph albums.[130]

In respect of marriage settlements favoured by the Irish middle class, additional insight can be gained from later generations of the Glynn family, including the agreement between Charles E. Glynn and Eileen Dorgan in 1918. That document described the process involved in achieving the most profitable return for the investment of Eileen's settlement of £1,000. The document was dated 23 April 1918 and recorded three family connections – William Lane-Joynt, Joseph Dorgan and Jack C. Ryan – as its trustees.[131] Charles E. Glynn had tasked his Dublin-based solicitor and his insurance agent with jointly researching the best manner in which to invest the money. Both firms advised Glynn to undertake a three-pronged investment: firstly, in the credit of Dublin Corporation; secondly, in the Great Southern Railways Company ('who have made enormous strides ... and is a high-yielding investment'); and thirdly, in the English Trustee Investment. However, in relation to the last one of these, the insurance agents Wright, Pim & Wallis noted that '[W]e cannot say that we are particularly keen on India stocks but no matter what the future of India might be, we do believe that the British government would never let holders go without their interest.'[132]

'BY THE BOOK – SUCCESSFUL SOCIALITE': ROSE GLYNN

In contrast to her sister's mixed marriage, Rose Glynn's union to John Charles Ryan adhered to the accepted conventions of the day. In 1901, she married John ('Jack') C. Ryan, a country solicitor and resident magistrate from Clonmel, Co. Tipperary. An amended note on Rose's marriage settlement said that £1,175 was

128 Alan Fernihough, Cormac Ó Gráda and Brendan M. Walsh, 'Mixed marriages in Ireland a century ago', UCD Centre for Economic Research, Working Paper Series (2014), p. 7. **129** Alan Falconer, 'Ecumenism in Ireland', *Bürgerkieg und Religion*, 10:1 (1997), pp 74–88. **130** William Joynt Glynn, will, 4 Feb. 1932; Glynn archive, box 13 (1930–40). **131** Letter from Charles to Harry Glynn dated 6 Apr. 1940; Glynn archive, box 13 (1930–40). **132** Copy of letter from Wright, Pim and Wallis to Joseph Dorgan, 30 June 1936. Also, series of letters between Charles E. Glynn and Messers Cussen and Keirnan with Messrs Richardson and Synnott (Cork- and Dublin-based solicitors, respectively) May to July 1936. Glynn archive, box 13 (1930–40).

due to Rose Glynn under the will of her father.[133] A lengthy account of their 'fashionable wedding' that appeared in the newspapers listed their guests and noted the gifts the couple received. The guest list, reflecting the social sphere in which the family moved, included members of the landed, professional and large merchant classes.[134] Jack Ryan had recently been promoted to the position of resident magistrate, which necessitated that the couple move around the country, and they lived in various places in Mayo, Carlow and Dublin.[135] By 1920, the salary of an RM was somewhere between £400 and £600 per year.[136] Their lifestyle was centred on respectability, sociability and rank and was fastidiously documented by Rose, an avid amateur photographer.

The photographs provide a window into the social realities of the time. Figure 13 illustrates the privileged lifestyle of the Irish upper-middle class at the beginning of the twentieth century. Rose Ryan's photographs reveal that the couple were closely aligned with the leading landed families of each county in which they resided and far from aspiring to the lifestyle of the landed gentry, they were in fact more identifiable as members of that class rather than of the professional class to which they actually belonged. They first lived in Westport, Co. Mayo, in a large house named Bellview, socializing with major local landowners such as the Ruttledge family of Westport and the Garvey family of Murrisk. From Mayo, the Ryans settled next in Co. Carlow and resided in a country house, Erindale, which was considerably larger than their previous residence in Mayo. It is most likely that the Ryans rented each of their houses, as their lifestyle was transient in nature owing to Jack's profession. However, they certainly had the means to purchase, as Jack was the joint beneficiary of his father's extensive will of over £46,735 in 1905.[137] In Carlow, readymade administrative networks may have enabled a swift and easy integration for the Ryans, as Jocelyn H.W. Thomas of the nearby Belmont House was a justice of the peace while Jack Ryan was his superior on the local bench.[138]

133 Draft marriage settlement, John C. Ryan esq. with Miss Rose Glynn, 'for approval of all concerned', 4 Feb. 1901. Rose invested the £1,175 in the family business and on the death of her husband in 1936 she became entitled to the full amount plus 5 per cent per quarterly since 1889, which after forty-seven years amounted to the considerable sum of £12,142. 134 Newspaper clipping, 12 Feb. 1901. The guest list included the Right Hon. John Meagher; the bishop of Clonfert; Sir Valentine Grace; and Miss Jameson of the whiskey distilling family; Glynn archive, box 10 (1900–10). 135 From 1901 to 1908, the Ryans lived at Jack's family home, Mountain Villa, Clonmel in Co. Tipperary. From 1908 to 1910 they lived in Bellview House, Westport in Co. Mayo, from 1910 to *c.*1922 they lived in Erindale House in Co. Carlow and from *c.*1924 to 1936 they resided at Mount Mapas House, Killiney in Co. Dublin. Jack Ryan died in 1936 and thereafter Rose lived at 38 Elgin Road, Ballsbridge, Dublin until her death in 1950; *Irish Times*, 6 Oct. 1950. 136 *Yorkshire Post & Leeds Intelligencer*, 20 July 1920. According to the newspaper report, class one received a salary of £625 p.a.; class two, a salary of £555 p.a.; and class three, a salary of £425 p.a. These three classes were amalgamated in 1920 to create a minimum salary of £500 p.a. rising to £700 p.a. It is unclear into which class Jack Ryan belonged. 137 National Archives of Ireland, Calendar of Wills and Administrations, 1858–1922, willcalendars.nationalarchives.ie/search/cwa/ details.jsp?id=1639421003, accessed 5 Jan. 2014. 138 Census of Ireland, 1901, Co. of Carlow, DED Carlow, townland of Mortarstown Upper.

13. Jack and Rose Ryan's cars outside their home, Erindale House. Rose Ryan is seated beside her chauffer.[139]

14. Tennis at Belmont House, Co. Carlow.[140]

139 Rose Ryan album; Glynn archive, box 11 (1900–10). 140 Rose Ryan album; Glynn archive, box 11 (1910–20).

15. Rose Ryan on her horse at Erindale.[141]

16. Jack Ryan on his horse in Carlow.[142]

141 Josephine Glynn of Kilrush, Co. Clare, interview (10 May 2013) **142** Rose Ryan album; Glynn archive, box 11 (1910–20).

Once more, the opportunity to build networks within the circles of the local gentry resulted in the formation of friendships with the principal landed families of the county, Rose's photographs recording tennis matches, games of cricket and summer soirées in the grounds of their Georgian mansion.[143] Perhaps the circles that the Ryans moved in caused Josephine Glynn to describe her aunt and uncle as being 'slightly British'.[144] A photograph taken at Belmont House of twenty women and five men illustrates the mixing of the sexes (fig. 14), but more than that it suggests the degree to which the professional and landed classes socialized with one another.

The house in which the Ryans resided, Erindale, was leased from the Carlow branch of the Ruttledges – a cadet branch of the same family with whom they had socialized in Mayo, and who now became their immediate neighbours and one of those families with whom they now socialized in the Carlow context. Another important aspect of the assimilation of the Ryans into Carlow society was their involvement in the county hunt, which was well documented in their photographic collection. As can be noted from figures 14 and 15, both Jack and Rose were accomplished handlers and riders of horses.

Both were avid members of the local hunt and this leisure pursuit, more usually associated with the upper class, typified their time in Carlow, which was a noted 'hunting county'.[145] Although the Ryans' involvement in the Carlow Hunt was not recorded in contemporary newspapers, a note in the *Dublin Daily Express* of 1908 stated that a 'Mr J. Ryan, Carlow' was awarded a prize for his hound in the associated Carlow Hunt Puppy Show.[146] While the newspaper article did not confirm the address of Ryan, it seems likely that it was Jack Ryan as the family kept a large pack of hounds at their home.[147]

Rose Ryan's photographic albums also documented their travels to Britain and Monte Carlo, and skiing trips in Austria.[148] Ultimately, Jack Ryan was sent to Dublin, where he purchased the large Mount Mapas House in the exclusive suburb of Killiney. Jack Ryan died in 1936 and left an estate valued at over £24,000, allowing Rose, who moved to the staunchly upper middle class enclave of Elgin Road, Ballsbridge, to lead quite a comfortable lifestyle.[149] According to her niece Josephine Glynn, Rose spent her days 'socializing with the elite of the city' following the death of her husband.

143 The photographs are an invaluable source to understanding the lifestyle of an Irish RM and his wife; included in the albums are leisure pursuits, holidays, family portraits, early models of motor cars and even an biplane in the lawn of their Carlow home in 1912; Rose Ryan album, Glynn archive, box 11 (1910–20). 144 Josephine Glynn of Kilrush, Co. Clare, interview (10 May 2013). 145 Though writing in the context of Clare, Sheedy's study of the hunt provides an excellent overview of the manner in which the landed gentry and upper-classes of the county patronized the hunt in nineteenth-century Ireland; Kieran Sheedy, *The horse in County Clare* (Dublin, 2001). 146 *Dublin Daily Express*, 11 Sept. 1908. 147 Rose Ryan album; Glynn archive, box 11 (1910–20). Three pages of Ryan's photograph album are dedicated to their packs of hounds and kennels of dogs. 148 Ibid. 149 *Irish Times*, 18 Aug. 1936.

'ONE MORE WEEK ON GRASS IN THE COUNTRY': EILEEN GLYNN

Although from the same background, Rose's sister-in-law Eileen Glynn presents a different face of the lives of the women of the self-made middle class in the early twentieth century. While Rose identified with the more genteel pursuits of her class, Eileen appears to have been a hardworking, industrious woman who received a higher education and raised a large family while actively engaged in local charitable work. Eileen Dorgan (1896–1978), the daughter of a Cork land valuer and farmer, married Charles E. Glynn in April 1918 after a three-month romance.[150] Their daughter, Josephine, later recalled how her parents first met:

> My grandparents (Dorgan) were comparatively young, they were a very good looking couple, my grandfather was a farmer and a land commissioner, he was asked to judge a gymkhana at Aylevaroo [outside Kilrush] my granny said to him 'Take your eldest daughter, take Eileen down to Kilrush,' because, she said, 'I used to know a fellow down there called Glynn … they're a nice family' … and they contacted the Glynns and said that Jerome Dorgan and his daughter would be judging the gymkhana and my father went out and fell madly in love with my mother as she was very good looking and sweet.[151]

Correspondence between Eileen and Charles provides glimpses of the patterns of courtship among the middle class in the early twentieth century and suggests a more egalitarian relationship than might be expected, with Charles confiding in his fiancée about business, financial and political matters. The correspondence also reveals the canny eye that Charles possessed – he suggested to Eileen in March 1918, that her sister, Úna Dorgan, 'must be fixed up with Narker … [H]e is one of the partners in Ross, Smyth and Co … [T]hey are the largest grain people in the world and act for the government in England, as regards to foodstuffs.'[152] It is clear that Glynn realized that any potential match between a member of the now extended family and the largest global grain company would strengthen the Glynn firm's position within the milling industry and provide additional markets, revenue and standing.

Eileen Dorgan received an elite education similar to the Glynn sisters' at the Loreto convent in Wexford, where she excelled at languages and botany. Her

150 Census of Ireland, 1911, Co. Galway, DED Tuam Urban, townland of Market Square. Jerome Dorgan was recorded as a 'land inspector'. See Joe Power, *Clare and the Great War* (Dublin, 2015), p. 199, where 'Mr Dorgan, the Department of Agriculture inspector is mentioned'. **151** Interview with Josephine Glynn of Kilrush, Co. Clare (10 May 2011). Eileen Glynn's marriage settlement of £1,000 was invested in railway stocks and shares on the advice of the family solicitors, Darley, Orpen & McGillicuddy, Dublin; Charles E. Glynn, 11 June 1936, Glynn archive, box 13 (1930–40). **152** Charles E. Glynn to Eileen Dorgan, letter, dated 3 Mar. 1918. Úna Dorgan (1897–1983) was Eileen Dorgan's elder sister. She married Frank Sutton in 1920 and had two sons. John Glynn stated that his godfather was Ralph G. Sutton SC who subsequently married Eavan Costello, daughter of

17. Charles and Eileen Glynn with family on the steps of Kilrush House. Photograph © the Glynn family.

lifelong interest in botany was reflected in her decision to keep into her adulthood a copybook from her school days. That treasured keepsake was a 'nature note book' and illustrates her attention to detail and her understanding of her subject.[153] According to her daughter, Josephine, 'she might have been of the scholarship class and I think maybe she got a scholarship to down there.'[154] While in Loreto, Eileen certainly displayed an aptitude for learning. In 1912, she won a medal for domestic science and £3 for French. The following year she was awarded a prize for French and German, claiming £4 for each subject. Eileen subsequently matriculated at UCC, where she is recorded as a student from 1914 to early 1918. However, she is not included in the graduates lists in the college calendars, which suggests that she did not finish her degree. Perhaps, owing to her father arranging her marriage to Charles E. Glynn, her university career finished prematurely.[155] It

John A. Costello, taoiseach (1954–7); John Glynn, email correspondence, 15 June 2015. **153** Eileen Dorgan, nature notebook, Loreto, Wexford, 19 Sept. 1911 to 4 June 1912; Glynn archive, box 11 (1910–20). **154** Interview with Eileen Glynn's daughter, Josephine Glynn, Kilrush, Co. Clare (10 May 2014). **155** Noreen Goggin, archivist, Loreto convent, Wexford.

appears though that Eileen continued her studies right up to her wedding, as Charles commented in a letter one month before the event that 'I am anxious to see how you got on at the college, tell the Latin professor that I shall pull her nose if she says a word to you!!'[156] Josephine Glynn noted that 'my mother would have been at college in Cork doing a BA in maybe French and English, I think and didn't finish it because she got married in April and the exams would have been in the summer.'[157] Charles and Eileen's forthcoming wedding was announced in the *Irish Times* in April 1918, which stated that the wedding 'would take place quietly towards the end of the month'.[158] The couple received numerous gifts, cards and congratulatory letters from individuals ranging from the principal of Eileen's former school in Wexford to a childhood friend of Charles' who wrote from his military posting on the island of St Helena.[159] It seems that the couple discussed potential wedding guests at length and numerous names cropped up, including William Martin Murphy, whom Eileen wanted to invite.[160]

THRIFTINESS AND HOUSEHOLD BUDGETS: LOCAL BUSINESS AND MAIL ORDERS

Unlike their landed counterparts, the Glynn women did not have large country mansions to manage, but Jane Glynn's household accounts from the 1880s reveal that a complex system of household management was firmly in place. Undoubtedly, Jane was influenced by her mother, who had been widowed when Jane was just 10 years old and had taken over and successfully operated the family pawnshop in Limerick. The domestic capability and the managerial role of elite women are documented in the Glynn papers. The use of account books suggested that the Glynn women followed the same rigorous and efficient system of record keeping that was in place for the family firm.[161] The accounts reveal certain responsibilities and control of the domestic sphere but also contain many non-domestic entries, suggesting that the Glynn women entered the traditionally perceived male sphere of a business management. They acted as rent collectors for some Kilrush properties in the ownership of the family and encountered and interacted with a large staff as well as members of the public. As an affluent middle-class woman with three domestic servants in her employment Jane Glynn required a number of practical abilities and skills in order to run a controlled household. For

156 Charles E. Glynn to Eileen Dorgan, 13 Mar. 1918; Glynn archive, box 11 (1910–20). **157** Interview with Eileen Glynn's daughter, Josephine Glynn, Kilrush, Co. Clare (10 May 2014). **158** *Irish Times*, 6 Apr. 1918. **159** Congratulatory cards were received from Sr T. Boyle, principal of Loreto convent, Wexford to Eileen Dorgan, letter, 2 Apr. 1918 and James Murphy, Jamestown, St Helena, 12 Aug. 1918; Glynn archive, box 11 (1910–20). **160** Eileen Dorgan to Charles E. Glynn, 3 Apr. 1918; Glynn archive, box 11 (1910–20). **161** Household ledger: Jane Glynn in account with H.R. Glynn, 17 May 1889 to 25 Feb. 1893. The accounts were included in the annual audit of the family firm M. Glynn & Sons, and as such were examined and approved by the family's accountants, Gardner & Co., Dublin; Glynn archive, box 8 (1880–90).

the mid-nineteenth-century bride, knowledge of managerial methods, the capacity for decision making, organizational skills and a basic understanding of business management were prerequisites for household management. Perkins has noted how 'a wife's economy and carefulness could contribute a great deal to the surplus income of a family, which then could be available for luxuries'.[162] The household ledgers suggest the Glynn women showed an authority and deftness in the running of their homes: the meticulous records coupled with the perfect handwriting attest to a sense of control and pride in their ability to 'run a tight ship' – a direct reflection of the manner in which the family firm operated. As the household accounts were scrutinized by the firm's accountants, there was an additional pressure to have everything in order. Jane Glynn's accounts mirrored that of her son's strict record keeping.

Evidence of Jane Glynn's financial management of the house is especially highlighted in a note attached to the household accounts for 1892. Writing to her son Mitchel, she noted, '[F]or every nine pounds that you pay towards the house account, I am satisfied to pay one, this is to apply from 17 May 1892 as well as for the future.'[163] By 1895, it seemed that even the indolent 35-year-old son Mitchel had to contribute to the household purse. His brother, Henry, the co-director of the firm, noted, 'Mitchel agreed today to be charged £1 per week for his keep.'[164] This suggests an understanding of the cost of living and upkeep on the part of Jane and an effort on her part to implement practical economy within her household. An ability to recognize what tasks needed to be carried out in a home and having the wherewithal to organize the servants to do them was also a consideration for Jane Glynn. To help with such endeavours, much literature in the form of pamphlets and advice books was available. The most popular of these instruction manuals was the staple of the middle-class house manager, *Mrs Beeton's book of household management*, a copy of which Jane acquired in 1862.[165] Jane Glynn clearly relied on the book for advice in a number of areas, the pages to which she gave attention being clearly marked in her hand: 'The mistress', 'The housekeeper' and 'Domestic servants and their duties'. Successive Glynn wives meticulously recorded every transaction, irrespective of its value, in household ledgers. Jane Glynn's daughter-in-law Eileen, the daughter of a wealthy Cork land valuer, also exercised a rigorous household regime. Records of her domestic management survive from the period 1919 to 1925 and document her skills as a very thrifty manager. Evidence of her early training in domestic economy was borne out in her skill at applying effective direction and control over her large house.[166] That house

162 Joan Perkins, *Women and marriage in the nineteenth century* (London, 1989), p. 245. **163** Jane Glynn to Mitchel Glynn, matters concerning household accounts for 1892; Glynn archive, box 9 (1890–1900). **164** H.R. Glynn, memorandum, 28 Sept. 1895; Glynn archive, box 9 (1890–1900). **165** Isabella Beeton, *Mrs Beeton's book of household management* (London, 1861). The book carries the inscription: 11 June 1862, Jane Glynn; Glynn archive, box 6 (1860–70). **166** Eileen Glynn, household account book, Kilrush House, Co. Clare, 5 Aug. 1919 to Mar. 1925; Glynn archive, boxes 11–12 (1910–30).

was surveyed for the installation of electricity in 1920 and was described as having a WC, servant's room, kitchen, larder, parlour maids' pantry, milk pantry, front hall, dining room, drawing room, study, eight bedrooms, storeroom and lumber room and cellar.[167]

Following her marriage and subsequent relocation to the west of Ireland, Eileen Glynn remarked that she wanted to 'feel useful'. Her new home in the small provincial town of Kilrush must have contrasted sharply from her life in Cork city.[168] Eileen had four children under the age of 10 when she 'learned how to drive, so that she could deliver wirelesses to the blind of west Clare. She was the first woman in Clare to hold a driving licence.'[169] Philanthropic undertakings such as those in which Eileen became involved were not uncommon for women of her class and had been much in vogue during nineteenth century. Maria Luddy has noted that '[T]he tradition of benevolence which middle- and upper-class women had developed by the mid [nineteenth] century became even more pervasive as the century progressed.'[170] Indeed, Eileen's new sisters-in-law had a long-standing history of similar local endeavours from the 1890s through to the 1920s. Florence and Alice Glynn organized concerts for the poor of Kilrush in 1895 and subsequently established the Kilrush Blanket Appeal in 1904.[171] During the First World War, a county ladies' committee established in Kilrush to boost morale and help with fundraising activities was spearheaded by Florence Glynn at the request of Sir Charles Barrington, the senior recruiting officer based in Limerick.[172] Perhaps their charitable endeavours were inspired by the similar actions of their mother, Jane Glynn, who as early as 1865 donated five shillings to an appeal 'towards the relief of the Protestant poor of Kilrush'.[173] While Jane's name was misspelled as 'Mrs Glynne' it is notable that she was listed with contemporaries from her own social and religious background, including the wives of the landed gentry, doctors, land agents and solicitors. A generation later, Eileen Glynn's strongly held charitable beliefs were evident even during the planning of her wedding in 1918. In an act of solidarity with those suffering from a shortage of food caused by the First World War, she decided against having a wedding cake after reading a letter in which her future husband had described the 'awful Kilrush bread made from cheap American flour'.[174]

Eileen's training in boarding school appears to have informed her household management decisions. Clear has noted that for almost thirty years, from about

167 Schedule of installation of electricity in Kilrush House by Ferguson and Bruty Ltd, Sanitary and Electrical Engineers, Dublin, 9 Jan. 1920; Glynn archive, box 12 (1920–30). **168** Interview with Eileen Glynn's daughter Josephine Glynn of Kilrush, Co. Clare (10 Apr. 2011). **169** Interview with Josephine Glynn (2011). Josephine showed the author many photographs from family albums of her mother driving a car around the Loop Head Peninsula in west Clare. Eileen Glynn was secretary to the Clare branch of the National Council of the Blind from the 1930s to the 1950s. The minute book from this period is in the Glynn archive. **170** Maria Luddy, *Women and philanthropy in nineteenth-century Ireland* (Cambridge, 1995), p. 1. **171** *Clare Journal*, 18 Feb. 1895; *Clare Journal*, 15 Feb. 1904. **172** Charles Barrington to Florence Glynn, letter, 15 Dec. 1915; Glynn archive, box 11 (1910–20). **173** *Clare Journal, and Ennis Advertiser*, 16 Jan. 1865. **174** Charles E. Glynn to Eileen Dorgan, letter,

1898 to 1928, government and voluntary bodies had attempted to encourage women to increase their knowledge of housecraft and cooking.[175] Luddy also stressed this point and has suggested that 'concern lay in ensuring that girls acquired the domestic skills necessary to manage their homes, or to work as servants in the homes of others'.[176] Eileen's account book certainly shows evidence of these skills and it includes entries for food, clothes, soft furnishings, charitable donations and servants' wages.[177] She also kept hens and geese. Her weekly budget was provided by her husband Charles, who gave her between £6 and £12 to spend. An additional £6 per week was set aside to pay the wages of the household staff. Input from her husband into household affairs was a feature of their marriage, and in 1918, Charles advised Eileen to 'buy a large hearth rug for the drawing room and decide on the enclosed wallpaper patterns'.[178] A picture of her household emerges: it was organized, controlled and frugal, but not mean. Eileen Glynn shopped in some of the most exclusive department stores such as the Munster Arcade in Cork, but at the same time ordered shirts for the boys from Walpole's, which appears to have been a mail-order white goods firm situated in Dublin. Similarly, there are various entries on new children's clothes, particularly for her sons, though she was paying a local dressmaker to make blouses for herself and work clothes such as aprons for her children's nurse.[179] Eileen Glynn also had access to English department stores. A note from Williamson & Cole of London, suppliers of art furnishings, blinds and cushion covers, advised her that '[W]e are pleased for you to hold the pattern ... and hope we may be favoured with your esteemed order.'[180]

Similar to Jane, her mother-in-law and the former matriarch of Kilrush House, Eileen Glynn seemed to understand the need for frugality in managing the household budget. An insight into the younger woman's thriftiness is evidenced in the purchase of items associated with the repair and reuse of clothing and soft furnishings – darning needles, mending wool, flannel and thread and covering for pillows – though it is unclear whether the servants or Eileen repaired the clothes. The account book also confirms that Eileen was a good employer in the context of the time and she paid her servants accordingly. It is unclear whether board and lodging formed part of their remuneration. Hearn has noted that the wages of servants in Ireland rose steadily between 1880 and 1920.[181] Eileen's staff included

19 Mar. 1918; Glynn archive, box 11 (1910–20). **175** Caitriona Clear, *Women of the house: women's household work in Ireland, 1922–1961* (Dublin, 2000), p. 28. **176** Luddy, *Women in Ireland*, p. 102. **177** Eileen Glynn, household account book 1919–25, some of the food items listed included: figs, plums, bananas, vegetables, chicken and duck, salmon and plaice; Glynn archive, boxes 11–12 (1910–30). **178** Charles E. Glynn to Eileen Glynn, 11 Oct. 1918; Glynn archive, box 11 (1910–20). **179** Eileen Glynn, household account book 1919–25: coat for Harry, 18*s*. 6*d*. and 'Mary Madigan came, paid Mary for blouses £1.8.9'; Glynn archive, boxes 11–12 (1910–30). Mary Madigan was recorded as a dressmaker in the Census of Ireland, 1901, county of Clare. **180** Williamson and Cole, 26 High Street, Clapham, SW, order note, to Eileen Glynn, 7 Oct. 1919; Glynn archive, box 11 (1910–20). **181** Mona Hearn, *Below stairs: domestic service remembered in Dublin and beyond, 1880–1922* (Dublin, 1993), pp 48–50.

two servants, Kate and Maggie, and one nurse.[182] By 1923, Eileen was advertising in the *Irish Times* for an 'experienced trained children's nurse to take entire charge of two children.'[183] The following year, Eileen employed a fourth servant, probably due to the birth of her third child in April of the same year.[184] The family home, Kilrush House, was a very busy environment. Living in the house were Eileen, her husband Charles, and their three children all under the age of 6. Also accommodated in the servants' quarters located at the top of the house were the four members of the household staff.[185] Apart from the nurse, the specific duties or job descriptions of these servants are unknown. However, Eileen's mother-in-law, Jane, employed the services of a cook, a housemaid and a general domestic servant.[186]

An insight into Eileen's benevolent nature is indicated by the intermittent donation of between six pence and five shillings to an anonymous 'poor woman' who features on the pages and thus was accounted for within the weekly household budget.[187] This personalized philanthropy was more usually associated with women from the landed and aristocratic classes who often provided blankets, comforting words and treats to the poor.[188] Added to this charitable act was a one-off payment of over £19 to the Peacock Lane Laundry in Cork, suggesting that prior to her marriage Eileen was also involved in charitable endeavours in her native city.[189] However, perhaps the greatest and most enduring cause Eileen Glynn championed was the establishment of the Clare branch of the National Council of the Blind of Ireland (NCBI) on 15 November 1933. This was the third county branch established and it was founded primarily through her efforts. The minute book from the branch attests to the many activities in which Eileen was involved through the association: fundraising events, visits to visually impaired people and advice on available welfare and state supports, such as the blind pension. One such case was that of local man Henry Blake. A note in the minute book described how 'Mrs Glynn visited this man and recommended him as a recipient for the wireless set' – this was both a popular and common act of the Clare Branch.[190] The NCBI reported in their history of the Clare branch: 'Eileen Glynn died in 1978 having founded and served the Clare branch for forty-six years. Because of transport difficulties she had travelled on foot, by bicycle and even on horseback; crossing

182 Eileen paid the household staff increases after three years: 1919, Kate: £1 10*s*. per month, Maggie: £1 5*s*. per month and nurse: £2 3*s*. 6*d*. per month; 1921, Kate: £1 15*s*., Maggie: £1 10*s*. and nurse: £3 10*s*.; Glynn archive, boxes 11–12 (1910–30). **183** *Irish Times*, 10 Sept. 1923. **184** Eileen Glynn, household account book 1919–25. Children of Charles Glynn and Eileen Dorgan are Henry, Charles, Eileen and Josephine. The boys were educated in Glenstal Abbey, Limerick and the girls attended Mount Anville, Dublin; Glynn archive, boxes 11–12 (1910–30). **185** The nurse was recorded in Eileen's household account book as 'Nurse Gertie Dineen, 18 Nicholas Street, Limerick'; Glynn archive, boxes 11–12 (1910–30). **186** Census of Ireland, 1901, county of Clare, DED Kilrush, urban townland of Frances Street. **187** Eileen Glynn, household account book 1919–25; Glynn archive, box 12 (1920–30). **188** Luddy, *Women and philanthropy*, pp 181–3. **189** The Peacock Lane Laundry was a Magdalene laundry operated by the Religious Sisters of Charity in Cork city. See Maria Luddy, *Prostitution and Irish society, 1800–1940* (Cambridge, 2007), p. 78. **190** NCBI, Co. Clare branch, minute book, 17 Feb. 1937, the process of supplying a wireless to a potential recipient is described in streams barefooted to reach isolated cases, carrying material to teach craftwork. Her home was always open to the blind of Clare.'

Eileen Glynn's interest in charitable endeavours was to remain with her for the duration of her life. As the energizer of a group of activist women who operated in Co. Clare from the 1930s to the 1960s, she acted as the intersection between the classes, she being of the well-established middle class and her fellow NCBI committee members being of the more genteel and higher professional classes. The position of the landowning class of which Lady Inchiquin and her cousin Mrs Vere O'Brien were prominent members had gradually changed over the latter years of the nineteenth century. This can be attributed to the changed political landscape which had ushered in the sale of their estates and dismantled their hitherto elite status so as to render them as little more than a fading remnant of the Ascendancy class. The professional class – represented by Mr Justice Gleeson, who acted as honorary president of a group essentially comprised of women – had emerged as an 'Irish bourgeoisie who had colonized local government and parliamentary representation'.[191] Yet despite their fundamentally different backgrounds in respect of their religious and political views, the first committee of the Clare branch of the NCBI had managed to come together and form a charity that paid little attention to their disparate origins. This informal but powerful group of women may have represented the affluent section of society, but their motivations were sincere and well-meaning. However, their contribution to the welfare of the blind does not form part of the wider narrative on early twentieth-century provincial philanthropy. Perhaps the limited narrative on the charitable contribution to the welfare of the blind by women of means can be explained by the lack of archival material or by the perceived hegemony framed by the socio-economic composition of members of the first committee.

All of the families involved in the committee resided within a 7 mile radius of one another. It is unclear how Eileen Glynn came to know or initially associate with these women, but as both the Glynn family and all the other families involved in the committee were members of the Ennis Hunt it is reasonable to assume that this is where they first met. Josephine Glynn recalled that the committee 'were a very powerful, hardworking group of women who helped the blind of the county'.[192] Eileen Glynn had managed through her networking abilities to bring together this group of empowered women in order to support, promote and represent the blind of Co. Clare and initiated a number of support strategies that enabled their integration into the general population. In addition to committee members from the landed class, the professional classes were represented by doctors, solicitors and members of the clergy. Also included in the first committee were more than nine middle-class women from throughout the county. Josephine Glynn described her mother Eileen's involvement in the NCBI: '[M]y mother and a couple of strong

detail. Glynn archive, box 13 (1930–40). **191** Matthew Potter, 'The Shannon estuary group' in Ciaran O'Neill (ed.), *Irish elites in the nineteenth century* (Dublin, 2013), pp 114–15. **192** Interview, Josephine Glynn of Kilrush, Co. Clare (19 Mar. 2014).

local ladies were on the committee, my mother was secretary … and a few Protestant ladies, Miss Elmhurst and "Miss this" and "Miss that" … they got the G.P. [Mrs Haugh] to take an interest in the blind and she'd see them [the blind] in Kilrush House.'[193] Josephine also described her mother as a 'hardworking, independent lady who rode side-saddle on her horse and held tea parties for the blind in our house'.[194]

The geographical spread of members from the Co. Clare branch of the NCBI covered the entire county, from the large town of Ennis to smaller villages and towns throughout the north and west coast. The actions of this group can be described as progressive and reforming in their approach to the welfare of the blind in the county. The fastidious record-keeping of Eileen Glynn, herself an outsider to the county, provides a useful insight into the charitable endeavours of a circle of women more usually associated with leisure and social pursuits than with the provision of welfare and relief to the less-well-off. Traditionally, middle-class women were motivated to provide assistance and welfare to the poorer classes in Irish society, and their importance and contribution, particularly in rural communities, cannot be underestimated. Besides social and cultural links that existed between members of societies and charities, Luddy has noted that 'many members also belonged to the same family and indeed in a number of instances a tradition of philanthropy was established within a family'.[195] Florence Glynn, Eileen's sister-in-law, was the committee's honorary secretary.[196] She was well versed in charitable activity and ably assisted Eileen as part of the first committee of the county branch of the NCBI. Familial contributions that benefitted the work of the NCBI in west Clare were also an element of the organization. Josephine Glynn recalled that helping her mother in her NCBI activities 'was our job when we came home from school, my sister and I would help our mother to deliver wirelesses to the blind back the west … [S]he was the first woman in the county to drive her own car.'[197] Josephine also noted that '[B]ecause my mother had a comfortable house and some help, this allowed her to concentrate on helping the blind'.[198]

Eileen Glynn may have been inspired by the earlier countrywide efforts of the Countess of Aberdeen in her campaign against the spread of tuberculosis among the poor.[199] Lady Aberdeen was involved in promoting home industry in Ireland,

193 Interview with Josephine Glynn of Kilrush, Co. Clare (19 Mar. 2014). Kilrush House was the Glynn family's main residence in the town and where Josephine spent her childhood. **194** Ibid. **195** Luddy, *Women and philanthropy*, p. 179. **196** *Clare Journal*, 15 Feb. 1904. **197** Rose Ryan photograph album; Glynn archive, box 13 (1930–40). **198** Interview with Josephine Glynn of Kilrush, Co. Clare (19 Mar. 2014). **199** There is evidence in the archive which suggests that as early as 1914 Charles E. Glynn (Eileen Glynn's future husband) was involved in the charitable endeavours of Lady Aberdeen. A letter from S.C. Hickman to Glynn stated, 'I have, at the request of Lady Aberdeen taken up the job of Honorary Secretary to the Soldiers and Sailors Help Society … [M]y wife is at present the only friend in this county … [W]ould you act for Clare and get the best lady or gentleman to assist you.' S.C. Hickman to Charles E. Glynn, dated 15 Dec. 1915; Glynn archive, box 11 (1910–20).

in particular lace-making, and she was supported in her endeavour by the Sisters of Mercy, who noted that '[S]he seemed very interested in the lace-making there [in Kinsale] and through her efforts the school received a large increase in orders, and so were able to keep about fifty girls constantly employed'.[200] Eileen must also have been aware of the charitable endeavours of Florence Vere O'Brien (1854–1936), who had established a lace-making industry in Limerick, which enabled women from the working class to earn a living from their craft.[201] She invited Vere O'Brien's daughter, Margaret, to become involved in the NCBI. In the early years of the twentieth century, both Lady Aberdeen and Florence Vere O'Brien were active in the promotion and development of public health care in Co. Clare and Clarke has noted that Vere O'Brien was

> a member of the Women's National Health Association founded by Lady Aberdeen, she was prominently involved in the establishment of a sanatorium at Ballyalla in 1912. She also started the Ennis District Nursing Association and for many years was directly responsible for the maintenance of the local district nurse. Throughout the war years and afterwards she assisted ex-servicemen in Clare through her association with the War Pensions Committee.[202]

The charitable nature of Florence Vere O'Brien must have run in the family: her daughter served as vice-president of the Clare branch of the NCBI on the 1934 committee.

The involvement of these women in charitable activities challenged the stereotypical view that women from the genteel class were little more than ladies of leisure, who were removed from the harsh economic realities of Ireland in the 1930s. Rather, this group of women were active and pioneering in their efforts to provide welfare and support networks to the blind of the county. Aside from traditional fundraising activities, such as raffles, garden fetes, bazaars and sales of work usually favoured by the committee, Eileen Glynn established a willow plantation in Kilrush in the 1930s. Though writing about charity bazaars in the nineteenth century, Prochaska has shown their effectiveness as a means to raise substantial amounts of money for local organizations, as they were being patronized by the women of the professional and genteel classes, who had the leisure time to make them work. Bazaars reflected the expanding influence of women in philanthropy.[203] Indeed, Josephine Glynn recalled that '[W]e ran flag days to collect money for the NCBI and mother had a small car and we would visit the blind in west Clare.'[204]

200 Nellie Ó Cleirigh, 'Lady Aberdeen and the Irish connection', *Dublin Historical Record*, 39:1 (Dec. 1985), pp 28–32. **201** Matthew Potter, *Amazing lace: a history of the Limerick lace industry* (Limerick, 2014), p. 44. **202** Frances Clarke, 'O'Brien (Arnold-Forster), Florence Mary', *Dictionary of Irish biography*, dib.cambridge.org, accessed 15 July 2014. **203** F.K. Prochaska, 'Charity bazaars in nineteenth-century England', *Journal of British Studies*, 16:2 (1977), pp 62–84. **204** Josephine Glynn of Kilrush, Co. Clare, interview (10 May 2013).

The result of the willow plantation was twofold, firstly it provided employment for blind people, and secondly, the funds raised from the sale of furniture produced by its employees enabled the committee to purchase necessary goods such as wirelesses, reading glasses and medical supplies.[205] Many years later, Eileen's daughter Josephine recalled that 'My mother got a blind teacher, Eileen O'Connor, who used to help the blind people to make stools and little chairs, and years later, I would often be in someone's house and I'd notice a stool that came from my mother's willow plantation.'[206] Eileen Glynn's charitable endeavours are embedded in the memory of Kilrush townspeople, much as they remember the Glynn men who employed large numbers over many generations. In terms of utilizing her contacts and those of her husband's company, Eileen Glynn's ability to network throughout the county with the support of its leading ladies, politicians and members of the clergy is reflected in the donations made to the Clare branch of the NCBI in the 1930s. These were meticulously recorded in the committee ledger and notebooks.[207]

Her respectability may have been guaranteed when she married into the local influential family, but Eileen Glynn cultivated an independent image away from the traditional Glynn identity. She is remembered as a charitable and hardworking individual and though she courted the landed gentry of the county through her charitable endeavours, she remained removed from the local elite of Kilrush and rarely entertained guests or held lavish gatherings in her large Georgian house in the town. Josephine Glynn summed up her mother in the following lines:

> When I was growing up we had a party for all the mill workers every Christmas. I don't think my mother was so much into parties; she would have had tea parties for the blind people and for the mill workers but she was more into having some of the cousins who weren't so well-off in Cork to stay and she would have been happier out riding her horse. I don't remember any more than tea parties. We would have been friendly (it was more my mother's generation) with Grania [*sic*] O'Brien (daughter of Lord Inchiquin of Dromoland Castle) and Captain Brady Browne (of the Clare Hunt), he got killed out hunting one day. The family would have mixed a bit alright but we wouldn't have been at very prestigious parties.[208]

The localism that gave strength to the Glynn business and family was reinforced by their 'looking outwards' – participation in elite education and cultivation of strategic marriage alliances, both of which were vital components in their success. Over the course of the nineteenth century, both were approached in a strategic and deliberate manner: they facilitated the family's social ascent, yet did

205 NCBI fundraising notebook, 12 Jan. 1935; Glynn archive, box 13 (1930–40). **206** Interview with Josephine Glynn of Kilrush, Co. Clare (24 Apr. 2014). **207** The second minute book of the NCBI from 15 Nov. 1933 to 27 Jan. 1958, selection of diaries, 1933–58; Glynn archive, box 13 (1930–40). **208** Josephine Glynn of Kilrush, Co. Clare, interview (10 May 2013).

not interfere with their commitment to business. The personalities of individuals played an important role in how the family operated. The strong will and work ethic of Jane Lane-Joynt seems to have left its mark on the business attitudes of her children. Indeed, her son Charles E. Glynn described her as a 'great and good woman who instilled into each of her children the principles of truth, honesty, sobriety and loyalty to each other'.[209] In a different context the open-mindedness and charitable commitments of Eileen Glynn boosted the family's reputation in Kilrush and beyond. The pragmatic attitude of the family towards mixed marriage in an age when more restrictive attitudes prevailed illustrated their ability to separate practical economic and personal realities from the restrictive position adopted by the Catholic church, and their pragmatism allowed the Glynns to brush aside any potential damage to the family's reputation. At the same time, the near religious commitment of Henry Glynn to the firm, characterized by discipline, thrift and above all hard work, in no way reduced his ambition to 'move upwards', as evidenced by his relentless quest for public office, which is discussed in the next chapter.

209 Charles E. Glynn to James McInerney, letter, 25 Feb. 1932; Glynn archive, box 13 (1930–40).

CHAPTER FOUR

Local politics and provincial personalities

BUSINESS NETWORKING BETWEEN the provincial middle class in Irish towns complemented informal social networks that had initially been established through an elite education.[1] Silverman's study of Thomastown, Co. Kilkenny (a town comparable in size to Kilrush) in the 1840s, noted that 'residents included professionals (doctors, solicitors, bank managers and teachers) and industrialists (tannery and mill owners)'.[2] A contemporary trade directory for Kilrush from the same period recorded a similar pattern in that four doctors, three solicitors, two bank managers and seven teachers were resident in the town.[3] This was in addition to forty-two other professions and occupations listed in the directory.[4] By the mid-nineteenth century, the Glynns were certainly of the merchant class, and, while their manufacturing concerns were relatively small in scale, they did put the family on the fringes of the industrial class. Provincial middle-class families certainly were ambitious of bettering their position and this included emulating the characteristics of the landed classes in a number of ways. So-called 'old boys networks' ensured that the elite education received by members of the middle-class protected them and informed their life decisions in terms of both career and marriage. Of course, good contacts, marriages and networking skills were not enough to ensure progress – a definite acumen was required to advance one's interests and concerns in the sphere of business. Of those who attended schools such as Clongowes, most progressed to professional careers or went on to inherit successful and established family businesses.[5] It was to this latter category that four of the Glynn boys belonged. Henry, Charles, William and Mitchel Glynn

1 Ciaran O'Neill, 'Rule Etonia: educating the Irish Catholic elite 1850–1900' (PhD, Trinity College Dublin, 2010), p. 288. The middle class in this present study comprised those from a secure farming background, wealthy industrialists and self-made merchants. For the purposes of this present study, the terms 'middle-class merchants' and 'industrial class' are treated as interchangeable, as the Glynn family are traditionally defined as middle class, that is self-made and entrepreneurial and major employers. This term 'industrial class' was how contemporary accounts referred to the family. See Charles E. Glynn's obituary in the *Clare Champion*, 20 Sept. 1941. 2 Marilyn Silverman, 'Custom, courts, and class formation: Constructing the hegemonic process through the Petty Sessions of a south eastern Irish parish, 1828–1884', *American Ethnologist*, 27:2 (May, 2000), pp 400–30. 3 *Slater's Directory*, 1846. 4 Ibid., for instance, the directory included publicans, drapers, grocers, apothecaries and hardware dealers as the core retailers in Kilrush. It stopped short of listing tanners and mill owners as industrialists, as Silverman did in her study of Thomastown. 5 An analysis of the school register of Clongowes was cross-referenced with *Thom's Directory*, 1870–90 and the diaries of Henry Richard Glynn (1865–1916) to confirm that friendships were maintained throughout an individual's

went directly from their secondary education at Clongowes Wood (1877–1893) into the family business. That business was M. Glynn & Sons, the flour mill established by their grandfather, Bartholomew Glynn, in 1811. It played a pivotal role in shaping the economic identity of Kilrush. The family also held numerous private and commercial properties in their home county and throughout Ireland, which confirmed that property remained one of the safest investments for businesspeople.[6] In addition, the business's customer base stretched throughout Ireland, England and Scotland.[7] Long after the completion of formal education, the opportunities of an elite education continued to benefit the individual and the resulting networking activities influenced local and regional economic development.[8]

Administrative networks along with those available through education presented an effective means for members of the aspirational middle class throughout provincial Ireland for much of the nineteenth century to ascend the social ladder. Civic titles and judicial appointments were progressively granted to middle-class individuals and they gradually began to encroach on hitherto unattainable positions such as justice of the peace and county lieutenant.[9] Entry into the local judiciary as a JP was often viewed as a stepping stone to a much more prestigious commission such as district lieutenant (DL) or Her Majesty's lieutenant (HML), sometimes referred to as the county lieutenant.[10] An appointment to the local bench was of considerable benefit to an individual's status in local society. Lisa Marie Griffith argued in her study of Dublin merchants in the eighteenth century that

> while elite merchants sought offices in civic institutions and while these positions elevated men above the mass population, the lower and middling sort, of Dublin, it consolidated them as leaders of their social rank rather than elevating them into a higher status.[11]

But this book argues that provincial merchants did in fact ascend to a higher rank, albeit with more limited prospects than their metropolitan counterparts. This was certainly the experience of the Glynn family from Kilrush, the elevation of some

lifetime; Glynn archive, box 11 (1910–20). 6 The family held eleven properties in Kilrush over the period 1811 and 1887; Glynn archive, box 8 (1880–90). 7 Michael Glynn, probate of will (1890). The will listed business contacts in Limerick, Dublin, Liverpool and Glasgow. Glynn archive, box 8 (1880–90). 8 Robin Pearson and David Richardson (eds), 'Business networking in the Industrial Revolution', *Economic History Review*, 54:4 (2001), pp 657–79. 9 The petty sessions court were the lowest courts in the country and dealt with minor local issues. They were often associated with corruption, as the bench usually comprised local landowners who acted as JPs and no juries were present. This led the government to install paid stipendiary magistrates known as resident magistrates. See Richard McMahon, 'The court of petty sessions and society in pre-Famine Galway' in Raymond Gillespie (ed.), *The remaking of modern Ireland, 1750–1950: Beckett Prize essays in Irish history* (Dublin, 2004), pp 101–37. 10 Matthew Potter, '"The most perfect specimen of civilised nature": the Shannon Estuary Group – elite theory and practice' in Ciarán O'Neill (ed.), *Irish elites in the nineteenth century* (Dublin, 2012), p. 121. 11 Lisa Marie Griffith, 'Social mobility and the middling sort: Dublin merchants, 1760–1800' (PhD, Trinity College Dublin, 2009), summary.

of its men to the county judiciary complementing and enhancing their status as influential local figures. While civic appointments were the sole preserve of men, one avenue where women often achieved recognition beyond the confines of the family home was through their benevolent activity, which courted the respect of the townspeople and elevated them to similar positions of civic responsibility and respectability.

Associational culture is an interesting way to examine an emergent merchant family because in this particular town with a population of 7,000 in 1881 it is not just about enterprise, there was a lot happening socially.[12] Associational activity provided yet another way of reinforcing and enhancing an individual's status in a provincial setting. The emergence of clubs, societies and sporting organizations in larger urban centres was by the mid-nineteenth century widely replicated in provincial towns. Such bodies were enthusiastically embraced by ambitious members of the middle class, who regarded membership as a public reflection of their status and rank. By mid-century, a plethora of clubs, societies and sporting organizations was established in Kilrush. Similar to other towns as far apart as Downpatrick, Kilkenny and Maryborough, Kilrush's emerging associations were backed by the civic elite – merchants, clergy, doctors and bankers – all of whom owned fixed property in the town.[13] As Kelly and Comerford have shown, 'the developing associational culture … voluntary activity, participation in clubs, societies and voluntary organizations' offered the middle class a favourable sphere in which to network on both a personal and business level with members of the landed gentry.[14] Moreover, membership of clubs and societies was a signifier of one's occupation, status and position in local society. The proliferation of sporting, musical, educational and social groups in Kilrush was broadly in line with the experience of other Irish towns.[15] In all, some thirty-seven clubs and societies catered for the sporting and cultural needs of Kilrush townspeople. Griffin's study of Irish cycling has shown that as early as 1879 up to eleven cycling clubs were in existence in Ireland.[16] The Kilrush Cycling Club was active in the 1880s, the *Clare Journal* reporting that '[T]he club turned out on Saturday last when the members had a most enjoyable spin to Kilkee'.[17] The report also provided the names of the committee members, a merchant, a solicitor, a money-lender, an auctioneer, a land

12 Census of Ireland, 1881, province of Munster, county of Clare, table XXX, 'Religious professions and education'. 13 As early as 1879, the committee of the Downpatrick Literacy Society reported that their annual event was attended by the 'most respectable and influential ladies and gentlemen of the neighbourhood'; *Irish Times*, 1 May 1879. The Kilkenny and South-east of Ireland Archaeological Society counted among its committee a number of MPs, barristers, clerics and landowners. See *Tralee Chronicle & Killarney Echo*, 13 July 1855. 14 Jennifer Kelly and R.V. Comerford (eds), *Associational culture in Ireland and abroad* (Dublin, 2010), introduction; see also Alice Johnson, 'Middle-class culture and civic identity in mid-nineteenth century Belfast' (PhD, Queen's University Belfast, 2010). 15 *Freeman's Journal* of 11 Dec. 1874. 16 Brian Griffin, 'Irish cycling clubs, 1869–1901' in Kelly and Comerford (eds), *Associational culture in Ireland and abroad*, p. 105. See also the *Irish Times*, 9 Aug. 1880, which advertised the 'fifty-mile road championship of Ireland'. 17 *Clare Journal*, 12 Apr. 1894. The census returns for 1901 were used to confirm occupations.

steward and a post office clerk. The absence of the Glynn family from the Kilrush Cycling Club may or may not be an indication of the lower status attributed to cycling as a leisure pursuit of the provincial middle class. The family are more readily associated with sailing, golf and tennis. As sports clubs developed, musical bands emerged in tandem, and McGrath has posited that 'the motivation behind forming such bands was to give young people a safe and orderly environment … which would help character development and help strengthen community bonds.'[18]

Kilrush played host to annual events such as horse racing and sail races, which were usually complemented by an associated ball. In the first fifty years of its existence, the Royal Western Yacht Club was solely patronized by a mix of the Ascendancy and professional classes. The membership lists of the Dublin-based club indicate that sailing was traditionally associated with the landed gentry, and several names on the list were those of Kilrush gentlemen such as Paterson, Unthank, Vandeleur and Studdert.[19] In 1828, the Royal Western Yacht Club established a branch in Kilrush and the personalities involved clearly follow a similar pattern.[20] The inclusion of two sons of Daniel O'Connell on the first committee suggests that the support for the club was cross-denominational and that religion was not a barrier to inclusion even on the committee. Sailing events such as regattas became prominent sporting occasions in their own right. While the sailing itself may have been the sole preserve of men, the ensuing soirées facilitated the mixing of men and women from varying ranks, fostering the development of social and economic networks. The *Clare Journal* reported in 1838 that '[T]he Shannon Regatta Ball was held in the Kilrush Assembly Rooms … under the patronage of Crofton Moore Vandeleur'.[21]

By the 1870s, the merchant and shopkeeping classes had begun to take an interest in sailing. The officers of the Kilrush Harbour Regatta in 1871 comprised the principal landholders and gentlemen of the county, along with individuals from the middle and professional classes, who acted as committee members.[22] By 1875, the *Freeman's Journal* listed a more recognizably middle-class committee of the Kilrush Harbour Regatta, a committee comprised of two doctors, two solicitors and seven merchants, along with the clerk of the union, one land agent, one bank manager and two local magistrates.[23] In 1892, Michael Glynn's son Henry sealed

18 John McGrath, 'An urban community: St Mary's Parish, Limerick and the social role of sporting and musical clubs, 1885–1905' in Kelly and Comerford (eds), *Associational culture in Ireland and abroad*, p. 131. **19** Royal Western Yacht Club of Ireland, 'Confirmed membership and yachts, 1827–1837', westernyachtclub.com/cms/index.php?page=club-history, accessed 1 Mar. 2015. **20** The first committee of the Kilrush branch of the Royal Western Yacht Club included members of the landed gentry: Crofton M. Vandeleur, Col. John Vandeleur, Maurice O'Connell, the Knight of Glin, John Bindon Scott, Poole Hickman and the Hon. J.P. Verecker. See Royal Western Yacht Club of Ireland, 'Club history', westernyachtclub.com/cms/index.php?page=club-history, accessed 15 Aug. 2014. **21** *Clare Journal*, 20 July 1838. **22** *Kilrush Herald and Kilkee Gazette*, 8 July 1871. The Kilrush Harbour Regatta officers of 1871 included members from the most prominent landed families in west Clare: C.M. Vandeleur MP (commodore), F.N. Burton, DL (vice-commodore), E.P. Westby, DL. **23** *Freeman's Journal*, 16 Aug. 1875.

the family's interest in upper-class leisure pursuits when he purchased a 50-foot racing yacht, which he named the *MV Rose*, from a boatyard in Falmouth, England for the sum of £178.[24] This purchase was a further indication of the gradual though steady move of the family towards gentrification. The extensive photographic albums of Rose Glynn, Henry's sister, after whom he named the yacht, provide additional and useful insights into the leisure pursuits of the middle classes in the late nineteenth and early twentieth centuries. Apart from the usual social occasions, tennis also facilitated a mixing of the middle and professional classes with the landed class, as was evidenced by an entry in Henry's diary in May 1885 describing how he played tennis at the Burtons' court in Carrigaholt (some 14 miles west of Kilrush) with 'Foley', 'Dowling' and 'Conyngham'.[25] Foley was a doctor and JP, Dowling was a pawnbroker and JP, and Conyngham was marquis Conynham of Co. Donegal, whose family had extensive estates in west Clare and Meath. Burton also held major estates in west Clare, where Carrigaholt Castle was his family seat.

The ascent of mercantile families such as the Glynns can also be traced through their membership of literary societies, which first emerged in Ireland in the early nineteenth century and offered places where members of the middle and landed classes could interact socially. Such was the popularity of literary and scientific clubs that the government introduced the Literary and Scientific Institutions Act, 1854, for the 'promotion of literature, science, or the fine arts, or for the diffusion of useful knowledge for improving the legal condition of such institutions'.[26] With a population of 4,593 in 1861, Kilrush was no different to other larger provincial centres such as Galway or Limerick, which also boasted literary and scientific societies.[27] The *Clare Journal* regularly reported on 'well-attended' lectures held by the Kilrush Literary and Scientific Institute in the early 1850s.[28] These activities progressively catered for the upwardly mobile residents of the town. The Institute was patronized by Vandeleur, and he provided meeting rooms and donated £5 to its lecture fund.[29] Ascendency patronage was still considered essential for this provincial self-betterment body, and although there is no mention of the Glynns in the 1850s, the gradual 'take-over' by the aspiring local middle class was evident in Michael Glynn's inclusion on the committee of the society in the 1870s.[30] Wider associational cultural activities of members of the Kilrush Literary and Scientific Institute were reported in the *Freeman's Journal* in 1857, when it noted that Patrick O'Connor esq., secretary of the Kilrush Literary and Scientific Institute, had joined the Dublin-based Ossianic Society.[31] O'Connor was of the shopkeeping

24 Invoice and notice of sale agreement between 'unknown individual' and Henry Richard Glynn, 15 Oct. 1892; Glynn archive, box 8 (1880–90). **25** Henry Glynn, diary entry, 11 May 1885; Glynn archive, box 11 (1880–90). **26** Literary and Scientific Institutions Act, 1854, CAP. CXII, Irish Statute Book, produced by the office of the attorney general, irishstatutebook.ie/1854/en/act/pub/0112/print.html, accessed 29 May 2015. **27** Census of Ireland, 1861. The Royal Galway Institution for the Promotion of Polite Literature, Science and Antiquities was established in 1839. The Limerick Philosophy and Literary Society was founded in 1840. **28** *Clare Journal*, 24 Jan. 1853, 13 Mar. 1854. **29** *Nation*, 12 June 1852. **30** *Clare Journal*, 15 Apr. 1872. **31** Robert Somervilleclass, whereas other provincial members of the Ossianic Society included the earl of Dunraven and Stephen de Vere, MP for Curraghchase, Limerick, among other members of the gentry and the clergy.[32] It is evident from the books still extant in his residence, Kilrush House, that Michael Glynn was a well-read individual; he served as a member of the Kilrush Library, which had been founded in the 1860s in the town.[33] However, the Glynns' cultural involvement does not appear to have extended to revivalist bodies such as the Gaelic League, which, by 1899, was well-established throughout Co. Clare and had branches in Miltown Malbay, Lisdoonvarna, Broadford and Kilmihil.[34] The social composition of Gaelic League members in the county was reflective of its national membership in that it was populated by clerics, bank managers, teachers and university students, but the business community appears to have been unrepresented.[35] Glynn's absence from the League, therefore, may be typical of his social background.

While the Glynn family appear not to have been involved with the Gaelic League, they certainly played some role within the Land League, as evidenced by the appearance of Michael Glynn on the platform at a demonstration in Kilrush in 1880. Glynn did not address the gathered crowd, estimated at over 10,000 supporters. The *Dublin Weekly Nation* noted the presence of a number of poor law guardians, newspaper proprietors, clerics and local businessmen who attended the meeting 'to organise a system of local branches of the League'.[36] Over the course of the 1880s, the Land League gained traction and support in Kilrush and by 1886, the *South Wales Daily News* reported that 'the walls of buildings in the town were covered with ejection notices by Vandeleur'.[37] The local nationalist branch had responded by issuing a poster inviting the people of Kilrush to become soldiers of Ireland under the banner of the National League.[38] Though the Vandeleur evictions were agitating the town at this stage, Glynn does not appear to have been openly involved, although his refusal to sign associated summonses shows that he was more than aware of what was happening. It appears that apart from his refusal to sign summonses, Glynn took up the mantle from the reasonably safe distance of the platform.[39] By 1888, the actions of the local Land League ultimately culminated in mass evictions on the Vandeleur estate. Successful local resistance

Woodward, 'The Ossianic Society 1853–1863', Department of Modern Irish History, University College Dublin, ucd.ie/pages/99/articles/somewood.html, accessed 16 June 2015. 32 *Transactions of the Ossianic Society for the year 1856*, 4 (1856). 33 *Clare Journal*, 27 Mar. 1873. A sample of some of the books from Michael Glynn's library include works by the poet William Wordsworth, the novelist Charles Dickens, as well as numerous travel books and texts of a religious nature. 34 Although there is no documentary evidence to confirm that the Glynns were members of the Gaelic League, there is perhaps one tantalizing piece of evidence in that Henry Glynn's greyhound was named 'Gaelic Leaguer'; *Irish Independent*, 3 Jan. 1914. 35 *Flag of Ireland*, 23 Mar. 1895. 36 *Dublin Weekly Nation*, 2 Oct. 1880. 37 *South Wales Daily News*, 20 Dec. 1886. 38 Ibid. 39 Glynn's association with the Land League was typical of his cautious nature: he was recorded as being present on the platform but did not take part in the proceedings. This was similar to his position as a poor law guardian. There are no references to his involvement with that body in the contemporary press, once more highlighting his seemingly deliberate method of shaping his persona – a form of self-censorship in the public arena.

led to Vandeleur requesting the presence of the 85th Regiment of Dragoons, who decamped to his demesne just outside the town.[40]

Glynn kept clear of divisive politics and was more likely to become involved in public activities linked with local economic advancement – for instance, the activities of the West Clare Agricultural Society. Perhaps reflective of the importance of agriculture to the economy and the county, the committee of the West Clare Agricultural Society, established in 1863, included members from both the landed and merchant classes. It was presided over by Colonel Vandeleur, who noted in 1866 that '[T]he establishment of agricultural societies in Ireland is one of the many proofs within the past few years of the increase and growth of that independent spirit of self-help which ought ever to help the tenant farmer.'[41] This optimistic note of harmony did not last. Despite the landed element's patronage of the association, the guest list at the 1868 banquet including such names as Vandeleur, Reeves, Studdert and Westby, the ascendant middle class was also creeping in. Michael Glynn was chairman of the society from its foundation and support was also given by the lord mayor of Dublin, William Lane-Joynt, solicitor and Michael Glynn's brother-in-law.[42]

LOCAL ADMINISTRATIVE NETWORKS

Michael Glynn ascended to the local bench in 1874 and the individual who granted his commission was Lt-Col. the Hon. Charles William White, who had held the position of county lieutenant since 1872.[43] White, himself the son of a self-made man, had risen so swiftly through the ranks of commercial and social respectability that he controlled a vast landed estate, spread across two counties, which by the 1870s amounted to approximately 24,000 acres.[44] In order to be considered for a position as a local magistrate, an individual had to satisfy stringent financial criteria, chief of which was the ownership of a landed estate and/or of property. In

40 Until the mid-nineteenth century, Kilrush was a traditional garrison town. However, following the 1850s, it became a sometime outpost of the military. Perhaps this was related to the presence of a significant police force, coast guard and naval ships. In 1845, the *Tipperary Vindicator* noted the presence of forty marines under Capt. Spalding in the former Revenue Square. In 1868, *Saunders's Newsletter* noted that a garrison of soldiers had departed Limerick for Kilrush and Carrigaholt, while in 1880 the *Irish Times* reported that the Second Battalion West Riding had departed Maryborough for Kilrush. It is suggested that none of these regiments or battalions had a permanent presence in Kilrush. 41 *Clare Journal*, 4 Oct. 1866. 42 *Irish Times*, 4 Oct. 1867. The committee in 1869 comprised three members of the landed class, two from the professional class and one from the merchant class. See also National Library of Ireland, EPH F446: 'West Clare Agricultural Society, the Sixth Annual Show of this Society will be held at Kilrush, on Tuesday, the 5th day of Oct., 1869 when the following prizes will be offered for competition. Kilrush'. 43 *Clare Journal*, 13 Feb. 1874. 44 Landed Estates Database lists Charles William White of 'Cahiracon', Kildysart and Annaly Lodge, Broadford, as the owner of Co. Clare estates that comprised of 18,226 acres plus 5,731 acres in Co. Tipperary; landedestates.nuigalway.ie:8080/LandedEstates/jsp/estate-show.jsp?id=1787, accessed

addition, the candidate had to submit an account of his business interests and the value of same and declare that he was financially solvent. However, satisfying these requirements alone was not enough, as a candidate's reputation beyond the constraints of his financial position was also vital to his obtaining a commission on the bench.

Another common feature associated with local magistrates was membership of a gentleman's club. These clubs offered formal networking platforms in a convivial environment, and membership of such organizations seems to have been another typical prerequisite for aspirant candidates to the bench.[45] Modelled on the private clubs of the eighteenth-century, gentlemen's clubs were originally set up by and for members of the upper class to provide them with a private space when they had business in a certain city or town. The formation of gentlemen's clubs seems to have extended from large cities to provincial towns from the late eighteenth to the late nineteenth centuries. In a small provincial town such as Kilrush, membership of a gentleman's club represented a deliberate statement of position and rank before the public. While no records of the Kilrush Club survive, supplementary evidence from newspapers can help identify the social composition of members of its committee. For instance, the *Cork Examiner* reported in 1905 that Mr Culligan JP was a member of the club, while the *Freeman's Journal* of December 1917 reported that Joshua Dowling was the club secretary; Dowling was a money lender and a draper.[46] The stated object of the Kilrush Club was to promote social intercourse between its members.[47] Clubs that provided their own private bar, for which a licence was required yearly, provided another opportunity for socializing.[48] The involvement of Glynn in elite clubs of this sort encompassed at least seven, including the Ennis Club, the Limerick County Club, the Stephen's Green Club and the Reform Club.[49] The Limerick County Club was founded in 1813 and it was the first provincial social club in the city, and was conducted on the model of Dublin's Kildare St Club.[50] In 1915, Glynn's Dublin-based solicitor, Synott, advised him to cancel his membership of the Stephen's Green Club in favour of the United Services Club on the grounds that the latter club 'was a far better choice for you'.[51] There is no extant material for the Ennis Club and little enough has been written

10 Mar. 2015. **45** The Glynns were members of clubs from London to Kilrush. See Milne-Smith, 'Clubland'. **46** *Nation*, 1 July 1848; *Cork Examiner*, 10 Mar. 1905; *Freeman's Journal*, 13 Dec. 1917. **47** *Irish Independent*, 7 May 1926. **48** *Irish Times*, 13 Dec. 1906. **49** A substantial amount of commercial and personal correspondence written on headed paper from clubs in Ennis, Limerick, Dublin and London survives in the family papers, the date range of which is 1870–1920. Similarly, telegrams were also sent from and delivered to these clubs, the names of which are the Reform Club, London, the Limerick County Club, the Limerick Junior Club, the Ennis Club and the Kilrush Club. **50** Committee of the County Club, Limerick, *The County Club, Limerick: a short history of a hundred years of club life* (Limerick, 1913). The Special Collections Library at the University of Limerick holds a notebook entitled 'Members of the Limerick Club'. However, it does not include any of the Glynn family. See Terence M. Dooley, *The decline of the big house in Ireland* (Dublin, 2001), pp 63–4. **51** Synott to Henry Glynn, letter, 16 June 1915. Synott did not provide any reason as to why he made this suggestion to Glynn. Glynn archive, box 11 (1910–20).

or documented about the Clare County Club, variously known as the Club House and the Bull Hall. One authority puts its date of opening at 1854.[52] Fitzpatrick has shown that the Clare County Club was more usually associated with Protestants who had business in the town.[53]

Mercantile representation on the local bench grew gradually in the years after the Great Famine and continued apace thereafter.[54] Previously, the membership of the local bench was drawn almost exclusively from among the landed gentry. Silverman has argued that throughout 'the period 1828–84, only landlords or their agents were appointed county magistrates [in Ireland]'.[55] Similarly, McDowell has noted that '[I]n England, Justices of the Peace were drawn from the landed class.' However, he made the distinction that 'in Ireland, where the landlord was often an absentee … there were obvious difficulties in making appointments to the bench'.[56] It would appear, therefore, that the make-up of the bench differed between Britain and Ireland. The British bench was more likely to be based on the lines of class, while the situation in Ireland appears to reflect a complicated religious-cum-class divide. One notable Co. Clare family to overcome that divide were the Catholic O'Loghlens from Ennis. Sir Michael O'Loghlen was appointed to the bench in 1811 and throughout his career held numerous top legal positions such as solicitor general of Ireland (1834–5), and was appointed master of the rolls in Ireland in 1837, and was elected MP for the borough of Dungarvan from 1835 to 1837.[57] The shift away from the traditional hegemony of the landed class who had dominated the local judiciary for many generations was further accelerated by the gradual break-up of their landed estates in post-Famine Ireland.[58] Control of the bench was utilized by the local landed gentry, who recognized its importance as an institutional tool of control over localities.[59]

Discontent relating to the non-appointment of Catholics to the bench was a common theme among letter writers to contemporary newspapers, and in 1864 a commentator to the *Cork Examiner* stated that '[I]t would be well to enquire how many petty sessions districts in the country have gotten Catholics on the bench and how many have not.'[60] The issue of the under-representation of Catholics on the

52 Peter Beirne of the Clare Library, email correspondence, 20 Apr. 2015. See the *Irish Times*, 22 Jan. 1873. The material related to the Reform Club includes correspondence written on headed club paper – this was complemented by the club records – membership criteria. The author is indebted to Laura Hogan for undertaking detailed research on his behalf in the library of the Reform Club, Pall Mall, London. 53 David Fitzpatrick, *Politics and Irish life, 1913–1921* (Dublin, 1977), p. 53. 54 The newspaper notes compiled by Senan Scanlan covering the period 1760–1830 proved an invaluable source in respect of locating JPs in the pre-Famine era. Of the ten mentions of the term 'JP', all the individuals identified were from the established landed class. 55 Silverman, 'Custom, courts, and class formation', pp 400–30. 56 R.B. McDowell, 'The Irish courts of law, 1801–1914', *Irish Historical Studies*, 10:40 (1957), pp 363–71. 57 *London Gazette*, 3 July 1838. 58 For a general analysis of the break-up of Irish landed estates see: Terence A.M. Dooley, 'Estate ownership and management in nineteenth- and early twentieth-century Ireland' in T. Dooley, *Sources for the history of landed estates in Ireland* (Dublin, 2000); Hugh Weir, *Houses of Clare* (Clare, 1984). 59 Byung Khun Song, 'Landed interest, local government, and the labour market in England, 1750–1850', *Economic History Review*, 51:3 (Aug. 1998), pp 7–8. 60 *Cork Examiner*, 23 Sept. 1864.

Clare bench was brought to the attention of the chief secretary of Ireland, Henry Campbell-Bannerman, as late as the mid-1880s. It was based on an issue raised in parliament by Matthew Kenny MP, who questioned the appointment of a minor Protestant landowner to the local bench.[61] While this case surfaced eleven years after Glynn's appointment to the bench, it provides some indication as to how individuals were considered for the judiciary. Colonel Lloyd, the controversial appointment of 1885, attained his position despite possessing a mere 60 acres in Knock (some 12 miles from Kilrush), whereas an unnamed Catholic gentleman, the owner of some 2,000 acres, was reputedly passed over for the same position.[62] The article alludes to the fact that Lloyd was not a full time resident of the locality, but 'a stranger and a Protestant ... and the district is almost exclusively Catholic', and the writer asked whether the Irish government 'proposed to redeem their pledge; to appoint a just proportion of eligible Catholics'.[63] The chief secretary responded by insisting that three out of eleven appointments in the previous two years had been Catholic gentlemen. He also defended Lloyd's appointment, pointing out that 'there is a very large Protestant population in the district and that Lloyd has in addition to the sixty acres, a large residence and farm that amounts to some 250 acres'.[64] The chief secretary was further pushed by Kenny, who informed him that '[T]he lord lieutenant of the county refuses to send forward the names of Catholic gentlemen [for consideration to the bench].' Kenny went on to claim that Catholics 'were refused appointments on account of their religion', to which the chief secretary replied, 'I do not know anyone – I am sure that no one would be – excluded by the Lord Chancellor on account of religion.'[65] The county lieutenant in this case was Charles William White of Cahercon, some 19 miles east of Kilrush. Although it had been suggested by Kenny that White was anti-Catholic in respect of his appointments to the bench, this clearly was not the case for Michael Glynn when he went forward in 1874.[66] Despite being an exceptionally prosperous merchant, he could not have been expected to compete with Catholic gentlemen who possessed thousands of acres. Nevertheless, Glynn had been appointed in 1874, some eleven years prior to the Lloyd controversy. If there was, as claimed in the Lloyd case, a bias against raising Catholics to the bench, how did Glynn

61 *Freeman's Journal*, 7 Mar. 1885. Matthew Joseph Kenny was a solicitor and nationalist politician from west Clare. He was elected to the House of Commons from 1885–95. 62 Ibid., 9 Mar. 1885. 63 *Freeman's Journal*, 7 Mar. 1885. 64 Ibid. Colonel Lloyd was a minor landowner in County Clare. See the Census of 1901, census.nationalarchives.ie/pages/1901/Clare/Coolmeen/ Prospect/ 1076644. The UK House of Commons record for the debate stated that 'Colonel Lloyd was placed in the Commission of the Peace for Clare on the recommendation of the Lieutenant of the county, a magistrate being much wanted in the locality where he will be available. His qualifications are stated to be (1) personal fitness; (2) residence in the county; and (3) property in this and a neighbouring county.' *The magistracy of Ireland, Colonel Lloyd, County Clare*, H.C. Deb., 3 Mar. 1885, vol. 294 c. 1896. Incidentally, when Michael Glynn died, Lloyd was included on a list of debtors to Glynn as he owed a debt of 17*s.* 6*d.* Probate of Michael Glynn, 17 May 1889; Glynn family archive, box 9 (1890–1900). 65 *The magistracy of Ireland, Colonel Lloyd, Co. Clare.* H.C. Deb., 3 Mar. 1885, vol. 294 c. 1896. 66 *Belfast News-Letter*, 12 Feb. 1874.

overcome this? His success was probably due to inter-familial networking as a means of countering institutional and class bias.

In addition to the religious make-up there was an interesting pattern emerging with the 'new money' of minor landed families now appearing on the bench in Kilrush.[67] Minor landed families, some of whom had earned their fortunes from trade associated with the river, began to distance themselves from their more humble origins. The landed members of the local magistracy appeared to possess a snobbery related to their new colleagues' background in trade, and Balchin noted a similar trend in Yorkshire's East Riding, where:

> between 1782 and 1836 at least forty-seven magistrates, some thirty-nine per cent of the Bench, possessed some previous or contemporary connection with business, commerce, industry, and trade … yet continued participation in such occupations was not encouraged.[68]

Other entrepreneurial families of the county also had a close association with business and commerce. As early as 1811, the *Clare Journal* reported that an oats ship had arrived in Kilrush from Liverpool, and the vessel was operated by Studdert and Gabbett, both members of minor landed families.[69] The Studdert family had purchased lands in Clare in the 1690s and established themselves as members of the landed gentry, while the Gabbett family were established in Co. Limerick by the end of the seventeenth century and from then on began to intermarry with local landed families until they rose to some prominence throughout much of Clare and Limerick. Cadet branches of the family established themselves in towns such as Ennis, Bunratty and Newmarket-on-Fergus, all in Co. Clare. In 1800, they intermarried with the important Limerick retail family of Spaight and settled into the more leisurely role of landed gentry.[70] A junior branch of the family operated flour mills in Corbally near Limerick city and resided nearby in a large country house.[71] Both the Studdert and Gabbett families, though considered to belong to the landed class, clearly relied on additional income from trade to supplement the income from their minor land holdings. Though writing in the context of Leeds in the 1830s, Wilson has noted that '[I]f the gentry provided occasional recruits to merchanting, the merchants in return provided the greatest channel of recruitment to the landed classes.'[72] It is clear from newspaper

67 The Studdert and Gabbett families, both of which had traded from Kilrush port, appear to have progressed from their import-export business and ascended the social ranks of society. From 1814, they are reported in contemporary newspapers as occupying the role of replevingers (agents authorized by the sheriff to recover property unlawfully seized), and by 1830 as justices of the peace; *Clare Journal*, 12 Apr. 1830. **68** Timothy A. Balchin, 'The justice of the peace and county government in the East Riding of Yorkshire, 1782–1836' (PhD, University of Hull, 1990), pp 91–2. **69** *Clare Journal*, 25 Apr. 1811. **70** Robert Gabbett, rector of Castletown, Co. Limerick, vicar-general of Killaloe, married Mary Studdert, daughter of Thomas Studdert of Bunratty Castle, Co. Clare on 5 May 1800, *Burke's Irish family records* (Britain, 1976), p. 456. **71** Landed Estates Database: landedestates.nuigalway.ie:8080/LandedEstates/jsp/property-show.jsp?id=2460, accessed 19 Jan. 2015. **72** Wilson,

18. Mill buildings and Kilrush House. Photograph © the Glynn family.

reports between 1811 and 1815 that both the Gabbetts and the Studderts were trading partners in a successful import and export business which operated from Kilrush to Plymouth, Liverpool and Glasgow.[73] In addition to their presence in Kilrush, both Studdert and Gabbett family members were recorded as merchants and members of Limerick Chamber of Commerce from approximately 1811. This suggests that their social progression was initially founded on trade followed by successful marriage contracts ultimately introducing them to the lifestyle of the landed gentry. The process of gentrification was typical for such families and more often than not, they readily welcomed their change in status and position.[74]

This was not the case for Michael Glynn, who, although he had amassed a considerable fortune through the success of his entrepreneurial endeavours, chose neither to purchase a large country estate nor to reside away from his flour mill. In fact, he purchased the large house attached to the mill and set up home on the doorstep of his enterprise. Many years later, his granddaughter Josephine described the scene: 'The family lived beside the noise [from the mill], the scraping of the metal gates on the ground, the loud machinery and the chimney puffing out thick black smoke.'[75]

Glynn was the second generation of the family and was an entrepreneurial, self-made member of the emergent new merchant class. He went a step further than his father, who had set up the thriving milling business: in 1855 he added to its already considerable interests, by investing in shipping and climbed into a social and administrative position hitherto unattainable for a person of his status. His acceptance of his appointment to the local judiciary in 1874 when he was 56 years

Gentlemen merchants, p. 220. *Holden's Directory* (Limerick, 1816) has an entry for Studdert and Gabbett but does not provide their trade. 73 *Clare Journal*, 25 Apr. 1811; *Limerick Chronicle*, 30 June 1813. 74 *Clare Journal*, 25 Apr. 1811. 75 Josephine Glynn, interview, May 2011. Josephine Glynn (b. 1928) is Michael Glynn's granddaughter.

of age marking the zenith of that ascent. His appointment also indicates that the traditional understanding of landed property ownership had now expanded to include owners of non-landed property.[76] Whereas Glynn's fellow magistrates in Kilrush had collective land holdings ranging from just under 620,000 acres, Glynn had no land but controlled a large and successful business enterprise that had commercial interests in counties Clare, Limerick, Kerry and Dublin and his firm also employed a considerable workforce.[77] In a further example of Glynn's elevated position, in 1874 he was also made an *ex officio* member of the board of guardians for Kilrush Union, another appointment that was formerly the sole preserve of local landed proprietors and professionals.[78]

All of this elevation led to Michael Glynn and his wife Jane being invited to the most prestigious society events in the calendar.[79] In addition to social gatherings and official balls, the appointment also offered unrivalled access to government bodies and boards and civic institutions. It is clear from the frequency of his trips to Dublin and the numerous newspaper clippings kept in the family papers that Glynn kept up to date with political and economic happenings in the capital.[80] Glynn possessed considerable social-networking skills and there can be little doubt that he turned these to good account in terms of furthering his commercial and personal interests. One such networking technique, which blurred the lines between the classes, was subscription to charities, testimonials and appeals, and especially the inclusion of one's name in the published list. In 1869, the *Freeman's Journal* featured an appeal for funds for the 'national testimonial to Sir John Gray' and listed among the subscribers were both Glynn and his brother-in-law, Andrew Madigan. The testimonial was in recognition of Gray's many 'eminent services' to his country; at the general election of 1865 he had been returned for Kilkenny, a seat he held until his death in 1875. Gray took a prominent and effective part in the passage of the church and land bills, and supported the home rule movement.[81] According to Norman, Gray was 'to become one of [Archbishop] Cullen's closest allies and one of the foremost in Catholic agitation after 1864'.[82] By supporting a man of such beliefs, Glynn was publicly making his position clear. When the full list of contributors is examined, the names reveal the extent to which families such as the Glynns had risen to prominence, included as they were within the ranks of high sheriffs, doctors and barristers.[83] The social composition of the subscribers to the Gray fund appears to have mostly comprised merchants (40 per cent), followed

76 Michael Glynn, probate of his will (1889) listed his assets; Glynn archive, box 9 (1880–90). 77 *Bassett's Directory* (Limerick, 1875). This source was cross-checked with the warrant for the commission of the peace for Co. Clare, which was presented to Glynn on his elevation to the bench, 9 Feb. 1874; Glynn archive, box 7 (1870–80). 78 *Freeman's Journal*, 6 Oct. 1874. In all, thirty-one guardians were listed, along with four doctors. 79 Ibid., 11 May 1876. 80 Series of press clippings from the *Nation*, the *Dublin Evening Mail* and the *Irish Times*, *c.*1850–85; Glynn archive, box 5 (1850–60); 6 (1860–70); 7 (1870–80); 8 (1880–90). 81 Alfred Webb, *A compendium of Irish biography* (Dublin, 1878), p 10. 82 E.R. Norman, *The Catholic church and Ireland in the age of rebellion, 1859–1873* (London, 1965), p. 80. 83 *Freeman's Journal*, 5 Oct. 1869. The high sheriff of Clare, J. Jameson, donated £50; William Foley MD gave 10*s*.; William Kenny, barrister contributed £1; Glynn

by the clergy (11 per cent) and professionals (7 per cent), with the remainder made up of women, newspaper proprietors and those of unknown professions. Taken as an internal gauge of status, the hierarchy of the list reveals that Michael Glynn was placed third on the list, close on the heels of the parish priest and the bank manager.[84]

Publicly subscribing to various popular appeals continued to build up Glynn's public profile in the last two decades of his life. Whether he felt 'safer' in doing so as his social elevation continued with his appointment to the bench in the mid-1870s is unclear, but both he and his son-in-law Andrew Madigan subscribed to the French Wounded Soldiers Fund in 1870, contributing one guinea each.[85] The popularity of this latter fund is obvious from the geographical and social range of subscriptions, causing the *Dublin Weekly Nation* to note that '[A] few warm sympathisers have donated over 17*s.* to the fund "La Grande Nation" ... including two labourers who contributed 1*s.* 6*d.* and 1*s.*, respectively'.[86] Support for such funds suggests that they transcended rank and position and appealed to all sections of society. Earlier in October 1870, the *Waterford Mail* reported that the Société de Secours aux Blessés Militaires had appealed for items including 'air-cushions, flannel to make vests ... shirts, port wine and Swiss milk' for the aid of the French Wounded Soldiers Fund.[87] Similarly, when the social composition of individuals from across the country is analysed to ascertain who donated to the Galway Vindication Fund in 1872, the results are broadly in line with the breakdown of those who contributed to similar funds. The list is comprised of landowners, professionals, and merchants, who contributed amounts varying from £40 to £80 each.[88] One such published list from the *Freeman's Journal* contained sums as low as four pence, indicating that those from less well-off backgrounds donated to public appeals for funds and testimonials.[89]

In a later testimonial to Gray that appeared in both the national and provincial press in 1875, the breakdown of the list of subscribers clearly reflected the dilution of the local judiciary by individuals from a non-landed background – merchants, doctors, solicitors, shopkeepers and even one tin-plate worker[90] – another indication of the growing prominence and status of the middle class. Perhaps, the reasons behind Glynn's sudden appearance as a highly public supporter of such causes and appeals was related to his ascent to the local bench – previous mention of the Glynn name in contemporary newspapers was more usually linked with advertising and offered little if any insight into the family's politics or other public

contributed £2 2*s.*; and Madigan gifted 2*s.* 6*d.* **84** Ibid. **85** *Nation*, 29 Oct. 1870. **86** *Dublin Weekly Nation*, 26 Nov. 1870. **87** *Waterford Mail*, 5 Oct. 1870. **88** *Freeman's Journal*, 19 June 1872. **89** *Dublin Weekly Nation*, 26 Oct. 1872. **90** *Irish Times*, 6 Nov. 1875. When the list was cross-checked with a local trade directory to provide the occupations of the subscribers, the results revealed that the local clergy (five in total – all denominations) donated an average of £1 each, the merchants (eleven) gave £1 5*s.*, the professionals (two doctors and two solicitors) gifted £1 4*s.*, respectively, and the local newspaper proprietor donated 10*s.* The tin-plate worker, John Culligan, donated 10*s.* The occupational data came from *Slater's Directory*, 1846.

affairs. However, some insight into Glynn's personality was offered by a prominent court case in Ennis in 1860. Glynn was accused by a newspaper proprietor of not paying for advertising in relation to advertisements placed on behalf of his brother-in-law, William Lane-Joynt, who was an election agent for a local politician during the municipal election of October 1860.[91] The article implied that Glynn had knowingly placed the advertisements without ever having had the intention of paying for them. On this occasion Glynn comes across as a shrewd, clever and somewhat crafty individual. He contended that he had not signed any agreement and the proprietor, Carroll, replied that Glynn 'was bound in honour' to settle the bill, and noted that 'I had experienced scurvy treatment from Mr Joynt in the previous election … he is a slippery gentleman.'[92] Glynn offered to pay a nominal amount of £10 – Carroll was demanding £150. While the outcome of the case was not reported in the newspapers, a conceited Glynn privately noted, '[W]e had a great contest with Carroll. He had two attorneys but was dismissed in court.'[93] Following the case, both Glynn and Lane-Joynt dispensed with the services of Carroll's newspaper, the *Clare Journal*.[94] This was recognized as a conservative newspaper, and its proprietor largely supported the landed class, although he also advocated for artisans' rights. The case highlighted the willingness of Glynn, acting on behalf of his brother-in-law (of just one year), to publicly align himself with the professional classes. This seemingly gradual shift away from their guarded private lives appears to be a calculated move on the part of Glynn and almost certainly was related to a need to increase his public profile.[95]

The crucial factor enabling Glynn to secure his appointment to the bench was inter-familial networking. For much of his legal career, William Lane-Joynt, Glynn's brother-in-law, acted as agent for the local landlord Col. William White, the son of Luke White, a self-made man who in the previous century had acquired a large fortune from selling books and operating a lottery.[96] Col. White held considerable estates in counties Clare, Limerick and Tipperary, which he represented in parliament from 1868 to 1875.[97] Typically, entry to the local magistracy was only possible following a recommendation from the county lieutenant, and in the case of Michael Glynn's elevation to the bench, it is

91 *Clare election: Minutes of evidence taken before the select committee on the Clare election petition, with the proceedings of the committee* (1860); *Irish Times*, 22 Feb. 1860. 92 *Tipperary Vindicator and Limerick Reporter*, 23 Oct. 1860. 93 Copy of letter between Michael Glynn and William Lane-Joynt, 10 Oct. 1860; Glynn archive, box 8 (1850–60). 94 *Clare Journal*, 28 Mar. 1870 and 3 June 1876, which noted the 'generous actions of the landlords – the White family of Ballyvaughan [Co. Clare]'. 95 Of the six causes to which Glynn donated, he gave to four before his appointment to the local bench in 1874. The subscriptions were as follows: Wounded French Soldiers Fund; Galway Vindication Fund; and two separate appeals for the John Gray MP memorial. It should be noted that Glynn was related to Gray through his wife Jane. 96 Rowena Dudley, *The Irish lottery, 1780–1801* (Dublin, 2005), pp 72–3. 97 The Landed Estates Database contains the following information: Charles William White of 'Cahiracon', Kildysart and Annaly Lodge, Broadford, inherited the Co. Clare estates, which comprised of 18,226 acres plus 5,731 acres in Co. Tipperary, landedestates.nuigalway.ie/LandedEstates/jsp/estate-show.jsp?id=1787, accessed 7 Oct. 2014. See also *Irish Times*, 9 Feb. 1874.

reasonable to assume that his family connection to White through the Lane-Joynts greatly aided his successful appointment. As White is not mentioned in the voluminous Glynn papers, there is no documentary evidence available to establish whether Glynn and White were on personal terms beyond the confines of the bench or whether they were simply professional acquaintances.[98] However, the landlord/agent relationship between White and Lane-Joynt certainly lasted until after the former's death. An advertisement for the auction of the contents of White's Co. Clare mansion, Cahercon House, indicated that William Lane-Joynt had graduated to the position of solicitor to the White estate, while his brother Robert acted as joint receiver along with the Limerick-based solicitor William B. Fitt.[99] While Glynn's appointment to the magistracy was a personal triumph, its importance in the wider context was not to be exaggerated, only appearing in one national newspaper.[100] A close reading of contemporary newspaper reports regarding the magistracy suggests that the less well-known provincial individual appointments to the bench were unlikely to be listed in national newspapers. This was certainly the case for Michael Glynn's, which was included in provincial newspapers such as the *Limerick Chronicle* and the *Nenagh Guardian*, yet did not appear in the *Freeman's Journal*.[101] The inclusion of the landed William Kenny of Cragleigh, Ennis, Co. Clare suggests a bias in favour of those of a higher rank.[102]

The increased status of a provincial merchant within a short space of time comes across in the fact that Glynn's death was reported in both national and provincial papers in May 1889.[103] He left an estate valued at over £24,000, which comprised the milling and shipping businesses and a considerable number of properties in counties Clare and Limerick. The value of his estate placed him firmly in the middle-class bracket, yet the family were not outwardly ostentatious in their lifestyle. There is evidence that Michael enjoyed the trappings of his success, but this was in an understated manner: his children attended elite boarding schools, and he and his wife Jane attended many official state balls and dinners.[104] Michael commissioned portraits of both his wife and himself, and these paintings adorned the walls of his large home. However, the following generation, though still not ostentatious, more visibly expressed their affluence in terms of both sociability and material culture.

INNOVATION AND INTRIGUE: HENRY RICHARD GLYNN

Henry Richard Glynn (1865–1916) and his brother Charles co-inherited the family business from their father in the 1880s.[105] The inheritance of the business by a new generation was viewed not with caution but as a catalyst for innovation and

98 Glynn archive, box 7 (1870–80). **99** *The Times*, 30 July 1892. **100** *Belfast News-Letter*, 12 Feb. 1874. **101** *Limerick Chronicle*, 17 Feb. 1874; *Nenagh Guardian*, 11 Feb. 1874; *Freeman's Journal*, 15 Feb. 1874. **102** *Freeman's Journal*, 15 Feb. 1874. **103** Ibid., 22 May 1889; *Limerick Chronicle*, 29 May 1889. **104** Ibid., 25 July 1884. **105** Henry and Charles appear to have taken control of the

diversification. The nature of networking in the early years of the twentieth-century had become unrecognizable since the appointment of Michael Glynn to the Co. Clare bench in 1874. By the time his second son, Henry Richard, sought a position on the bench, all manner of networking – social, business and inter-familial – were equally necessary in order to secure what was for the most part an unpaid, troublesome position in the petty sessions court. Yet the relentless manner in which Henry Richard pursued his appointment to the bench suggests the prestige associated with it had waned little since his father's time. The strategies adopted by Henry Richard Glynn in securing a countywide position on the provincial magistracy were many and complex. His attempt at securing it was aided by leading members of the British establishment. Glynn's persuasive networking strategies reveal the reach and access enjoyed by a relatively minor west-of-Ireland merchant, suggesting that early twentieth-century social connectivity was not hampered by geographical location. Glynn, resident in Kilrush, proved that however distant his main residence was from Dublin and London, he was privy to gossip from the inner circles of the Irish government and the British court. This was evidenced in a revealing letter to Glynn from May 1910 stating that

> King Edward's death was very sudden ... [T]he elimination of the German-Jewish financiers and bookmakers and the bulk of the horsey fraternity ... greater recognition of the commercial and business interests and no doubt the navy will, under George V, be placed in the favourite position hitherto enjoyed by the army[. H]e has always been very nice to our worthy peer [Pirrie] and I predict that this relationship will develop.[106]

Henry was the third generation of the dynasty to succeed to the business. Educated at Clongowes Wood by the Jesuits, he joined the family firm in 1878 and set about diversifying its interests.[107] He was a hard-working, shrewd businessman who abstained from alcohol and was deeply religious. Huggins has shown that '[T]here is plenty of evidence that much middle-class life was relatively sober, hard-working, law abiding and pious.'[108] Henry's business acumen was instilled from an early age but he furthered his knowledge of enterprise by studying contemporary business-instruction manuals. In 1888, he ordered the book *Money: how to get, how to keep and how to use it: a guide to fortune*.[109] The inclusion of what

business while William and Mitchel played lesser roles in its running. The evidence to support this claim is based on the large amount of commercial material in the archive produced by the former two brothers. A fifth brother, George, attended Trinity College Dublin and qualified as a medical doctor in 1898; Glynn family archive, box 9 (1890–1900). **106** Letter from Isaac Johnson to Henry Richard Glynn, 22 May 1910; Glynn family archive, box 10 (1900–10). Lord Pirrie was chairman of Harland & Wolff, the Belfast ship-building firm. **107** Corcoran, *The Clongowes Record, 1814–1932*, p. 184. **108** Mike J. Huggins, 'More sinful pleasures? Leisure, respectability and the male middle classes in Victorian England', *Journal of Social History*, 33:3 (2000), pp 585–600. See also the diaries of Henry Glynn, in which he described his daily routine: 'be up at 6.30, prayers until 7.00'. The Glynn family bible also contains notes written by Glynn: 'I promise to abstain from alcohol until the end of the year [1889]'; Glynn family archive, box 8 (1880–90). **109** Henry Richard Glynn, diary, 10 Apr. 1888;

were in effect 'get-rich/self-help' books suggests that Glynn was progressive and open-minded in terms of his approach to his business practices. In 1899, he was elected to the county council's Kilrush division.[110] However, although Glynn was a respected businessman from a well-established family, he was not listed among his peers in trade directories under the heading 'Gentry, Clergy, Principal Residents, etc.'[111] This was not the first time that a Glynn family member had been excluded from such lists and again one must question the method employed in compiling such data. Under Glynn's watch, the business expanded to include a woollen factory in 1879, it invested in up-to-date milling technology in 1888 and Henry became a 'baronial director' of the West Clare Railway in 1892. Aside from commercial pursuits, Henry was active in Kilrush society and there is evidence of his involvement in the Kilrush horse-racing scene. He acted as a steward for a race meeting which occurred in the Vandeleur demesne in 1912, which may have been a conciliatory gesture following the conclusion of a lengthy court case between the two families.[112]

The close relationships that the leading Irish industrial families enjoyed and the manner in which their networking practices created opportunities for enhancing social and business position was underlined by the Glynn family's close relationship with John Eustace Jameson, who was MP for West Clare and a member of the famous whiskey-distilling dynasty. It is unknown how the families became acquainted. There is no evidence to suggest that Glynn supported Jameson in his 1895 bid to be elected for the Nationalist Party, and Glynn was not reported to have attended the selection meeting.[113] A more plausible explanation is offered by the involvement of both individuals in railway development. Glynn was a director of the West and South Clare Railways and in 1897 Jameson requested to 'join the deputation to the Chief Secretary to aid the furtherance of the extension of the South Clare Railway to Carrigaholt'.[114] Such connections presented an opportunity for Glynn to advance his position among the leading businesses of the day, and following the conclusion of their lengthy AGM in 1898, the shareholders of Jameson & Sons appointed Glynn to their board.[115] The meeting had discussed the fall in revenue and the problems associated with the supply of Irish barley to the company. The *Irish Times* reported that 'the farmers of the South of Ireland were determined to drink no spirits unless it was produced from Irish barley'.[116] As a prominent miller who had a working relationship with barley producers, it is reasonable to assume that Glynn was in a strong position to advise the board about developments in the agricultural sector. The relationship Glynn shared with Jameson also extended beyond the sphere of business and into their private lives.

Glynn family archive, box 8 (1880–90). The book, *Money, how to get, how to keep and how to use it: a guide to fortune* was first published in Philadelphia in 1848. **110** *Clare Journal*, 24 Apr. 1899. **111** *Guy's Directory of Clare* (1893). **112** *Freeman's Journal*, 21 Aug. 1912. The remaining stewards were drawn from the landed, professional and middle classes of the town. **113** *Freeman's Journal*, 17 July, 25 July 1895; *Flag of Ireland*, 20 July 1895. **114** *Freeman's Journal*, 7 Dec. 1897. **115** *Irish Times*, 29 Nov. 1898; *Freeman's Journal*, 10 Dec. 1898. **116** *Irish Times*, 29 Nov. 1898.

In 1901, Jameson was a guest at the wedding of Henry's sister, Rose.[117] The Jameson family presented Rose with a 'silver cream jug, a sugar bowl and gold and turquoise bangle'.[118]

Henry remained unmarried and hence this traditional avenue of networking was unavailable to him. Therefore, he had to rely on his strength of character and ability to network. Family lore suggests that 'Henry was well able to hold his own, he was charismatic and friendly with the right people and he was invited to some of the most prestigious events in the social calendar.'[119] The ability of an individual from a mercantile background to be invited to the most prestigious society events in Ireland further demonstrated the manner in which the middle classes had penetrated the upper echelons of contemporary society. Glynn was invited to a number of such events including three levées held by various lord lieutenants at Dublin Castle between 1903 and 1913. Included on the 'who's who' guest list were members of the principal Irish landed families such as the earls of Westmeath, the lords of Oranmore and various privy councillors. For the 1903 event, under the lieutenancy of William Humble Ward, 2nd earl of Dudley, Glynn was listed along with members of the professional classes, including doctors, solicitors and magistrates, and under the term 'general circle'.[120] Interestingly, it appears that only two individuals from the merchant class attended, and one of these was Glynn. Most of the guests were from south Co. Dublin and the adjoining counties of Wicklow, Meath and Kildare. The more distant counties were represented by Kerry, Clare, Galway and Derry.

Such evidence suggests that for Glynn, state balls acted as an important avenue in terms of business and social networking and reinforced his identity and place within the principal merchant and professional families in early twentieth-century Ireland. Moreover, behind the frivolous nature of such social occasions important business connections and acquaintances were formed. Take, for example, William Anderson from Dublin's Merrion Road, who attended the state ball in 1903 and was later to be connected to the Glynn family through marriage.[121] It is unclear if it was this meeting that precipitated that later marriage, though when Glynn's commercial interests are taken into account, it is reasonable to assume that he was probably familiar with Anderson's background. He was the manager and secretary of the Dublin United Tramway Company, whose investments, under the direction of William Martin Murphy, stretched throughout Ireland, Britain, Argentina and Ghana.[122] Anderson's later connection to the family also heralded a union between

117 Photograph from Rose Ryan (née Glynn) photograph album of her wedding day in Kilrush, June 1901; Glynn family archive, box 10 (1900–10). Jameson was also included on the guest list, 14 Feb. 1901. **118** Unknown newspaper, 12 Feb. 1901; Glynn family archive, box 10 (1900–10). **119** Josephine Glynn, interview, May 2011. Josephine Glynn (b. 1928) is Henry Glynn's niece – though he was dead before Josephine was born, she remembers her parents describing his outgoing personality. **120** *Irish Times*, 21 Feb. 1903. **121** Ibid., 7 Feb. 1903. **122** Letter from Johnston to Glynn, 15 June 1910 in which he stated, 'I see that William Martin Murphy had to pay £8,000 damages in the action his engineering friend took against him over the West African railway contract.' Glynn family archive, box 10 (1900–10).

the leading contemporary Irish industrialist, Murphy, and the Glynns. In 1936, Murphy's grandson Billie married Norah Roantree, the sister of Gwendoline Glynn (née Roantree) thus uniting a prosperous provincial merchant-class family with two of the leading Irish industrial-class families.[123] As Dudley's tenure in Dublin Castle came to an end, Lord Aberdeen was appointed lord lieutenant of Ireland in December 1905. He was a noted supporter of home rule and a strong promoter of Irish industry, and the landed gentry largely avoided his official soirées at Dublin Castle. Robins noted that '[A]ttendance at the Castle was widely disdained by the nobility and the gentry and became ineffably middle-class ... the list of 2,000 guests for the St Patrick's Day ball in 1907 shows that only fifty or sixty titled persons were present.'[124]

It was Henry's ability to comfortably network with leading industrialists that set him apart from previous generations of the family. He was on personal terms with members of the provincial landed gentry and enjoyed professional and personal relationships with leading members of the Irish and British landed gentry.[125] An example of the latter was his close friendship with William James Pirrie, 1st Viscount Pirrie, chairman and proprietor of Harland & Wolff, the largest contemporary global ship-building company.[126] It is unclear from the available documentary evidence how Glynn established his friendship with Pirrie. However, both men were members of the Reform Club of London and both had shipping interests, although Glynn's were miniscule in comparison to Pirrie's. According to Moss and Hume, Pirrie was never quite accepted in London society and perhaps he recognized Glynn as also being on the margins, given his position as a merchant.[127] Their friendship also raises questions about class – how was a wealthy industrialist from Ulster acquainted with a minor merchant from west Clare? However it developed, Glynn turned his relationship with Pirrie to good account in respect of his obtaining a commission to the bench. It was telling of his self-confidence that he bypassed the junior local position of justice of the peace and applied directly for the senior county-wide commission of county lieutenant. Crossman has pointed out that '[S]enior civil offices in the county were largely

123 Glynn family pedigree was compiled by the late Charles W. Glynn (1945–2008). **124** Joseph Robins, *Champagne and silver buckles: the viceregal court at Dublin Castle, 1700–1922* (Dublin, 2001), p. 155. **125** Glynn counted landed families such as the Hickmans of Ennis, Co. Clare, the Barringtons of Glenstal, Co. Limerick, the Fitzgeralds, Knights of Kerry and the Carews of Ballinmona, Co. Waterford among his close network of friends. Private correspondence between these families and Henry Glynn confirms these relationships. Much of this correspondence relates to Glynn's activities as a recruiter for the army during the First World War (1914–18); Glynn family archive, box 11 (1910–20). **126** Apart from the study of Pirrie by Herbert Jefferson, no biography of this Protestant home ruler and industrialist and the dynamic force behind Harland & Wolff has appeared. See R.D.C. Black, 'William James Pirrie' in Conor Cruise O'Brien (ed.), *The shaping of modern Ireland* (London, 1960), pp 174–84; Patrick Long, 'Pirrie, William James' in *Dictionary of Irish biography*, dib.cambridge.org, accessed 27 Aug. 2014. **127** M. Moss and J.R. Hume, *Shipbuilders to the world: 125 years of Harland & Wolff, Belfast, 1861–1986* (Belfast, 1986), p. 128; John Bradbury, *Celebrated citizens of Belfast* (Belfast, 2002), pp 77–88.

honorific … county lieutenants' roles were not clearly defined, their functions included providing names of suitable deputy lieutenants and conveying to the lord chancellor opinions on the local magistracy.'[128] The role of the magistracy had remained a contentious issue for many years and although commenting on its role from the early part of the nineteenth century, Bartlett's description is still relevant: '[I]ts members were universally recognised to be inefficient, often corrupt and frequently reluctant to undertake any measure that might jeopardise their election prospects.'[129]

In order to secure such a prestigious commission, Glynn had to satisfy a number of criteria, such as being financially solvent and accepted within certain circles. This respectability was something that Glynn had earned throughout his lifetime. Many of his friendships and business relationships reflected the circles in which he moved. In a sense, canvassing for a commission to the bench began early on in an individual's life. It is not clear whether his father's successful tenure on the bench had any influence on his appointment. Certainly, in the case of the landed gentry, inter-generational appointments were more or less guaranteed. However, whether this applied to the sons of merchants or professionals remains to be researched. There is no documentary evidence to suggest that Henry Glynn relied on his father's reputation as a magistrate in order to secure his appointment, and in any case his father had been dead for over fifteen years before Henry made a move in respect of the local bench. Commenting on the frequency of appointments to the bench in respect of religious persuasion, Crossman noted that '[T]he proportion of Catholic magistrates which stood at just over ten per cent in 1834, had only risen to twenty-five per cent by 1886.'[130] The occupational background of the Irish county judiciary requires further research. However, Zangerl has shown that in England and Wales, middle-class magistrates continued to be active in commerce and manufacturing, a situation that would have been unthinkable fifty years earlier but in the closing years of the nineteenth century, individuals from the middle class were entering the magistracy in greater numbers.[131] Zangerl has noted that

> The landed classes were unwilling to admit individuals to the county bench who had close ties with commerce and manufacturing … the process of assimilation was a gradual one, usually requiring several generations for a middle-class family to attain a superior social status.[132]

128 Crossman, *Local government*, pp 15–18; see also Marilyn Silverman and P.H. Gulliver, '"Common sense" and "governmentality": local government in south-eastern Ireland, 1850–1922', *Journal of Royal Anthropological Institute*, 12 (Mar. 2006), pp 109–27. **129** Thomas Bartlett, *Ireland: a history* (Cambridge, 2010), pp 249–50. **130** Number of magistrates by county including the number of Roman Catholics, Jan. 1834 (Staffordshire Co. Record Office, Hatherton papers, D260/M/01/2058), cited by Crossman, *Local government*, p. 21. **131** Carl H.E. Zangerl, 'The social composition of the county magistracy in England and Wales, 1831–1887', *Journal of British Studies*, 11:1 (Nov. 1971), p. 124. **132** Ibid., p. 119.

Michael Glynn served for fifteen years, from 1874 to his death in 1889.[133] He was also serving as chairman of the Kilrush petty sessions by 1888.[134]

Henry Glynn was an avid diarist and meticulously recorded his thoughts in his pocket diaries. Entries concerned his commercial interests, and were peppered with personal crises and occasional questions of his faith in God. In a diary entry recorded on 15 April 1909, Henry noted that '[U]ncle Willie [William Lane-Joynt] will secure the DL position for me if I help him with *that* matter.'[135] While there is no evidence contained therein about which matter he was referring to, what is clear here is that appointments to the bench were open to influence from well-connected individuals. Lane-Joynt, as crown and treasury solicitor for Ireland, was perfectly placed in terms of access to top-ranking government officials.[136] Glynn also pointed to the fact that his sister Rose was married to Jack C. Ryan, who was a resident magistrate (RM) in Westport, Co. Mayo. Ryan was a career solicitor who was elevated to the position of RM in 1891 and enjoyed a privileged lifestyle. He was transferred to Co. Carlow in 1910, and a framed note handwritten by his colleagues on the Mayo bench stated that '[T]he magistrates of the Westport Petty Sessions District … desire to place upon the record our deep regret at the departure of Mr J.C. Ryan RM, to Carlow.'[137]

In terms of patronage, Pirrie was another powerful ally for Henry Glynn. He was raised to the peerage in 1906 and the following year was appointed comptroller of the household to the lord lieutenant of Ireland, who at the time was Lord Aberdeen. Pirrie was often referred to as a self-made man (although he was from a prominent family whose lineage included a prime minister and a lord chief justice of Northern Ireland), so it is hardly surprising that he and Glynn became close friends.[138] Their personal correspondence covered a wide range of topics, from Glynn's civic appointment to discussing the recruitment of men to the armed forces. Both men were prolific letter writers and many examples are extant in the Glynn archive.[139] Glynn was also on close personal terms with Lady Pirrie, and they enjoyed a regular correspondence. Glynn was a regular visitor to Pirrie's extensive estate of Witley Court, Goldaming, Surrey, England, and their exclusive London residence located at 24 Belgrave Square, one of the grandest and largest houses in the city. Glynn was on even closer terms with Pirrie's land agent and

133 Warrant for the commission of the peace, Co. Clare, 9 Feb. 1874. This extensive manuscript was presented to Michael Glynn on his entry to the judiciary. It contains the names of the individuals who held office in the judiciary of Co. Clare. One hundred and fifty-five names are included on the manuscript. Glynn family archive, box 7 (1870–80). 134 *Kerry Weekly Reporter*, 14 July 1888. 135 Henry Richard Glynn, diary entry 15 Apr. 1889. It was not the first time that a member of the Glynn family had relied on their family connection to Lane-Joynt, and Henry recorded in a note that 'father would have lost his job (as a JP) if William Lane-Joynt was not Crown and Treasury Solicitor at the time'; Henry Richard Glynn, handwritten note, 26 Nov. 1909; Glynn family archive, box 10 (1900–10). 136 *Irish Times*, 4 Jan. 1906. 137 The note is signed by Col. J.H. Buchannan, Lt. Col. B. Hamilton-Burke, W.H. Daley, J. Wington and J.M. Gray; Glynn family archive, box 10 (1900–10). Also included is an announcement from the *Connacht Tribune*, 11 Feb. 1910. 138 Jefferson, *Viscount Pirrie of Belfast*, p. ix. 139 Paul O'Brien, 'Provincial recruiting in the First World War: the Glynn's

secretary, Isaac Johnston. Little is known of Johnston's origin, although he rose to some prominence and was included on the king's birthday honours list of 1910. He mentions his inclusion on this list in an aside in a letter to Glynn: 'I will be able to say more tomorrow as my appearance on the birthday list of honours may detain me.'[140] He married Enid E. Griffiths, a sister of Richard Griffiths, manager of the largest suppliers of railway plant and rolling stock in the United Kingdom. Johnston and his wife chose Glynn as godfather to their daughter Kathleen.[141] In respect of securing his appointment to the bench, it was Johnston who relayed all of Glynn's correspondence to 'Lord P.', as both men referred to Pirrie.

Glynn's attempt to secure his appointment to the local bench can best be described as relentless. It is astonishing to note the reach that one individual had in terms of access to the senior levels of the British government and Dublin administration. The ability of Henry Glynn to network within circles that were inaccessible to most others is illustrated by a handwritten note from 1909. The note is addressed from the Viceregal Lodge, but it is unsigned: 'I was speaking to the Prime Minister about him [Henry Glynn] when last in London and the P.M. questioned me particularly about his landed estate, because, as he (the P.M.) remarked this is the point on which stress would probably be laid.'[142] The prime minister in 1909 was Henry Herbert Asquith, and according to historian Éamon Phoenix, 'Pirrie's Liberal credentials would have given him considerable clout with the Asquith Liberal government after 1908 and with the Lloyd George coalitions of 1916–18 and 1919–22.'[143] Glynn's letter-writing to both Johnston and Pirrie took full advantage of the latter's position as comptroller of the household of the lord lieutenant, Lord Aberdeen. In a glowing account of Glynn, Pirrie informed Aberdeen that

> The landed estate of Mr Glynn is not large … 100 acres, the approximate value of £4,000 … [T]his is quite apart from town properties in Kilrush, including two mills … valued at £50,000 … [H]e owns the Shannon Steamship Co. valued at £40,000 and is, as was his father, a large shareholder in the Great Southern and Western Railway, of which he is the director … [H]e possesses considerable houses in Limerick and Kerry, the milling business was founded by his grandfather in 1811 … [He] is a man of considerable substance and I need not point out how much more important are his claims [to be appointed to the bench] by reason of the position he holds.[144]

of Kilrush Co Clare', *Military Heritage Trust of Ireland* (July 2013). **140** Letter from Johnston to Glynn, 23 June 1910. The king's birthday honours with awarded on the birthday of the sovereign usually to senior politicians, military personnel, businessmen and members of the court and government; Glynn family archive, box 10 (1900–10). **141** Enid Johnston was married to Isaac Johnston and they had one daughter, Kathleen, to whom Glynn was godfather. The letters between Glynn and Mrs Johnston are of a friendly, frivolous nature and chiefly relate to acknowledgment of gifts and cards; Glynn family archive, box 10 (1900–10). **142** Handwritten letter (unsigned), Viceregal Lodge, Dublin, 15 Nov. 1909; Glynn family archive, box 10 (1900–10). **143** The author is indebted to Éamon Phoenix for his valuable insight into Pirrie, email correspondence, 5 Feb. 2014. **144** Copy of letter addressed to Lord Aberdeen, lord lieutenant of Ireland from Lord Pirrie, 17 Nov.

The extent to which Glynn had contacts willing to speak on his behalf and further his attempt to be included on the local bench was astounding, stretching from senior members of the Irish peerage to the prime minister of the United Kingdom. There can be little doubt that Glynn was well positioned to take full advantage of his business reputation. He seems to have paid scant attention to the strict conventions that were related to the process of applying for a commission on the local bench. He bypassed the lesser offices of JP and DL in favour of the prestigious county-wide lieutenancy. Previously holders of this office were nearly always landed and/or titled and had been for many generations, and most were Protestant. However, this began to change from the 1890s when John Morley, chief secretary of Ireland (1892–5), appointed 554 Catholic JPs out of a total of 637.[145] Morley's reforms drew negative commentary from the traditional members of the bench, and one individual suggested that the impartiality of local magistrates in the administration of justice was undermined by the appointment of 'men dependent on the people for their living – shopkeepers, farmers, publicans and the like'.[146] It was within this category that Glynn was firmly placed, and perhaps this goes some way to explaining why established Clare families such as the Kelly-Kennys and the O'Loghlens moved to block his commission.[147] The Kelly-Kennys in particular seem to have been the prime movers behind the attempt to prevent Glynn from securing the county lieutenancy. There seemed to have been no love lost between Johnston, Glynn and Kelly-Kenny, whom the former referred to as 'that old ruffian'.[148] The background to the fractious relationship between these individuals remains unexplained despite exhaustive research in the Glynn papers and an examination of Kelly-Kenny's diaries.

The occupational profile of the magistrates who comprised the Clare bench was beginning to shift from hereditary landowners to men of the industrial and merchant classes. For instance, of the fourteen Co. Clare magistrates recorded in the 1901 census, just four were born in the county, six included an alternative occupation in the description of their profession, four noted their religion as Roman Catholic and the average age was 64.[149] By the time of the 1911 census, the changes in the composition of the county bench were notable. Of eleven magistrates, six were born in the county, eight listed an additional occupation, seven identified as Roman Catholic and the average age was 54.[150] By the time of Henry Glynn's appointment, the social background of the magistrates had

1909; Glynn family archive, box 10 (1900–10). **145** Penny Bonsall, *The Irish RMs: the resident magistrates in the British administration in Ireland* (Dublin, 1997), pp 79–80. **146** Ibid., p. 80. See Matthew Potter, 'The rise and fall of local democracy', *History Ireland*, 19 (Mar.–Apr. 2011), pp 40–3. **147** *British Medical Journal*, 10 Oct. 1874, p. 480. General Sir Thomas Kelly-Kenny (1840–1914) was one of five children born in Kilrush to Mary Kenny and Matt Kelly. Educated in Carlow and later Sandhurst, he joined the army in 1858 and served in the Cape of Good Hope, Bombay, Afghanistan and China. In 1887, he became assistant adjutant general in Aldershot until the outbreak of the Second Anglo-Boer War of 1899–1901. **148** Letter from Isaac Johnston to Henry Glynn, 22 May 1909; Glynn family archive, box 10 (1900–10). **149** Census of Ireland, 1901, population records, Co. Clare. **150** Census of Ireland, 1911, province of Munster, Co. Clare.

changed beyond recognition. Magistrates from a professional background and a landed class had been overtaken by ambitious, wealthy industrialists and aspirational, prosperous merchants. Of the sample analysed, occupations such as farmer, rate-collector, miller and shopkeeper all featured prominently among the JPs on the bench in 1914.[151] Added to this group were individuals from the professional classes, including doctors and solicitors. With the exception of one magistrate, all of the individuals included in the sample were Catholic.

The method used by Johnston to enable Glynn to secure his appointment to the bench included a certain fabrication and deliberate exaggeration of Glynn's financial position. In correspondence between Glynn, Pirrie and Johnston, it is apparent that Glynn was coached as he attempted to secure the position. In November 1909, Johnston wrote to Glynn and stated that 'I hope you understood my telegram about *fully* [this word is underlined] valuing the properties as it is important to make a good showing … [W]e purposely lumped the "landed" with other property.'[152] By manipulating the facts concerning Glynn's financial buoyancy, both Johnston and Pirrie were complicit in duping the authorities in respect of Glynn's fully meeting the criteria to be considered necessary for the position of lieutenancy. A second letter, written two days later, stated that 'your letter was very good … I drafted a reply to his Lordship, who duly signed it this evening … [W]ho the devil is Rynne of Ennis and how dare he?'[153] The inclusion of Rynne in the contest does suggest that other individuals were working to block Glynn's appointment. Glynn and Rynne shared similarities as both individuals were from non-landed backgrounds. Rynne operated a hardware shop in Ennis, Co. Clare.[154] This was a further indication of the shift in the social background of potential members to the local magistracy.

Glynn maintained the pressure on Johnston to the point where there was an almost daily exchange of letters, postcards and telegrams between the two parties. The large number of telegrams, in particular, attest to Glynn's relentless pursuit of his appointment to the bench. A series of telegrams from January 1909 best illustrate this point. The messages seem frantic in nature: '[F]orgot to tell you … my father was magistrate of Clare … a cousin was on the grand jury … my uncle was Lord Mayor of Dublin …'[155] Part of the strategy employed by Johnston was the introduction of Glynn to Lord Aberdeen, the lord lieutenant of Ireland. Johnston insisted that Glynn visit the Viceregal Lodge in Dublin and become personally acquainted with Aberdeen and his household. In doing so, Glynn was

151 Warrant for the commission of the peace, Henry Glynn, 1914; Glynn family archive, box 11 (1910–20). It should be noted the term 'industrialist' is how Henry and his brothers referred to themselves, which was a distinct move away from either merchant or middle class, which the previous generation had used to describe themselves. **152** Letter, from Johnston to Pirrie, 15 Nov. 1909; Glynn family archive, box 10 (1900–10). **153** Letter, from Johnston to Pirrie, 17 Nov. 1909; Glynn family archive, box 10 (1900–10). Rynne of Ennis was subsequently appointed as a JP. **154** Mark Humphry, 'The possible royal descent of Dr Michael Rynne', humphrysfamilytree.com/OMara/rynne.html#royal.descent, accessed 23 Apr. 2015. **155** Three telegrams to Isaac Johnston c/o Harlandic, London, all dated the 18 Jan. 1909; Glynn family archive, box 10 (1900–10).

granted access to many of the most influential members of the Dublin administration. Coupled with the invitation to the Lodge, Johnston arranged for Glynn to attend the annual levée at Dublin Castle – one of a number of prestigious events in the Dublin social calendar.[156] Following his successful introduction to Aberdeen, Glynn, at Johnston's suggestion, invited the lord lieutenant to visit Clare and stay at his house in Kilrush. The documentary evidence confirms that Aberdeen at least acknowledged Glynn's invitation by return of a letter of thanks: 'I appreciate your courteous offer of hospitality … next time you find it convenient to be in Dublin I would be pleased to see you here, when we could talk over any possible plans for an expedition.'[157]

This was not just altruism but a trading of favours: Johnston used his considerable influence to secure lucrative contracts for his brother-in-law's company, MacKenzie & Holland. He called on Glynn to ensure that MacKenzie & Holland won a contract for the supply of signalling material for Lahinch Station in north Co. Clare, closing his request by reminding Glynn that 'Griffiths will be grateful and will see that you will get a satisfactory job … his father is director of the company.'[158] It is therefore suggested that whatever favour Johnston provided to Glynn, he expected in return certain preferential treatment from Glynn in respect of assisting his brother-in-law's business. Glynn was in a position to influence the outcome of the tendering process for the signalling equipment as he was a director of the West Clare Railway and also occupied a position on the Co. Clare finance committee.

Despite the concerted effort by Johnston, Pirrie and Glynn to secure the county lieutenancy, Glynn was ultimately passed over for the position, which was instead awarded to Sir Michael O'Loghlen, who held it from 1910 to 1922.[159] There is little doubt that Glynn was disappointed with the outcome. It would appear that the primary reason provided for his failure to secure the appointment was rumours of his 'shaken financial position' following the lengthy and expensive court case with Vandeleur, which went all the way to the House of Lords. Vandeleur seems to have informed the decision to some degree. Although Glynn had provided detailed accounts of his income, the high-profile nature of the case, which he lost, had given rise to gossip that he could not overcome. One of the main criteria for admittance to the county lieutenancy was evidence of an individual's financial security, and the rumours suggested that the legal action had cost him approximately £10,000 – in fact, the cost was closer to £500, but the damage had been done.

The choice of O'Loghlen as county lieutenant reflects conservative thinking if the economic criteria used to select a candidate is taken into consideration. Glynn

156 Dr Matthew Potter has suggested that 'for Glynn to be invited to state balls, he along with his siblings must have been presented at Court in Dublin Castle'; email correspondence, 29 June 2014. Despite an exhaustive search of newspapers and society magazines such as *Irish Life* and *Irish Society*, as well as the Glynn family archive, there does not appear to be documentary evidence to support this assumption. 157 Letter from Lord Aberdeen to Henry R. Glynn, marked private, 2 Feb. 1910; Glynn family archive, box 10 (1900–10). 158 Letter from Johnston to Glynn, 17 June 1910; Glynn family archive, box 10 (1900–10). 159 *Irish Independent*, 23 Sept. 1910, and *Freeman's Journal*, 9 Nov. 1910.

fitted the criteria, but one could describe him as 'new money'.[160] The influence of the local landed class in deciding the candidate is evident as they awarded it to a traditional candidate from a long established Catholic landed family. This would suggest that long-held local rivalries and the fact that Glynn had the audacity and financial capability to challenge the status quo such as the position of Vandeleur in the courts may have given the impression that he had risen above his station. Johnston referred to the court case when he wrote to offer his commiserations to Glynn: '[B]etter luck next time but you had a lot of worry and trouble over the long drawn out struggle and I sympathise with you on our failure.'[161] Interestingly, Johnston noted that 'I am glad that O'Loghlen rather than Kelly-Kenny or Inchiquin got it.'[162] This comment suggests another layer of intrigue between local landed candidates. Johnston also included a draft of a note for Glynn to send to Pirrie in order that he might thank him for the support in his failed candidature to secure the county lieutenancy.

Ultimately, Glynn secured the less-prestigious position of DL in Co. Clare in January 1915.[163] As the Glynn family were recruiters for the British army during the First World War, this undoubtedly influenced his appointment. Glynn received numerous congratulatory letters and one in particular is quite revealing – it was from John Meagher in Australia. Meagher had emigrated from Kilrush in the wake of the Famine and established a hardware empire in his adopted country. He imported drapery, grocery, ironmongery, wines, spirits and furniture. By extending customer credit on the advice of their store managers, John Meagher & Co. assisted the development of the central and south-western districts of New South Wales.[164] In the letter addressed to Henry Glynn, Meagher wrote:

> [A]s far as I am aware you are the first Catholic D.L. to receive this distinction … it is thirty years since my mother and father visited my native town, your attention and hospitality was very much welcomed in London and Kilrush.[165]

The entrepreneurial spirit that characterized merchant identity in the nineteenth century was even evident from abroad, and Glynn benefitted from the support offered by Meagher. International links such as those Glynn enjoyed with Meagher reflected the importance of business and social networking to the Victorian merchant class. By the time of Glynn's appointment, Meagher had enjoyed a swift rise in position and rank and was a member of the upper house of the New South Wales legislature from 1903 and he was honoured by Pope Leo XIII with a Knight

160 Zangerl, 'The social composition of the county magistracy', pp 113–25. **161** Letter from Johnston to Glynn, dated 23 Sept. 1910; Glynn family archive, box 10 (1900–10). **162** Ibid. **163** *Clare Champion*, 14 Jan. 1915. **164** Bruce Pennay, 'Meagher, John (1836–1920)', *Australian dictionary of biography*, adb.anu.edu.au/biography/meagher-john-7545, accessed 15 May 2012. **165** Letter from John Meagher, Bathurst, New South Wales, to Henry Richard Glynn, Kilrush, Co. Clare, 12 Apr. 1915; Glynn archive, box 11 (1910–20).

Commandership of St Gregory the Great. Meagher was a supporter of home rule and visited Ireland a number of times, his final trip being 1919–20. He was a close friend of leading political figures John and William Redmond, John Dillon and Michael Davitt.[166] In terms of networking, Henry Glynn was a contemporary of John Redmond at Clongowes Wood College, and the fact that Glynn and Meagher maintained a close friendship must have been known to Redmond.

Henry Glynn died suddenly in 1916 and the archive shows the network reach of the family from their small beginnings in 1811 to his death. The correspondence offering condolences amounts to over four hundred letters, which came from Australia, Canada, America, Malta, England and Ireland, from people including leading figures from the worlds of business, finance, politics, religion and education.[167] Even though the content of the letters was highly romanticized and nostalgic, what is important is that key figures in the Australian Catholic church were acquainted with Glynn and informed as to what was happening in Ireland. This included individuals such as the bishop of Bathurst, New South Wales, John Dunne, who described a 1902 visit to Kilrush, calling Glynn 'our warm-hearted friend ... from the Old Land, with its noble river, beautiful scenery, pious people and Catholic institutions'.[168] John Meagher's letter addressed to Florence Glynn, whom he described as 'mother, wife and sister' to Henry, mentioned that he received the *Limerick Chronicle* newspaper in Australia, which for Meagher, a staunch home ruler, seems strange.[169] The world of commerce was represented by William Martin Murphy, who described Henry as 'your greatly esteemed brother'.[170] Numerous business contacts from the United Kingdom offered their sympathy to the family, including Norman & Thomas of Liverpool, grain merchants, and Ross T. Smyth, also extensive grain merchants with offices in Liverpool, London, Hull and Manchester. Henry's alma mater, Clongowes Wood College, offered their sympathy.[171] Individuals from the landed class also sent their condolences, including Lord and Lady Pirrie and Lord Wimborne. Vera Matterson of the prominent Limerick business family also penned a letter. This illustrated that an active network existed between provincial business families – Matterson

166 Pennay, 'Meagher, John'. **167** The letter totals break down as follows: Kilrush (75), Ennis (21), Limerick (80), Dublin (75), rest of Ireland (77), London (19), England (13), Scotland (3), Australia (4), USA (1), Canada (1), Malta (1), France (1), Belfast (3), Salonika (2), others (2). The family also received eight-six telegrams of sympathy. Most of the letters refer to newspapers as their source, e.g. John Walsh, 26 Dec. 1916 from Salonika, Roland Pears esq., Belfast, 24 Nov. 1916, Vera Matterson, 28 Nov. 1916, Mayfair, London; Glynn archive, box 11 (1910–20). **168** Bishop John Dunne to John Meagher, letter, 22 Jan. 1916. This letter was posted to the Glynn family at the request of Dunne. Dunne was from Mitchelstown, Co. Cork and served as bishop of Bathurst, New South Wales, Australia from 1901 to 1919. A second Australian bishop of Irish descent, Patrick Joseph O'Connor (1848–1932) of Armidale, Sydney also wrote to the family in a letter dated 20 Jan. 1917; Glynn archive, box 11 (1910–20). **169** John Meagher to Florence Glynn, letter, 18 Jan. 1917; Glynn archive, box 11 (1910–20). **170** William Martin Murphy to Messrs Glynn, telegram dated 20 Nov. 1916; Glynn archive, box 11 (1910–20). **171** O'Connor to Florence Glynn, letter (date unknown); Glynn archive, box 11 (1910–20).

gave her address as Mayfair, London.[172] Likewise, Alfred Arthur Lynch, MP for West Clare, sent a letter to the Glynn family.[173] The legal profession was also widely represented and the firm used by the Glynn business offered their sympathy. The letters provide an in-depth example of Glynn's ability to network far beyond the confines and headquarters of his enterprise in the west of Ireland. Many of the letters were penned by his former schoolmates from his time spent in Clongowes Wood College, and this supports the idea of an 'old-boys' network'. Former Glynn employees who had joined the armed forces and were stationed in France for the First World War also posted letters of sympathy to the Glynn family.

By the 1860s, the Glynns epitomized the ambitions of an emerging business class, fulfilled through access to a broader arena of power, especially in membership of associational groups and local committees that previously had been the preserve of the landed and professional classes. This apparent acceptance of the family in more landed circles is perhaps what contributed to a newfound confidence on the part the next generation. Henry Glynn's apparent belief in his entitlement to the county lieutenancy amply illustrates this confidence and equally significant is his realization that networks of far-flung allies had to be utilized on this upward journey. The fact that these individuals were available to him (especially Lords Pirrie and Aberdeen) shows just how far the family had come in influential circles. That his quest was unsuccessful suggests that perhaps it had not come quite far enough. But successful or otherwise, the Glynn capacity to keep its eye on business matters during this time ensured that the firm continued to prosper and the family maintained its prominent position in local society and beyond.

172 Vera Matterson to Charles E. Glynn, letter dated 28 Nov. 1916; Glynn archive, box 11 (1910–20).
173 Letter from Arthur Alfred Lynch to Charles E. Glynn, dated 21 Nov. 1916; Glynn archive, box 11 (1910–20).

CHAPTER FIVE

'All we want is fair play': changing ways of doing business

THE GROWTH OF THE Glynn business from the 1850s to the 1890s was steady, but it remained more static after this period. Many of the family's characteristics remained the same, but in terms of upward mobility, they appear to have reached their peak. They had 'made it', but it was in a changing world and 'making it' by 1920 was a different animal. The forty-year period between 1850 and 1890 represented a gradual but consistent chipping away at the power and position of the landed gentry and underlined the advancement of the middle class, who comprised merchants, shopkeepers, industrialists and large farmers. By the 1920s, this disparate group were more readily recognized as the stalwarts of provincial Ireland than the landed gentry, who had trundled on from the disaster of the Famine through to the Land War of the 1880s. Their heirs were decimated by the First World War, and the establishment of the Irish Free State in 1921 led to the break-up of their vast estates and ultimately to the exodus of many of their number. Dooley noted in his study of the decline of the landed gentry that '[I]n Ireland the gentry were detested because the culture they represented was the one that the new order in Ireland was attempting to suppress ... [W]hile their isolation in the past had been voluntary, it now became enforced.'[1]

Meanwhile, the Glynn family had risen rapidly from humble masons and corn merchants to well-connected flour and meal millers, railway investors, ship-owners and coal importers; they had entered civic office and married well. Henry R. Glynn was a member of Clare County Council following his election on the nationalist ticket in 1899.[2] His brother William was a member of Kilrush Urban Council, which was formed after the introduction of the Local Government Act in 1898; he had been elected under the local banner of 'trade and commerce'. As part of the election campaign, they had pledged to 'do their best for the improvement of the town.'[3] The entrepreneurial skill of the Glynn family was demonstrated through their readiness to diversify their commercial interests and their ability to network and build relationships with local merchants, some leading Irish industrialists and even figures within the administration. By the early twentieth century, the Glynns were at the apex of their influence.

1 Dooley, *The decline of the big house in Ireland*, p. 243. 2 *Freeman's Journal*, 7 Apr. 1899. 3 Kieran Sheedy, *The Clare elections* (Dublin, 1993), pp 779–80.

The Glynn family was in the mainstream of respectable, aspirant Catholic Ireland, which was content enough to stay within the union. They were not actively involved in politics for most of the nineteenth century and although there is a signed commemorative plaque of O'Connell in the archive, it was probably little more than an emotive connection to him or perhaps was gifted as part of a will, there being mention of Lady Gray – a cousin of Jane Glynn (née) Lane-Joynt.[4] O'Connell was upwardly mobile and Catholic – much like the Glynn family. While there is no evidence that the family contributed to the Catholic rent,[5] a contemporary account informs us that the Revd Corbett had collected '£6 which was the amount of Catholic Rent collected for the town [Kilrush] and parish for July'.[6] However, in 1845, Bartholomew and John Glynn were listed as supporters of the O'Connell Tribute in Kilrush – they contributed five shillings each – and by the latter half of the century, the family supported popular causes with a Catholic undertone, subscribing in 1870 to a public testimonial for injured French soldiers (but not appearing on pro-French platforms).[7]

The family did a balancing act between supporting popular political causes and maintaining their position within the establishment. Michael Glynn's appointment as a local magistrate in 1874 was a legal rather than a political appointment, and his ready acceptance of it indicated that he was concerned with acting within rather than undermining the existing system. However, it was impossible to avoid political entanglement completely. Though designed to be apolitical, the magistracy, like other local government bodies, was often associated with political issues. For instance, in 1882, the Kilrush Board of Guardians expressed its 'great satisfaction at the liberation of the imprisoned members of parliament and Michael Davitt as being conducive to the peace and welfare of our country', and there is no record of Glynn, who was a member, dissenting from that motion.[8]

Five years later, Glynn was more visible in land-related political activities when a branch of the National Land League was established in Kilrush and a resolution passed at its first public meeting called for the 'establishment of a peasant proprietary … the only means of rooting the people in the soil and preserving them from being mendicants upon the charity of nations'.[9] Michael Glynn was on the platform and his speech was tailored to support the resolution. He stated that '[F]or forty years I have witnessed the condition of tenant-farmers in west Clare

4 Commemorative plaque signed by Daniel O'Connell, MP for the county of Cork, Richmond Bridewell, 5 Sept. 1844. It has the following inscription: 'Written for the fair and most respected lady of my friend, John Gray, also Thomas W. Ray, secretary of the Royal National Repeal Association of Ireland, Richmond Bridewell, 5 Sept. 1844; John Gray, editor of the *Freeman*; John O'Connell MP, Kilkenny city, 5 Sept. 1844, the last day in Richmond Bridewell, the first of Ireland's triumph; Charles G. Duffy, editor of the *Nation*; Richard Barrett, editor and proprietor of the *Pilot*; Thomas Steele, O'Connell's head pacificator'; Glynn family archive, box 4 (1840–50). 5 The Catholic rent was one penny per month and was designed to fund O'Connell's attempt to win Catholic emancipation. 6 *Proceedings of the Catholic Association in Dublin*, 13 May to 11 Feb. 1823 (London, 1825), p. 485. 7 *Nation*, 29 Oct. 1870. 8 *Irish Times*, 25 May 1882. See also Noel Mulqueen, *The Vandeleur evictions and the plan of campaign in Kilrush* (Clare, 1988). 9 *Irish Times*, 27 Sept. 1887.

and the hardships they suffered … [W]here was the landlord that came forward and helped them [?] … [T]he shopkeepers and traders stood by them.'[10] Clark has argued that businessmen and farmers were intertwined in their enterprises and that they relied on one another for their economic survival.[11]

From its establishment in 1885, Kilrush Town Commissioners often discussed political events, something that seemed to contradict its remit, though this was by no means uncommon in later nineteenth-century Ireland. These discussions clearly raised tensions and dilemmas for its members, as was evidenced by the resignation of the landed Michael S. Brews (a former poor law guardian) in May 1886. Brews resigned his position owing to the adoption of a resolution passed which accused the Clare Grand Jury of 'blaming loyalists for maintaining public order'.[12] Brews stated that he had only become a commissioner on the understanding that it would be a non-political body, though in the context of the times this was a near impossibility.[13] Throughout its lifetime, the Kilrush Town Commissioners unanimously passed a number of politically related resolutions including one in 1887 that protested against the Coercion Act.[14] Two years earlier, in 1885, the Kilrush Town Commissioners had welcomed Michael Davitt to town prior to his 'monster demonstration' in Kilkee.[15] The business of the commissioners also addressed the Vandeleur evictions, in particular in 1888 when James S. Clancy condemned Vandeleur's actions.[16] The Vandeleur evictions were widely condemned in the contemporary press, both in Ireland and Britain, and the *Hartlepool Mail* noted that 'the evictions are fast becoming a scandal … as an army with battering rams and wicker shields force tenants to obey the Queen's writ'.[17]

Although there is no documentary evidence available from the meetings of the Kilrush Town Commissioners confirming whether Glynn agreed with the passing of political resolutions, family tradition seems to suggest the family's involvement with the local Land League from its inception, and while the date he cited is incorrect Henry Glynn's note of nearly thirty years later does underline the importance of the land question to the family.[18] He described the first Land League meeting that was held in Kilrush, in his father's mill in 1883: 'I was there, father gave the room at that time and afterwards I saw crowds of men marching up and down Frances Street and saw them dispersed by the police.'[19] Contemporary

10 Ibid. 11 Sam Clark, 'The social composition of the Land League', *Irish Historical Studies*, 17:68 (Sept. 1971), p. 450. 12 Sheedy, *The Clare elections*, p. 772, Kilrush Town Commissioners operated from 1886 to 1898, when it was replaced by Kilrush District Council, which operated from 1899 to 1993. Michael S. Brews (1838–1916) was a farmer and landed proprietor; Census of Ireland, 1901. See also *Bassett's Directory*, 1875–6. 13 *Irish Times*, 25 May 1882. 14 Ibid. 15 *Freeman's Journal*, 5 Oct. 1885. 16 Sheedy, *The Clare Elections*, p. 774. 17 *Hartlepool Mail*, 27 July 1888. See also the *Aberdeen People's Journal* of 28 July 1888, which noted 'exciting scenes at Irish evictions, the bayonet and the battering ram', and the *Sheffield Independent* of 27 July 1888, which carried the headline 'Sickening Spectacle at the Vandeleur Evictions: Fighting for the Old Home'. 18 Sheedy's extensive study of the Clare elections does not mention if the Glynn family were involved in the planning and implementation of the local plan of campaign. See Sheedy, *The Clare elections*, pp 267–302. 19 Henry Richard Glynn, handwritten note, 26 Nov. 1909; Glynn archive, box 10 (1900–10). There is

newspaper reports seem to contradict his account. For instance, the *Dublin Weekly Nation* described the rather low key visit of Michael Davitt (the founder of the Land League) to Kilrush in August of 1883. It noted that 'his coming through Kilrush was almost wholly unknown'.[20] Henry, also noting his father's actions during the Land War, described how

> in 1886 and 1887, father prevented nearly two hundred Vandeleur tenants being evicted by signing summonses against Vandeleur and Studdert ... the dispute was referred to arbitration and all of the tenants who were evicted were reinstated. Father would have lost his JP [position] if only for ... William Lane-Joynt who was Crown and Treasury Solicitor at the time.[21]

This note concerned the action that Michael Glynn initiated against Vandeleur's agents during the Land War. In 1888, a series of mass evictions took place on the Vandeleur estate in west Clare. One of those evicted tenants, Mathias McGrath, took a case against Turner, a local magistrate, Croker, the sub-sheriff and Studdert, the land agent, in respect of his forced eviction, which he contended was illegal. Glynn, a district magistrate, granted a summons on foot of McGrath's affidavit.[22] Glynn's action was without precedent and caused much hostility and resentment towards him. The *Freeman's Journal* reported that Glynn had signed the summons in a district in which he was not authorized to do so.[23] His unpublished reply to the editor of that paper attempts to explain his actions and to counter the damage he felt was unjustly caused to his reputation. Glynn drafted several replies – all of which survive in the family papers, and they provide some insight into his reasons for taking that course of action. Glynn noted that

> my refusal to sign the summonses especially as they had been asked for in the sworn presence of a solicitor ... would have shaken the faith of the people of this extensive district in the just and impartial administration of the law and would lead them to believe that there was no protection for the poor and the humble when they came into conflict with the rich and the powerful.[24]

Glynn's unconventional action led to an official caution from the lord chancellor, who reminded Glynn of his magisterial duties:

> Such action is clearly not in accordance with the general practices of magistrates and would appear to be opposed to the courtesy of conduct

no other evidence to confirm this date, although the *Irish Times* of 27 Sept. 1880 noted 'a meeting of the National Land League was held in Kilrush ... to denounce land robbers and landlordism'. **20** *Dublin Weekly Nation*, 11 Aug. 1883. **21** Ibid. William Lane-Joynt was Michael Glynn's brother-in-law and intervened on his behalf. Hallam Studdert (1841–1905) acted as Vandeleur's land agent. **22** *Irish Times*, 5 Sept. 1888. **23** *Freeman's Journal*, 22 Aug. 1888. **24** Michael Glynn, unpublished letter to the editor of the *Freeman's Journal*, 22 Apr. 1888; Glynn archive, box 8 (1880–90). It is worth noting that the proprietor of the *Freeman's Journal*, Sir John Gray, was a cousin of Michael Glynn's which should exist between magistrates and which is necessary to due administration of justice and the maintenance of respect for the law.[25]

Glynn also noted that he had signed summonses in neighbouring districts for over fourteen years and that it was not an issue. That Glynn shared sympathy with the evicted tenants in west Clare at the risk of losing his place on the local magistracy highlights the manner in which the family held a respect and understanding for the condition of the smallholder in the region. Glynn was a landlord in his own right in the urban context, although he agreed to a rent abatement in 1886 and the *Irish Times* reported that '[A]t the meeting of the Kilrush House League ... reductions of rents were made by Mr Michael Glynn, J.P., to his tenants in Henry Street and Moore Street.'[26]

Perhaps Glynn's action against Vandeleur and his agents influenced the later bitter and protracted legal dispute that emerged between the two families, which centred on the latter's attempt to recover the tolls and charges for the use of Kilrush Creek which Glynn had withheld. At the establishment of the Kilrush branch of the Land League in 1887, Glynn apportioned blame to Vandeleur for the declining state of trade in the town, which he suggested was related to the neglected condition of the harbour.[27]

Though the family seemed clearly positioned within the political atmosphere of the day, it was not without its critics, and in 1887, notices appeared in the newspapers from Clare and Limerick merchants who called for a boycott of the Glynns' Shannon Steamship Company for 'conveying political prisoners to Limerick Gaol'.[28] Following the death of Michael Glynn in 1889, his son William J. Glynn was co-opted onto the Kilrush Town Commissioners.[29] The Glynn family continued to increase its presence in local and county affairs and the *Clare Journal* reported in 1899 that Henry R. Glynn was elected a Nationalist county councillor for the Kilrush Division and received a hearty ovation on his arrival home on Friday evening.[30] The following year Glynn was elected as chairman of the county council.[31] During his tenure on the county council, he was active in relation to a number of issues, most notably the cost of policing. In 1908, the *Irish Times* reported that owing to an increase in cattle-driving and agrarian disturbances, additional funds to cover extra policing costs were to be raised locally. As a ratepayer himself, Glynn protested at the 'enormous cost to the county' and suggested that 'it was the whole cause of the government putting this extra charge on the people of the county'.[32] Glynn also took an active role in bringing to an end a railway strike in September 1910. This was, however, a more personal matter, as he was co-director of the West Clare Railway and a member of the county council

wife, Jane. **25** Copy of letter from lord chancellor's office, Four Courts, Dublin to Michael Glynn esq. JP, 25 Aug. 1888; Glynn archive, box 8 (1880–90). **26** *Irish Times*, 7 Sept. 1886. **27** Ibid., 27 Sept. 1887. **28** *Sheffield Daily Telegraph*, 17 Nov. 1887. **29** Sheehy, *The Clare elections*, p. 774. **30** *Clare Journal*, 24 Apr. 1899, *Irish World and American Industrial Liberator*, 6 May 1899. **31** Ibid., 14 June 1900. **32** *Irish Times*, 16 Dec. 1908.

executive.[33] Perhaps, Glynn's increasing public profile instilled a confidence in him to openly challenge the Vandeleurs. Either way, it was a highly symbolic move on the part of a merchant – who had enjoyed a momentous rise.

Not content just to invest their fortunes in traditional interests, the merchant class diversified its business investments beyond the confines of the local and national arena. For example, the Glynns invested in a number of emerging colonial and imperial companies such as Nestlé, Marconi and Unilever.[34] When William Joynt Glynn died in 1932, he had the considerable amount of £7,571 invested in thirty-three Irish Free State, English and 'foreign and colonial' companies.[35] The willingness of the merchant class to expand their commercial interests beyond the traditional sphere of railways, gas companies and bank stock suggested that they were willing to take risks with their fortunes. However, the potential risks were well-researched in advance and Glynn did not tie up vast amounts of capital in emerging international companies. He may have been prompted to invest in certain shares by Isaac Johnston, who asked Henry Glynn 'if you or your brother had purchased any Pneumatic shares, the shares are 2*s.* and 6*d.* … but I do not know whether this is normal.'[36] The readiness of Glynn to invest in new companies was not a strategy adopted by Vandeleur – apart from some limited interests in the railway, there is no evidence to suggest that he invested in new technologies or emerging global companies. However, other Irish landed families did invest in stocks and shares, and according to Dooley, the investment portfolio of the Leslie family of Glaslough, Co. Monaghan 'soon bulged … with the most fanciful stocks and shares'.[37] This is broadly in line with the experience of the landed gentry in England, who 'were willing to diversify their investments into mining, railways and a range of other urban and industrial ventures as economic conditions came to permit such behaviour'.[38] Vandeleur's reluctance to diversify his investments firmly represented the traditional landlord, whose land-based enterprise was generally his only means of generating revenue, and this contrasted sharply with the new entrepreneurial merchant class to which Glynn belonged.

'THE CHAMPION OF THE PUBLIC INTEREST': LANDLORD VS. MERCHANT

Prior to the legal action, there seems to have been a cordial relationship between the Vandeleur and Glynn families. Members of both families served on local committee boards, namely the West Clare Agricultural Society and the Harbour

33 *Irish Times*, 8 Sept. 1910. 34 The Glynn family purchased shares from international brands such as Nestle, Marconi and Unilever and Irish companies such as Dublin Distillers, the *Irish Press* and Great Southern Railways. 35 William J. Glynn, deceased, shares valued by Messrs Rawlinson, Allen and White as on 1 Sept. 1932; Glynn archive, box 13 (1930–40). 36 Isaac Johnston to Henry Richard Glynn, 22 June 1910; Glynn archive, box 11 (1910–20). 37 Dooley, *The decline of the big house in Ireland*, p. 243. 38 F.M.L. Thompson, *English landed society in the nineteenth century* (1963); idem,

19. Kilrush Creek, with the Glynn milling complex in the background. Photograph © the Glynn family.

Regatta, which promoted business and leisure pursuits in Kilrush. In 1874, Michael Glynn was appointed a local magistrate and Crofton Moore Vandeleur was the chairman of the same court. This relationship was representative of the wider mixing of the middle and upper classes that began to occur in the years following the Great Famine, especially in respect of associational culture and the local magistracy. The determination of the Glynns to protect their business concerns and their position in Kilrush was highlighted by a lengthy legal action that spanned the final years of the nineteenth and the early years of the twentieth century. The action centred around the Glynns' withholding of duties and payments from the Vandeleurs – the money, £15 16*s*. 5*d*. was nearly inconsequential – the important point to consider was that upwardly mobile merchants now found themselves in a secure enough position to openly challenge the authority of the landed gentry.[39] The altercation between Vandeleur and Glynn, while it took place during the Land

'English landed society in the twentieth century', I–IV, *Trans. Royal Historical Society*, 5th ser., 40–6th ser., 3 (1990–2), cited by Mark Rothery, 'The wealth of the English landed gentry, 1870–1935' in *Agricultural History Review*, 55:2 (2007), pp 251–68. 39 John Cullinan, solicitor for Hector S. Vandeleur, plaintiff to Michael Glynn & Sons, defendants, ordinary civil bill, 23 Dec. 1896; Glynn archive, box 9 (1890–1900).

War, had nothing directly to do with it. The case concerned an action taken against M. Glynn & Sons by Hector Stewart Vandeleur in relation to the Glynns' withholding of quayage, wharfage and tolls in response to Vandeleur's reputed negligence in relation to the upkeep of Kilrush Creek and the harbour.[40] The case taken by Vandeleur was centred on his claim to the ownership of the foreshore rights in Kilrush Creek. It was primarily about economic competition, as Vandeleur was extracting considerable income from the control of imports and exports through the creek.[41] For instance, in the year July 1893 to June 1894, three of the Glynn vessels (one steamer, and two packets) paid more than £28 in tolls and charges to Vandeleur. Considering that 496 vessels discharged cargo in Kilrush in 1885, the turnover must have been considerable.

The Glynn family's growing business depended on the distribution network stretching from west Clare up the Shannon to Limerick port. The coming of the railway greatly increased the market for Glynn's produce and from the early 1890s the firm traded with more and more businesses located both in Ireland and the United Kingdom. The creek was vital to the smooth running of this distribution network and to the success of Glynn's extensive business. In addition, both the Shannon Steamship Company, controlled by Glynn and the West Clare Railway, under his directorship, were both dependent on access through the creek and the Glynns claimed that their ability to conduct business was severely limited by Vandeleur's negligence in the basic upkeep and dredging of the creek.[42] Their assertive approach to the dispute clearly indicated that new social and economic forces were at work in the late nineteenth century, and that, at least in the context of Kilrush, landlordism was losing ground in the face of an assertive merchant class. The issue of Vandeleur arbitrarily raising rent was another concern of the Glynns and formed an additional argument in the case. According to Henry Glynn, his father had taken possession of Donovan's Field in the 1880s 'with the intention to erect a factory building'.[43] However, this had not materialized as no lease for the site was provided and '[T]hus the poorer classes of the town could not avail of constant employment.'[44] Glynn's comments raise questions about whether he was expressing a genuine altruism or was more focused on the loss of a source of potential profit. In addition, the rent was raised from £1 to £6 per year, and the landlord

40 Quayage was a charge for the use of a quay, whereas wharfage was a charge assessed by a shipping terminal or port when goods are moved through the location. 41 Glynn family archive, box 8 (1890–1900). See *Royal commission appointed to inquire into the manner in which railway communications can be most advantageously promoted in Ireland*, [145] 449, vol. 35. 42 High court of Ireland, chancery division, master of rolls, Vandeleur v. Glynn, minutes of evidence taken, 30 Oct. 1902. Vandeleur challenged this assertion and stated that he had deepened the creek at a cost of £80, following a request from Glynn. This was denied by Glynn, who annotated the minutes with the word 'wrong'; Glynn archive, box 10 (1900–10). 43 Henry Richard Glynn to Hallam Studdert, typed copy of letter, 7 Apr. 1909. Michael Glynn acquired part of this field shortly before his death. It originally belonged to (or was let from the Vandeleurs by) Dr Richard Hungerford Donovan (d. 1856) and then his widow, Elizabeth Sophia née Parker (d. 1881); Griffith's Valuation, 1855. 44 Henry Richard Glynn to Hallam Studdert, typed copy of letter, 7 Apr. 1909; Glynn archive, box 10 (1900–10).

demanded back rent for the previous twenty years. Glynn blamed Vandeleur's apparent inaction for thwarting large-scale investment designed to benefit the town through the employment of a large numbers. The frustration levelled at Vandeleur was succinctly summed up by Henry Glynn in 1914 when he remarked,

> [O]ur steamers were injured, our men suffered great hardship in the winter for want of shelter, the cargo was injured and steamers delayed almost every trip, we were put at great expense and almost driven distracted and could not understand why Vandeleur refused our requests.[45]

The sense of Glynn's frustration at the situation is clearly visible from the copious documents concerning the case. Glynn requested that basic but necessary facilities be installed at Merchant's Quay to aid his growing trade. He asked that Vandeleur install a crane and suitable lighting and arrange for special berths at the quay. Vandeleur refused Glynn's request but instead granted special berths to a Glasgow company 'whose steamer does not come here for two or three months'.[46] To support his claim that the creek was hazardous to enterprise, Glynn furnished detailed receipts to the Vandeleur estate office that recorded extensive damage to his vessels.[47]

It is significant that individuals from the landed class supported Glynn in his action against Vandeleur, one of their own. In 1909, Peter David Fitzgerald, a younger son of George Fitzgerald, 1st Baron Fitzgerald of Valentia, and grandson of the Knight of Kerry, wrote to Henry Glynn and assured him that '[T]he question is being looked into … [C]an you give me a little time to look into the matter for you [?] … [S]end me a wire if urgent.'[48] This suggests that a unified landed elite was not a reality by the late nineteenth century, and that the course of action taken by Vandeleur appears not to have been entirely reflective of his class, as Glynn had noted in 1893 that '[O]ther landlords on the Shannon have offered us special advantages if we dock at their town so as to encourage industry there.'[49] Glynn also had the support of the wealthy industrialist Viscount Pirrie, who shared an understanding of the obstacles put in place by Vandeleur. Pirrie's agent, Johnston, wrote to Glynn in 1910 and stated that Pirrie

> noted the obvious attempts by Vandeleur to hamper your shipping business which reminded him of the great struggles he had with Belfast Harbour … for over twenty years to make them keep pace with us in the provision of deeper berths and dredging the channel etc. and it appeared to be the same thing in smaller scale.[50]

45 Henry Richard Glynn, draft of letter, 17 Apr. 1914; Glynn archive, box 11 (1910–20). **46** Henry Richard Glynn to Hallam Studdert, typed copy of letter, 21 Apr. 1909; Glynn archive, box 10 (1900–10). **47** Copy of bill of repairs to Glynn vessels, which amounted to £1,025, 11 Feb. 1909; Glynn archive, box 10 (1900–10). **48** Peter David Fitzgerald to Henry Glynn, letter (marked private and addressed as Mondellihy), 18 May 1909; Glynn archive, box 10 (1900–10). **49** M. Glynn & Sons to unknown party, 23 Dec. 1893; Glynn archive, box 9 (1890–1900). **50** Isaac Johnston to Henry

Jefferson acknowledged some instances of the trouble that Pirrie experienced with the Belfast Harbour Commissioners, who 'gave him no encouragement ... and told him that his ideas [to develop the harbour] could not be realised'.[51] Glynn had a powerful ally in Pirrie, who at the time was the wealthiest global shipping magnate, in 1909 reportedly controlling capital of £30,000,000.[52] Johnston closed the letter with the assurance that '[Y]ou may rely upon him to force it [the outcome of the case] strongly in your favour.'[53]

Some of Glynn's fellow Kilrush merchants, described many years later in the Glynn correspondence as 'jealous parties', sided with the landlord.[54] One of them was O'Doherty, the timber and coal merchant who had been a business rival of Glynn since 1890. He swore in an affidavit that he was 'willing and able to pay for the use of Merchant's Quay the same tolls and charges ... [I]f the plaintiff deepened the quay as to admit larger tonnage vessels, I would be satisfied to pay double the existing dues.'[55] But whether the emergence of these local rivalries, which benefitted Vandeleur's legal case, was a sign of their allegiance to the landlord, or whether it was motivated by the desire to increase the individuals' share of business and trade in Kilrush is not clear. After all, business and enterprise had been dominated by successive generations of the Glynns. Vandeleur was not alone in securing the support of individuals associated with the creek and in 1896 the traffic manager from the South Clare Railway, speaking on behalf of the Glynns, noted that '[T]he interests of Kilrush are inseparable from the benefit that will accrue to the railway company by the dredging of the creek.'[56]

A clear image emerges of a frustrated businessman who sought improved conditions to enable his commercial pursuits to develop but was hindered by what he saw as an unreasonable landlord who appeared as an outdated reminder of the gentry from the previous century. Glynn represented the commercial interests of the town, whereas Vandeleur seemed to be typical of his class – only interested in extracting more profit from the townspeople of Kilrush. Ultimately, the House of Lords ruled that Vandeleur was entitled to the quay but that the foreshore was the property of the crown.[57] Glynn's co-defendants were Kilrush Urban District Council, which desired that Kilrush Creek be vested in its authority, and the crown, which was represented by the attorney general of Ireland and which contested that no part of the shore was ever granted to Vandeleur. In any case, the Vandeleur days in Kilrush were drawing to an end, and in 1897 the family's large mansion, Kilrush House, was accidently destroyed by fire, which hastened their

Richard Glynn, letter, 13 Feb. 1909; Glynn archive, box 10 (1900–10). **51** Jefferson, *Viscount Pirrie of Belfast*, p. 15. **52** *Scotsman*, 26 Feb. 1909. **53** Isaac Johnston to Henry Richard Glynn, letter, 13 Feb. 1909; Glynn archive, box 10 (1900–10). **54** Charles E. Glynn to Revd Fr Clancy, 24 Apr. 1941; Glynn archive, box 14 (1940–50). **55** High court of justice in Ireland, chancery division, master of the rolls, Hector S. Vandeleur, plaintiff v. Henry R. Glynn and others, defendant, affidavit of Francis J. O'Doherty, 3 Feb. 1908; Glynn archive, box 10 (1900–10). **56** P.K. Sullivan to Vandeleur, 1896 (full date unknown); Glynn archive, box 9 (1890–1900). **57** Question on Merchant's Quay, Kilrush, *Hansard Parliamentary Debates*, H.C. Deb., 15 May 1906, vol. 157 c. 365. See also *Freeman's Journal*, 30 Oct. 1902; *Irish Times*, 30 Oct. 1902.

departure.[58] They purchased Cahercon House, the former seat of the White family and never again resided in Kilrush itself. Though Glynn did not record his private thoughts on the departure of the Vandeleurs from the town, Irish Parliamentary Party member Arthur Lynch MP stated that it 'signified the wiping out of the last traces of the foreign domination of Cromwell in the Kilrush district'.[59] However, not to miss an opportunity to gain the upper hand, almost immediately Glynn changed the name of his own family residence from Merchant's Quay House to Kilrush House, thereby confirming in a highly symbolic and public manner that the provincial middle classes had superseded the landed classes as the de facto leaders of at least this quarter of provincial Ireland. The lengthy case had deeply affected Henry R. Glynn. Over thirty years later, Charles E. Glynn still harboured bitter memories of the affair – echoing those penned by his brother in its immediate aftermath:

> The peasants own their land,
> Michael Glynn has come to their aid
> But many of them who fought
> have passed into the shade
> The railway runs to Kilrush
> Our shed is on the quay
> The dues are fixed by court
> But my hair is grey.[60]

Although Glynn had challenged the authority of one local landlord, that was not to say that he was anti-establishment. His court case with Vandeleur was based on a practical economic argument that sought to increase trade and commerce in Kilrush. While his unsuccessful legal action represented a further weakening of the position of the landed gentry, it was not designed to be an oblique political statement in favour of the home rule movement. Murphy has noted that '[I]n respect of loyalty to the crown and the United Kingdom … their existed a plurality of allegiance.'[61] Glynn still very much identified with the Dublin administration, so it was not surprising that he should express a willingness to assist the authorities in their efforts to recruit individuals to the armed forces during the First World War.

NETWORKING AND RECRUITING IN THE FIRST WORLD WAR

At the commencement of the British war effort in 1914, the Glynn family reflected the enthusiasm of much of the Irish population for enlistment in the army.[62] Aided

58 *Irish Times*, 27 Mar. 1897. 59 Horace Plunkett, *Noblesse oblige: an Irish rendering* (Dublin, 1908), p. 5, as cited by Fitzpatrick, *Politics and Irish life*, p. 51. 60 Charles E. Glynn to Revd Fr Clancy, 24 Apr. 1941; Henry Richard Glynn, diary entry, 3 Nov. 1912; Glynn archive, box 11 (1910–20). 61 James Murphy, *Abject loyalty: nationalism and monarchy in the reign of Queen Victoria* (Cork, 2001), p. 244. 62 Adrian Gregory, 'Ireland and Britain' in John Horne (ed.), *A companion to World War One* (Chichester, 2012), p. 405. Horne has suggested that war enthusiasm was socially limited by class.

by his brother Henry, Charles Glynn acted as local recruiter for the British army during the war. So immersed was the family in the war effort that through an analysis of their personal and commercial papers, it is possible to examine the response to the recruitment drive at a broad local level.[63] In the provincial context, the recruitment campaign eventually hinged on the ability of the merchant class to network with the professional and landed classes in order to secure recruits for the cause. Without the interdependence of all three groups, the pooling of their resources would have been in vain. A further group, local priests, were strongly urged to encourage their flocks to enlist.[64] Here again the decimation of the influence of the landed gentry can be seen. Even though the head of the Vandeleur family enlisted in the war (and was killed in action), the family does not appear to have lent its support to the efforts of the 'gentlemen of the county' in their campaign to encourage the recruitment of men to the war effort.[65] Therefore, networking among the merchant, the professional and a limited number from the landed classes was the essential factor in the provincial recruitment campaign.[66]

The town of Kilrush had a population of approximately 3,666 inhabitants at the outbreak of the First World War, and as a deep-water port it was a transport hub for people and produce for much of the south-west of Ireland. The total number of Kilrush men who enlisted was 476: 414 in the army; 55 in the navy; and 7 in the merchant navy.[67] These figures represent nearly 13 per cent of the population of Kilrush. At national level, many of the early recruits to the war effort were members of the Irish National Volunteers, whose aim was to obtain home rule for Ireland, but the enthusiasm for recruitment among this body was relatively short-lived. According to Staunton, Kilrush, like the rest of Co. Clare, reflected similar patterns in initially securing army recruits from among the Volunteers, but by late November 1914, enthusiasm from within the local branch had waned.[68]

Almost immediately, Charles E. Glynn declared his support for the war effort and he wrote to Sir Michael O'Loghlen, lord lieutenant of Co. Clare, that

> in view of the grave statement made by the Secretary of State for War [Lord Kitchener] in the House of Lords, will you allow me as an employer of extensive labour in this county to say, it will give me much pleasure if I can be of any assistance to you in anyway whatsoever during this crisis.[69]

63 Glynn archive, propaganda, newspaper articles, personal accounts, minutes of meetings and personal correspondence; Glynn archive, box 11 (1910–20). 64 Power, *Clare and the Great War*, p. 122. See Patrick Callan, 'Recruiting for the British army in Ireland during the First World War', *Irish Sword*, 17:66 (1987), pp 42–56; and Martin Staunton, 'Kilrush and the Munster Fusiliers: the experience of an Irish town in the First World War', *Old Limerick Journal*, 30 (1993), pp 35–8. 65 'Gentlemen of the county' was a common phrase that appeared numerous times throughout the official wartime literature and generally referred to merchants, professionals, justices of the peace, magistrates, the clergy and landowners. 66 There is no documentary evidence to illustrate that Charles Glynn chose to wear his optional dress uniforms. He received an allowance towards the uniform but no photograph has survived with him wearing it. 67 Charles E. Glynn, *List of Kilrush men who served with colours during the Great War, 1914–1918* (Waterford, 1919). 68 Staunton, 'Kilrush, County Clare and the Royal Munster Fusiliers', p. 271. 69 Henry Richard Glynn, letter

The Glynn family's status as local leaders was firmly rooted in west Clare. They had long been the largest employers in the region, generations of the same families had been employed by their firm, and the Glynns sought to tap into this for the recruitment campaign.[70] The West Clare Recruitment Committee was formed in February 1916 and consisted of nineteen members. It was chaired by Lord Inchiquin and Sir Charles Barrington, with the remainder drawn from the merchant and professional classes. All nineteen members held positions on the county judiciary, and seven served on town and county councils.[71] In Kilrush, the recruiting committee appealed to 'influential people in the district', with the object of 'obtaining their assistance and co-operation'. Glynn zealously courted the local elite – magistrates, merchants, shopkeepers and large farmers – and he organized meetings throughout the county.[72] In February 1916 a public meeting was held in Kilrush town hall, chaired by Charles Glynn. It was attended by a large and enthusiastic crowd. According to Glynn's account, '[F]ollowing the conclusion of the meeting, eleven men agreed to enlist, and a further fifteen agreed to think about their position.'[73]

The recruiting literature highlighted what was arguably the most attractive inducement: army pay that included a pension – a rarity for the labouring class. A booklet published in 1915 for voluntary helpers encouraged recruiting officers to make known the contents to any 'willing and spirited man who wished to enlist'.[74] Most of the Kilrush recruits came from labouring-class backgrounds and there was a general consensus that joining the army and accepting the 'King's shilling' was an opportunity to increase one's pay packet as opposed to remaining at home with very limited prospects of a wage increase or even a job.[75] This pragmatic approach to volunteering suggested that for many individuals soldiering was simply another job with a steady income and a pension guarantee. Thomas Dooley has noted in the Waterford context that '[P]ay and allowances … provided many working-class families with a regular income for the very first time.'[76] The emphasis placed on the value of army pay and conditions was clear in official documentation, which stated that '[T]he liberal terms offered to men and their dependents, and the arrangements made for the convenience of Irish recruits, should always be explained.'[77] Employers further enhanced the attractions of recruitment by adding an 'employer's

addressed to Sir Michael O'Loghlen, lord lieutenant of Co. Clare, Aug. 1914; Glynn archive, box 11 (1910–20). **70** Glynn archive, employee ledgers, 1914–1918, estimated number of men employed stands at 186 from throughout their business interests; Glynn archive, box 11 (1910–20). **71** Charles E. Glynn, copy of circular, 'Recruiting conference held in Ennis on 9 Mar. 1916'; a deputation was appointed to wait in the county council with the object of securing their assistance and cooperation in the recruiting scheme, 15 Mar. 1916; Glynn archive, box 11 (1910–20). **72** Glynn archive, letter from C.E. Glynn to Charles Barrington, sub-director of recruiting, Limerick, 17 Nov. 1915; Glynn archive, box 11 (1910–20). **73** *Kilrush Herald & Kilkee Gazette*, undated newspaper cutting; Glynn archive, box 11 (1910–20). **74** Central Council for the Organization of Recruiting in Ireland, letter to C.E. Glynn concerning *Instructions for voluntary helpers* (Dublin, 1914); Glynn archive, box 11 (1910–20). **75** Glynn, *List of Kilrush men*. **76** Dooley, *Irishmen or English soldiers?*, p. 126. **77** Department of Recruiting, *Attitude of the Department of Recruiting towards the raising of recruits* (Dublin, 1916); Glynn guarantee', which protected their workers' pre-war employment. Instances of the adoption of the employer's guarantee are evident in the policy of the Limerick City Council and the approach of some companies in Cork.[78] The Glynns were quite vocal in their support of this clause and willingly signed up to the guarantee.

The success of this approach is evidenced in the large numbers of Glynn employees who enlisted. At the conclusion of the war, and from a total workforce of 186, 57 per cent of Glynn employees had enlisted, which represented over a quarter of the total of Kilrush recruits.[79] All appear to have held non-commissioned rank and, with the exception of four men from the Church of Ireland community, were almost all Roman Catholic.[80] There is also some evidence regarding the class structure of the men who enlisted. The under-representation of men from Henry Street, the main commercial area of Kilrush, coupled with the marked absence of any men from Frances Street, where local solicitors and doctors resided, stands in marked contrast to the large numbers of men who enlisted from the working-class areas of the town.[81]

Economic advantage created by the need for increased agricultural productivity resulted in recruitment among the farming class being slower than among the general population, a government circular stating that '[R]ecruiting was very good in Co. Clare among the labouring class in the towns but there was no recruiting at all from the farming classes.'[82] According to Fitzpatrick, '[R]epublicans noted with disgust the complacency of Irish farmers, prospering from rising prices as the disruption of international shipping drove their competitors from the British market.'[83] This division between the farming and labouring classes in the Clare context was borne out in a court case in Kilrush that involved a young farmer attacking a soldier. In 1915, the local court heard that a respectable farmer was charged with 'drunkenness and riotous behaviour'. He accused a young soldier of 'being a mean man to fight the Germans' and added that '[I]t was all the scruff and corner boys of Kilrush that were in the army and that only for being rowdies they would not be in it at all.'[84] Such local equation of recruitment with membership of the lower class continued well into the twentieth century. Family memory corroborates this: the author's grandfather declared several times that '[W]hat those lads, those corner-boys, needed was a good war to sort them out.' This man's father and his three brothers had all served in the war with the Royal Munster Fusiliers.[85]

archive, box 11 (1910–20). **78** Tadgh Moloney, 'The impact of World War One on Limerick' (MA, Mary Immaculate College, University of Limerick, 2003), p. 16. **79** Glynn archive, employee ledgers, 1914–18, estimated number of men employed stands at 186 from throughout their business interests. **80** Glynn, *List of Kilrush men*. **81** Total number of men from each street was as follows: Pound St. /Hector St. etc. (89), The Glen (70), Henry St. (11), Moore St. (31), Stewart St. (10), Vandeleur St. (8), John St. (4), Alley Lane (13), Chapel St. (45), Grace St. (38), Malt House Lane (17) and miscellaneous (25). No member of the immediate Glynn family joined up. They were all over the age limit for recruitment, which was set between 18 and 38. **82** T.P. Gill, Department of Recruiting for Ireland, 'Ireland and the war: the farmer's position' (Dublin, 1915). **83** David Fitzpatrick, *The two Irelands, 1912–1939* (Oxford, 1998), pp 56–7. **84** Martin Staunton, 'Kilrush, County Clare and the Royal Munster Fusiliers', *Irish Sword*, 16:65 (1986), pp 268–72. **85** John O'Brien (1919–99),

The Glynn papers include a wealth of letters that recorded their thoughts and ideas about the conflict.[86] In a thorough understanding of the importance of propaganda, Glynn suggested that a report in the *Irish Times* be reprinted in all Irish daily and weekly newspapers as it was a 'magnificent recruiting speech' and asked for permission to 'reprint same in the Clare papers which are largely read by farmers in this county' – an obvious nod to the local farmers' lack of interest in volunteering.[87] Furthermore, Glynn suggested a number of methods to increase the numbers of men enlisting. Chief among these the withdrawal of the threat of conscription:

> [W]e have learned of the loss of the Irish mail steamer *Leinster*, if the government withdraws the threat of conscription and leave it to the Irish people ... the *Lusitania* brought in the Americans and the *Leinster* will bring in the Irish.[88]

The issue of conscription was a topic that featured regularly throughout Charles Glynn's personal letters to his fiancé. Charles confided in Eileen that '[T]he war news is not good and it looks as if we are to have conscription but they cannot take Willie's [his brother and business partner's] men if we object.'[89] Just three weeks later, he informed Eileen that '[W]e hear all kinds of wild rumours about a shooting in Cork, and it looks as if we are going to have trouble very soon, all over the country, the government is mad to attempt conscription.'[90] His growing disillusionment with the war may have been informed by the death of his fiancée's nephew, James H. Nash, son of Sir Vincent Nash of Limerick, doctor and prominent land agent. James was killed in action on 27 March 1918, some three weeks before Charles was due to marry Eileen.[91] The correspondence between Charles and Eileen suggests they enjoyed a more egalitarian relationship than might have been expected for the period.

The fundraising activities of voluntary women's groups were intrinsic to the war effort and numerous national and provincial groups were established, including the organization Comforts for Troops from Irish Friends, which collected items such as socks that were dispatched to the soldiers at the waterlogged front.[92] In Clare the West Clare Ladies' Recruitment Committee was formed, which encouraged the 'leading ladies of the town' to promote and assist with recruiting in that county and it was chaired by Florence Glynn.[93] Power noted that '[U]pper-class women of

author's grandfather. **86** The material related to the First World War amounts to approximately 2,500 documents and it spans in date the entire length of the war. The correspondence was not one-sided: it also included the replies from Captain R.C. Kelly of the recruitment office, Nassau St., Dublin; Glynn archive, box 11 (1910–20). **87** *Irish Times*, 13 Nov. 1915. **88** Letter from C.E. Glynn to F.W. Dawson, secretary, Ministry of Food, 12 Oct. 1915; Glynn archive, box 11 (1910–20). **89** Charles E. Glynn to Eileen Dorgan, 6 Apr. 1918; Glynn archive, box 11 (1910–20). **90** Ibid., 18 Apr. 1918. **91** *Irish Times*, 20 Apr. 1918. **92** John Horne (ed.), *Our war: Ireland and the Great War* (Dublin, 2008), p. 176. **93** Department of Recruiting for Ireland, circular, co-signed by Florence Glynn, president, and Charles Barrington Bt., provincial sub-director, dated 11 Apr. 1916; Glynn

Clare, mainly Protestant, had a huge role in fundraising for charities such as the Red Cross … Belgian soldiers and prisoners of war.'[94] The sentiment of the literature aimed at the female recruiters was broadly similar to that aimed at the male recruiters: 'The women's message' placed an emphasis on the intertwined themes of manliness and cowardice and stated:

> O ye who might have been soldiers, and yet have stood aside,
> What is your place in this kingdom for which our men have died?
> Shall ye share in the day of triumph the peace that dawns afar,
> Ye who have hidden your manhood under a coward's star?[95]

This group reflected the elitism that characterized the exclusively male West Clare Recruiting Committee and was comprised primarily of prominent local women who sought to 'encourage young men to take their places … to defend our country and the defenceless women and children who are left behind'.[96] A sceptical reading of these sources might suggest that while it is clear that the Glynns genuinely supported and co-operated with recruitment activities, there was a degree of pragmatism inherent in their actions, since the family firm had secured a Ministry of Food contract to supply flour to the army.[97] Astute businessman that he was, Glynn also offered his mill as a facility for the production of munitions, though the recently established Ministry of Munitions did not accept.[98]

The degree to which the Glynn family had become closely identified with the contemporary political elite and with the war effort and army recruitment was emphasized by the decision of the lord lieutenant of Ireland, Wimborne, to visit Kilrush in 1915 and dine with them. The viceregal visit was part of a countrywide tour designed to rally support for the recruitment drive. The trip took in Cork, Limerick and Clare and the *Irish Times* reported that the viceregal party was to be entertained at Kilrush House, the home of the Glynn family.[99] What is remarkable is that of all the places on the official itinerary, their stop in Kilrush was the only time where the lord lieutenant and his entourage engaged in a reception hosted by a member of the merchant class. The tour did encompass official engagements, such as a reception hosted by the mayor of Cork. But the decision that Wimborne should dine privately with the Glynn family served as recognition of their improved rank and status. The honour paid to the Glynns by their being chosen to host the dignitaries from the Castle was carried in an article in the society magazine *Irish Life*, a large photograph clearly showing the viceregal party leaving the Glynn residence, surrounded by local dignitaries and onlookers, and the family's

archive, box 11 (1910–20). **94** Power, *Clare and the Great War*, p. 274. **95** 'The woman's message', Parliamentary Recruiting Committee, 12 Downing St., London, SW, leaflet 26; Glynn archive, box 11 (1910–20). **96** *Cork Examiner*, 11 Apr. 1916. **97** Ministry of Food, flour order form B.12. Stamped 'M. Glynn & Sons, Kilrush', dated 1917; Glynn archive, box 11 (1910–20). **98** Ministry of Munitions to C.E. Glynn, letter, 13 Mar. 1916; Glynn archive, box 11 (1910–20). See Niamh Puirséil, 'War, work and labour' in Horne (ed.), *Our war*, pp 184–5. **99** *Irish Times*, 14 Aug. 1915.

consciousness of their importance in the war effort was perpetuated in the displaying since 1915 of this photograph in a prominent position in Kilrush House.[100]

In preparation for the visit of the lord lieutenant, members of the Kilrush Urban District Council directed that 'the bridewell be lime-washed and that streamers be suspended where suitable [...] and that trees be put down in the centre of Frances Street, a platform be erected and that W. O'Shea be asked to send out the Temperance Band for the occasion'. A dual political identity was obvious on the platform for the public reception of the viceregal party. It was draped with the Union Jack, adorned with a harp motif and the local band played 'God save the king' and 'A nation once again'.[101] Glynn's enthusiasm for the visit was undeniable, and in addition to hosting the viceregal party in his house he paid for the temporary installation of trees to 'improve the appearance of the town' for the visit. He was clearly impressed by the efforts of the local band, who he cheerfully complimented in a letter to his sister Rose.[102] Henry Richard Glynn's obvious delight for the occasion was clearly shared by the select vestry in the town who decided to raise a flag on the church tower in 'honour' of the visit to Kilrush.[103] Save for an isolated and minor incident in Miltown Malbay, Co. Clare, where the mother of a girl who had been selected to present flowers to Lady Wimborne had refused permission to allow her 'little daughter present the bouquet', there is no documentary evidence of any local opposition to the viceregal visit to Kilrush and the provincial or national press certainly did not carry comment to that effect.[104]

While there is limited evidence of hostility to the activities of those individuals engaged in recruiting activities in west Clare, one such incident in July 1915 does provide an insight to such opposition. The *Dublin Daily Express* reported on the case of a young woman, Miss Adelaide E.E. Palmer from Dublin, a teacher at the O'Curry College, Carrigaholt. It was reported that following her decision to volunteer at the front as a nurse, '[S]he had become immediately unpopular due to her commitment to the war effort and was denounced as a recruiting agent by the College authorities.' Palmer described how a man 'dragged her off her bicycle and threw her into a bog-hole … [H]e endeavoured to force her head, front under the water but she resisted and escaped.' The judge, Bodkin, awarded her costs and damages to cover the destruction of her bicycle and Burberry coat.[105] Palmer's treatment at the hands of those individuals who resented her support for the war was in contrast to the appearance, in provincial newspapers, of a number of locally penned poems, which encouraged 'the young men of Ireland to go forth and join the fight'.[106] Although Henry Glynn was a sitting magistrate at the Kilrush petty

100 *Irish Life*, 17 Sept. 1915. **101** Henry Richard Glynn to Power, 27 Oct. 1915. Samuel L. Power was a clerk in the Irish Office, Old Queen Street, London, SW; Glynn archive, box 11 (1910–20). **102** Charles E. Glynn to Rose Ryan, letter, 2 Sept. 1915; Glynn archive, box 11 (1910–20). **103** Fitzpatrick, *Politics and Irish life*, p. 64. **104** Fr Hannon to Henry Richard Glynn, letter, 24 Aug. 1915; Glynn archive, box 11 (1910–20). **105** *Dublin Daily Express*, 6 July 1915. **106** *Limerick Chronicle*, 22 May 1915; 5 June 1915. Both of these poems were initialled 'J.W. Kilkee'.

sessions, the circumstances of the Palmer case were not mentioned in his diaries and the event did not disrupt the subsequent visit of the lord lieutenant to Kilrush.

Henry Glynn's account of the visit reveals a certain resentment at not being fully acknowledged as the instigator of the lord lieutenant's excursion to west Clare. Instead, Wimborne's private secretary appears to have got the credit. Writing in October 1915, Glynn noted,

> I am in fact pretty sore over their Excellencies visit … I was the only Liberal D.L. in the county, I invited them and had to put up with a lot, I canvassed the county for three weeks to make sure that his Excellency did not address the people of Kilrush off a soda-water case.[107] [I]f there had been any unpleasantness we would have got the blame.[108]

A few weeks previously, in a typically ambitious move, Henry R. Glynn had inquired about the possibility of being appointed as a senator after the passage of the Home Rule Act.[109] A friend, Samuel L. Power, chief clerk in the Irish Office in London, confidently replied that '[A] note has already been made of your suitability for the position of Senator under the Home Rule Act and I will bear you in mind when the time comes.'[110] It was not all politics and war news they discussed though: Power also extended an invitation to Glynn to visit London and suggested that he might possibly see a 'Zepp' (Zeppelin).

The viceregal tour coincided with and was motivated by a national decline in the numbers of men enlisting. From a height of over 50,000 who had enlisted countrywide from August 1914 to February 1915, numbers had fallen to just over 25,000 from February 1915 to August 1915.[111] The tour was a public-relations exercise designed to arrest that decline. However, the situation in Kilrush was in direct contrast to the national trend: five months before the viceroy's visit the *Limerick Leader* reported that '[O]ver 200 recruits left Kilrush by train and were seen off by an enormous crowd.'[112] Although Staunton questioned the actual number of men who enlisted – '[P]ossibly many were rejected at a more thorough medical examination, the important fact is that enthusiasm for the war locally was obvious in the men's enlistment in the first instance.'[113] It is not clear why the pace of recruiting did not lose momentum in Kilrush. Perhaps the image the Glynns had cultivated as respected and decent employers meant that as they fervently supported the war effort, their men supported their actions.

It is apparent that while most men in Kilrush enlisted for economic reasons, they also considered family, friends and political influences in arriving at their decision. The government recruiting drive that pulled out all the stops in order to

107 Henry Richard Glynn to Power, 27 Oct. 1915; Glynn archive, box 11 (1910–20). **108** Ibid. **109** Ibid., 17 Oct. 1915. **110** Ibid., 21 Oct. 1915. Power to Henry Richard Glynn, 9 Nov. 1915; Glynn archive, box 11 (1910–20). German Zeppelin airship raids first occurred over London in May 1915; *London Times*, 2 June 1915. **111** Keith Jeffery, *Ireland and the Great War* (Cambridge, 2000), p. 7. **112** *Limerick Leader*, 31 Mar. 1915. **113** Staunton, 'Kilrush and the Munster Fusiliers', p. 36.

persuade men to enlist cannot be overlooked.[114] The initial mobilization of men was followed by a carefully targeted and highly organized campaign orchestrated and controlled by the department of recruiting. However, the emotive language and terminology contained in the recruiting literature that flooded provincial towns such as Kilrush would have been less effective without the fervour and support of large local employers such as the Glynns. Willing co-operation and an overriding sense of duty and loyalty from provincial middle-class merchants were central to the success of the recruitment effort.

The prospect of an allied failure also permeated the recruiting literature, which warned that if the Germans were not defeated they would seize banks and confiscate all cash balances; 'they would levy off such places as Nenagh [Charles Glynn crossed out 'Nenagh' and replaced it with 'Kilrush'], charge a huge cash fine, arrest clergy men and local politicians, demand a ransom and if this is not forthcoming, the hostages would be shot'. The booklet described the German soldiers as a 'Hun General and his Pomeranians'.[115] These overtly racist attacks were designed to exploit popular prejudices.

While the statistics associated with the war have been well documented, the long-term effects of enlistment are more difficult to trace in towns such as Kilrush. Personal memories have all but disappeared, but one feature of the town suggests that a long-term legacy of the war remained. There is an area close to the town where the homes of returned soldiers are located. While the townland is officially named Ballynote-West, it is significant that even in the twenty-first century it is locally referred to as 'Shellshock'.

'MASTERS OF THE SYSTEM': ELECTORAL CHANGES, 1910–18

While not directly involved in political activities, the Glynn family showed a clear awareness of the manoeuvres within parliamentary politics. The 1910 general election campaign was discussed at length between Henry Richard Glynn and Isaac Johnston. Over the course of several letters, Johnston, agent for the Protestant home ruler Lord Pirrie, described the election as a 'stormy affair'.[116] He reported that he was going to the Albert Hall to attend a meeting for Asquith and

Staunton did not offer any reason as to why the recruitment campaign in Kilrush seemed to buck the national trend. **114** A selection of the recruitment literature is as follows: 'Ask your conscience' (leaflet), issued by the Central Committee for the Organisation of Recruiting in Ireland, printed by Alex Thom & Co. Ltd, Dublin; 'The soldier who wrote' (leaflet); 'The astonishing record of Ireland's armies' (booklet), Powell Press, Dublin; Glynn archive, box 11 (1910–20). **115** Gill, 'Ireland and the war: the farmer's position', p. 10; Glynn archive, box 11 (1910–20). **116** Isaac Johnson to Henry Richard Glynn, 18 Dec. 1909; Glynn archive, box 11 (1910–20). Historian Éamon Phoenix described Pirrie as a 'Protestant home ruler' who disliked sectarian unionism and contributed to a booklet entitled *Religious intolerance under home rule: some opinions of leading Irish Protestants* (1911) compiled by the nationalist Jeremiah MacVeagh MP. In this booklet Pirrie declared that he had no fear of discrimination against Irish Protestants under a home rule parliament. The author is grateful to that '[E]veryone tells me that it is arranged that my chief [Pirrie] will be the lord lieutenant should the liberals return to power.'[117] In late December, Johnston wrote to Glynn that '[I]t is expected that the Liberals will lose about forty to forty-five seats … [T]his will leave them a good working majority apart from Irish support … of which they are fully assured.' His projections were remarkably near the outcome.[118] Their correspondence reveals that both Glynn and Johnston were enthralled with the election, and they kept up to date with the political movements and changes in Britain and Ireland. Johnston appeared to treat Glynn as a confidante and trusted him with private information about Pirrie, the British government and in some instances the British royal family. For instance, following the 1910 election, Johnston wrote to Glynn and informed him that Pirrie had travelled to Belfast and thought that 'Walter Long ought to be locked up for recent incitements to rebellion and Civil War.'[119] On which point Johnston remarked, 'Long seems to be the only Tory leader with any fight left in him, nearly all the others are moderating their language.'[120] The discussion around the election and politics consumed most of their correspondence for January 1910 and the debate concerning home rule featured heavily, with Johnston noting that '[Conservative MP John E.] Jameson called round the other day and told me he was a good nationalist and that he was satisfied with Asquith's declaration in regard to home rule.'[121] Johnston also noted that he told Jameson that he was a friend of 'the Glynns from Kilrush'. An insight into Pirrie's politics is offered by Johnston, who claimed that '[M]y chief told me that he was coming round to my view (which was Gladstone's) that the Liberals in Ireland should throw in their lot with the Nationalists and go for the whole policy instead of opposing home rule.'[122]

FAMILY OR POLITICS?

Although the family's focus in 1918 was the wedding of Charles E. Glynn to Eileen Dorgan, the political fallout from the general election, coupled with issues related to the war, also featured prominently in their personal correspondence. In a series of letters to his fiancée, Glynn expressed his concerns about the impending threat of conscription and the activities of Sinn Féin in west Clare.[123] Glynn's dislike of Sinn Féin reveals, for the first time, some real insight into his politics. There were frequent discussions with his brothers, brother-in-law and acquaintances about Sinn Féin's activities in Kilrush and west Clare. Perhaps his concerns were

Phoenix for this source. **117** Historian Éamon Phoenix suggested that 'Pirrie's Liberal credentials would have given him considerable clout with the Asquith Liberal government after 1908 and with the Lloyd George coalitions of 1916–18 and 1919–22'; email correspondence, 5 Feb. 2014. **118** Ibid., 30 Dec. 1909. Glynn archive, box 11 (1910–20). **119** Isaac Johnston to Henry Richard Glynn, 9 Jan. 1909; Glynn archive, box 10 (1900–1910), Walter Long, 1st Viscount Long, chief secretary of Ireland (1905). **120** Ibid. **121** Isaac Johnston to Henry Richard Glynn, 12 Jan. 1909; Glynn archive, box 10 (1900–10). **122** Johnston to Glynn, 30 Jan. 1910; Glynn archive, box 11 (1910–20). **123** Glynn archive, box 11 (1910–20).

justified, as almost immediately after their election victory Sinn Féin wrote to all Irish millers and demanded information about the productivity of their mills. In January 1918 the Sinn Féin demand was hand-delivered to Glynn by the Revd Fr Moloney, who instructed Glynn to sign the return, giving particulars of the capacity of the flour mill. It stated that 'we are particularly interested in Oat Meal and Oat Flour Mills, and desire a definite and exhaustive report regarding the possible output of each mill in Ireland.'[124] Interference in the private workings of his enterprise was not entertained by Glynn, and his curt reply made his political allegiance clear as he 'declined to sign, without first getting the consent of Ministry of Food'.[125] In a related incident, according to Charles Glynn, '[A]rmed Sinn Féiners called to his brother's house and demanded that he hand over any guns on the premises.' They only searched one room and '[O]n Mrs Glynn's assurance that there were no guns in the house, they all left quietly.'[126] An additional note described the actions of the men as they left. They 'presented a document signed Capt. Moonlight to Willie and demanded he sign it, it stated that there were twelve men around the house and they would stay there until 4am. Willie advised them that no guns were present and they left the premises.'[127] The inclusion of a reference to 'Capt. Moonlight' suggests that the objectives of some provincial Sinn Féiners were not necessarily political but rather a continuation of nineteenth-century agrarianism which was primarily concerned with immediate local objectives generally revolving around land and land disputes.[128] Campbell broadly agrees with this sentiment, noting that

> Sinn Féin emerged from the radical agrarian and republican tradition ... In Galway, the early Sinn Féin movement mobilised the support of the members of a pre-existing secret society, and the new Sinn Féin ideas were incorporated into the republican and anti-grazier ideology of the secret society.[129]

Glynn's was not the only premises in Kilrush that was raided for arms. The *Sunday Post* reported that '[S]everal Sinn Féin raids for arms have been made around Kilrush, they seized guns at Widow Lyon's, Mrs Fitzpatrick's and Mr Costelloe's.'[130] Reports on the raids for arms in Kilrush were sent to the chief secretary for Ireland in monthly lists that detailed the countrywide activities of organizations such as the Ancient Order of Hibernians, the Irish Volunteers and Cumann na mBan.[131]

124 Sinn Féin, Harcourt St., Dublin, blank mill productivity form, 21 Jan. 1918; Glynn archive, box 11 (1910–20). **125** Ibid. Charles E. Glynn, note written on blank form, 24 Jan. 1918. The Ministry of Food had controlled mills in Ireland since 1917; Glynn archive, box 11 (1910–20). **126** Account of raid for guns on Pella House, home of William Joynt Glynn, 26 Jan. 1918; Glynn archive, box 11 (1910–20). **127** Ibid. **128** James S. Donnelly Jnr, *Captain Rock: the Irish agrarian rebellion of 1821–1824* (Cork, 2009), p. 62. **129** Fergus Campbell, 'The social dynamics of nationalist politics in the west of Ireland 1898–1918', *Past & Present*, 182 (Feb. 2004), p. 202. **130** *Sunday Post*, 27 Jan. 1918. **131** Colonial Office Records, district inspectors' reports, 1914–21, CO 904, boxes 32–122 and 148–156A.

The report dated 16 February 1918 detailing incidents for Kilrush noted that a house was broken into and a gun and revolver stolen.[132]

Glynn wrote to his brother-in-law Jack Ryan RM in Carlow and advised him of the situation in Kilrush, suggesting that he surrender his guns to the local barracks. Ryan replied that 'I don't think that there will be trouble up here [in Carlow] but there is small doubt that you may expect trouble in Clare.'[133] The support for Sinn Féin was not limited by gender, and two local women called to Glynn's mills and asked Charles and Willie to 'lend £5 to the Sinn Féin Club to start a fund to buy up corn potatoes'.[134] The two women were Alice Counihan and Miss Queally, the former a doctor's daughter and the latter a shopkeeper's daughter. The Glynns declined and stated that '[W]e do not want to have anything to do with the movement.'[135] Glynn was in a potentially precarious situation, as he was a recruiter for the British army and entertained senior military personnel in his home on many occasions.[136] From March to April 1918 there were more than nine occasions when the Glynn family entertained military personnel in Kilrush House. Glynn's wider family seems to have been present on several of these: 'Alice cooked dinner for eight guests, including Sergeant O'Sullivan, his wife, two colonels and some others.' There seems to have been local support for Sinn Féin, as the *Irish Times* reported in 1918 that in Kilrush Sinn Féin 'flags were flown from telegraph posts'.[137] Increasing Sinn Féin activity in Kilrush prompted Glynn to request 'the local Dean to call to the Bishop [Fogarty] who is the recognised head of the Sinn Féiners in Clare … to publicly denounce such conduct or otherwise we must assume he approves of it'.[138]

In March 1918, Charles Glynn described the actions of the 'Sinners [*sic*]': '[A]t Doonbeg yesterday, the Sinn Féiners pulled down the mourning flag for John Redmond, the soldiers chased them and smashed their band instruments including their big drum, we had no trouble in Kilrush and it looks as if we won't either.'[139] Both Sinn Féin and Glynn were anti-conscription, although as recruiters for the British army, the latter could not publicly denounce the government's plans to introduce it. Instead, Glynn voiced his concerns privately to his fiancé, Eileen, and noted that he had attended a 'great sermon advising fellows to resist conscription, the priest told them to lie down on the ground and just say meow, meow, meow'.[140] This was typical of the Glynn outlook – they supported the war effort but prioritized their own business concerns. The Catholic clergy had been quick to support Sinn Féin, so it is hardly surprising that they included such rhetoric in

132 Ibid. **133** Jack Ryan to Charles E. Glynn, 28 Jan. 1918; Glynn archive, box 11 (1910–20). **134** Account of raid for guns on Pella House, home of William Joynt Glynn, 26 Jan. 1918; Glynn archive, box 11 (1910–20). **135** Ibid. **136** Letter from Charles E. Glynn to Eileen Dorgan, 10 Oct. 1918; Glynn archive, box 11 (1910–20). **137** *Irish Times*, 6 Dec. 1918. **138** Bartholomew Culligan to William Joynt Glynn, letter, 29 Jan. 1918. Note also that Michael Fogarty, bishop of Killaloe, was accused by Glynn of being the local leader of Sinn Féin leader; Glynn archive, box 11 (1910–20). **139** Charles E. Glynn to Eileen Dorgan, 11 Mar. 1918; Glynn archive, box 11 (1910–20). **140** Charles E. Glynn to Eileen Dorgan, 15 Apr. 1918; Glynn archive, box 11 (1910–20).

20. Charles E. Glynn. Photograph © the Glynn family.

their sermons. In the context of Galway, Campbell has noted that the support of the Catholic clergy for Sinn Féin was a major factor for the politicization of young men who until then had been little attracted to the movement.[141] Glynn was kept up to date with events in Dublin and noted in April 1918 that he had 'heard today that several Kilrush girls who are at school in Dublin got the tip to leave and come home, there are all kinds of rumours flowing … I hope in the interests of the country that the government will drop the conscription question for the present.'[142]

'ALL WE WANT IS FAIR PLAY': CENTRALIZATION, COMPETITION AND LOCAL RIVALRIES

The main issue for Charles Glynn during this period was not politics but the more practical problem of control of the local railway. The coming of the railway to west Clare had been a long, drawn-out process, and when it eventually opened in 1892, it presented a fresh set of problems related to the manner in which the company was managed. Henry Glynn, in his capacity as baronial director and representative of the local ratepayers' association in Kilrush, consistently challenged and lambasted the management practices of the board of the West Clare Railway which was run by the South Clare Railways from their offices in Dame Street, Dublin. Glynn asked that he be appointed a 'shareholders' director' on the West Clare Railway's board, but his request was denied. There followed a bitter and protracted dispute with the company that was played out in the local and national press. The company suggested that 'Mr Glynn's demands were to the benefit of himself and not the district … to get more favourable terms than those already obtained.'[143] The public spat between Glynn and the railway board highlighted the issue of centralization in relation the daily operation of the company at a local level. Kilrush Urban District Council and the local ratepayers' association supported Glynn's position, although admittedly many of the ratepayers were also members of the district council, which had a vested interest in the proceedings as it subsidized the railway. The ratepayers' association suggested 'that the County Council pay no money to the Railway Companies until the shareholders appoint as [directors] … gentlemen who are in touch with the county'.[144] They further stated that '[W]e back up H.R. Glynn on his endeavour to have the ratepayers properly represented on the Board of Directors, the railway worked in the interests of the county and the secretary to live in Ennis.'[145]

From the outset in 1892 the West Clare Railway proved to be a profitable venture for the Glynns and Kilrush, and this was reflected in the request of Daniel

141 Chief inspector's monthly report, East Galway, Feb. 1918: PRO, C.O. 904/10, as cited by Fergus Campbell, 'The social dynamics of nationalist politics', pp 175–209. 142 Synott to Charles E. Glynn, 15 Apr. 1918; Glynn archive, box 11 (1910–20). Synott was Glynn's solicitor. 143 *Kilrush Herald & Kilkee Gazette* (unknown date); Glynn archive, box 11 (1910–20). 144 *Saturday Record*, 30 Apr. 1910. 145 Ibid.

Ryan, a local competitor of the Glynn enterprise, for 'sixteen wagons for a consignment of a thousand bags of flour to be distributed on the line'.[146] The railway enabled Glynn to distribute vast amounts of cargo to merchants and traders throughout Co. Clare, which included Guinness caskets, wheat, animal feed and coal.[147] However, Glynn seems to have been in constant disagreement with W.J. Kennedy, the secretary of the Great Southern and Western Railway, over what appeared to be trivial matters. For instance, Glynn's request to erect a shed to cover his coal in the railway station was not entertained and a vast amount of related correspondence was generated in a two-year period.[148] The disagreement between provincial merchants and Dublin-based management reflected the wider issues of centralization and the manner in which it affected the operation of a business that was vital to the economic development of Kilrush and west Clare. The provincial merchants insisted that the railway company being managed from such a great distance hampered their trade and stymied the growth of the district.

Aside from trying to negotiate competitive rates and protect their interests in the railway while preventing interference from local rivals and the Dublin-based management of the West Clare Railway, the Glynns had to contend with the vastly changed Irish political landscape and carefully reposition themselves so as not to alienate themselves from the new administration. The Irish Civil War (1922–3) had a direct and negative impact on the ability of the Glynns to carry out their business. Almost immediately, their vessels the *Turk* and the *Corona* were requisitioned by the Free State army for the transport of their troops and military stores, which prevented the Glynns from supplying their mills with maize and resulted in the temporary lay-off of most of their employees.[149] Their vessels were used by the military for the duration of the war and the frustration felt by the Glynns in respect of their much delayed claim of compensation of £5,000 for loss of business is clearly visible in the large dossier of documents related to their fruitless efforts to obtain the payment.[150] It was not uncommon for civilian vessels of all sizes to be requisitioned during the Civil War, even cross-channel ferries were commandeered to ensure that planned landings went ahead.[151] The Glynns stated that during the Civil War the military utilized its Lower Shannon Steamship service 'for the conveyance of troops, prisoners, dispatches and military stores … we estimate that we transported over 1,000 troops or an average of about one hundred per month'.[152] They compiled detailed accounts which they supplied to the army finance officer in Dublin in support of their claim.[153] The accounts reveal

146 Andrew Ryan to P. Sullivan, manager of the West Clare Railway, letter, 19 May 1911; Glynn archive, box 11 (1910–20). **147** Messrs Glynn & Sons, invoices for outwards goods, 2 Feb. 1914; Glynn archive, box 11 (1910–20). **148** Messrs Glynn & Sons, series of letters, notes, demands and maps, estimated at 1,200 documents, 27 Mar. 1914 to 13 Apr. 1917; Glynn archive, box 11 (1910–20). **149** *Irish Times*, 9 Aug. 1922. **150** The dossier contains approximately 1,500 documents related to their lengthy appeal and are dated from 1922 to 1928; Glynn archive, box 12 (1920–30). **151** Padhraic Ó Confhaola, 'The naval forces of the Irish State, 1922–1977' (PhD, NUI Maynooth, 2009), p. 27. **152** Letter entitled 'Schedule to statutory declaration' from M. Glynn & Sons to the army finance officer, Dublin, 10 Mar. 1926; Glynn archive, box 12 (1920–30). **153** The Glynns that as well as commandeering their vessels, the Free State army also took petrol, sandbags, coal and parts for vehicles. Agreements between employer and trade union also had to be respected and the Glynns noted that '[T]hirty labourers, employed at £80 per week had to be paid as owing to our arrangements with the Transport Workers Union, they could not be discharged without a week's notice.'[154] The detailed letter concluded with a reminder that their claim was over three years outstanding and that they were claiming a further £500 for 'additional services rendered in connection with the conveyance of military during the Civil War of 1922–3'.[155] In support of their claim, they supplied a copy of the anti-treaty publication *Sgeal Chata Luimnighe* (*Limerick War News*), which clearly placed the Glynns on the pro-treaty side:

> with regard to the [ship] 'E.D.J.' I understand that Ryan of Kilrush, who has large shares in her is, and has always been, friendly to us, and that another merchant named Glynn who is not friendly, has two boats – 'the Corona' and 'the Turk.' Will you arrange with the bearer that if the 'E.D.J.' is not of any great use to us that she be returned as soon as possible, and make arrangements that one of the others be taken.[156]

Charles Glynn certainly cooperated with the Free State army during the Civil War, and a request for assistance from 1922 stated: 'I would be very much obliged if you would take our released prisoners to Limerick … in one of your boats.'[157] Their readiness in assisting the Free State army was reminiscent of their previous willingness to support the British army during the First World War.

The conviction and determination employed by the firm in seeking that their claim be paid reveals their unending self-belief in their cause. The Glynns refused to let the matter go and utilized their extensive network of contacts to help fight their case. Support from within government and clerical circles was enlisted, and the bishop of Killaloe, Michael Fogarty, assured the Glynns of his support in their compensation claim.[158] Glynn contacted Timmy McInerney, a native of Cooraclare (a village 6 miles north of Kilrush), who appeared to be a well-placed accountant in the Board of Works. McInerney pushed Glynn's compensation claim within government circles. Ultimately though, this failed, and the family were forced to

calculated the daily loss of earnings for each of their two vessels: an average loss of £46 per day for the *Corona* for twenty-seven days amounted to £929; the *Turk* was calculated to have lost £315 (including the repair of a boiler). Other charges included the loss of maize at £150. In all they calculated the total loss to be £4,929; Glynn archive, box 12 (1920–30). **154** Letter from M. Glynn & Sons to the army finance officer, Dublin, 10 Mar. 1926; Glynn archive, box 12 (1920–30). **155** Ibid. **156** *Sgeal Chata Luimnighe*, produced by the Free State army in Limerick during the Irish Civil War, 5 Aug. 1922; Glynn archive, box 12 (1920–30). **157** Handwritten note on Óglaigh na hÉireann-headed paper from unidentified individual to M. Glynn, Kilrush, 28 July 1922; Glynn archive, box 12 (1920–30). **158** Letter from Charles E. Glynn to Michael Fogarty, bishop of Killaloe, 20 Jan. 1924. In 1918 Glynn had accused the same bishop of being leader of Sinn Féin in west Clare; Glynn archive, box 12 (1920–30).

accept a much lower amount. That award of £75 was made under Section 15 of the Damage to Property (Compensation) Act, 1923.[159]

Another example of Charles Glynn utilizing his extensive contacts within government circles was a case from 1925 concerning a dispute with the Board of Works in relation to his shed located on Saleen pier in Co. Kerry, just across the Shannon estuary from Kilrush. Again Glynn called on McInerney for help with the matter. Glynn noted that the secretary of the Board of Works had requested the shed's removal. An insight into the manner in which Glynn did business is included in his letter – '[A]ll we want is fair play,' he wrote.[160] Seemingly trivial matters that hampered business appear to have been associated with the Free State government and not with the previous administration as, apart from disputes related to the local landlord, such matters did not feature in the Glynn archive up to 1922. Within three weeks McInerney replied and informed Glynn that 'the Saleen shed case has been satisfactorily settled … lest there be any hitch I am giving you a letter to give to Mr Cassidy, who is private secretary to the minister for defence and will gladly help'.[161]

After 1932 the family supported de Valera's government and, as large providers of employment in a country characterized by excessive poverty, emigration and lack of employment opportunities, their place was assured. In 1935, Glynn reminded the president that '[W]e are giving employment to one hundred men and have been paying about £13,000 per year in wages.'[162] It cannot be ignored, however, that their rank and position was greatly diminished in comparison to the situation before independence, as civic titles and appointments under the previous administration were not continued by the new regime and the official clout they had once enjoyed was largely restructured and confined to the past.

TURF: 'FATHER WAS SICK OF THOSE ENGLISH' WHO WOULD NOT GIVE HIM THE COAL

In the 1930s, the Glynns continued to create employment, which the fledging state desperately required. They may have lost the civic power they had previously enjoyed, but their milling enterprise was a necessary element in the stabilization of

159 P. Kelly, department of finance, Dublin, to Philip J. O'Sullivan, solicitor, 88 O'Connell St., Limerick (acting on behalf of Glynn), 8 May 1926; Glynn archive, box 12 (1920–30). **160** Charles E. Glynn to T.M. McInerney, Board of Works, Dublin, 18 Nov. 1925; Glynn archive, box 12 (1920–30). **161** T.M. McInerney to Charles E. Glynn, 16 Dec. 1925; Glynn archive, box 12 (1920–30). **162** Copy of letter from M. Glynn & Sons to President de Valera, 27 Apr. 1935. Clerical staff were paid £1,000 per year; commercial travellers, £400; corn, flour and meal employees, £6,250; bakers, £286; retail shop workers, £104; delivery people for the bakery, £125; farm labourers, £416; smith at the mill, £125; shipwrights, carpenters and engineers, £598; casuals, £200; captains and crew of river steamers, £1,040; office staff at Shannon Steamship Company, £400; store man, £130; and coal-delivery men, £500. In addition, the Glynns' Limerick depot received £700 for wages for staff there; Glin was paid £373; Tarbert claimed £230; and Ennistymon was paid £100. The total wages paid by the Free State economy. The Glynns had always utilized the availability of turf in west Clare and in times of coal shortages, this locally sourced fuel had proven to be a viable alternative to power their mills. A consistent supply of coal had been an ongoing issue for Irish millers since the years of the First World War, and by the 1930s coal shortages were common. There were numerous instances of the Glynns attempting to obtain coal from suppliers both in Ireland and Britain, only to be met with the reply: '[R]egret at moment no coal to offer.'[163] Interference from local government was viewed as an unnecessary hindrance to their business and Charles Glynn was at odds with the Kilrush Urban District Council on the matter of a steady coal supply.[164] In 1919, Glynns were summonsed to a special meeting of the town council to produce 'invoices, freight dockets, showing the cost price of the different qualities of coal and the freights to Kilrush'.[165]

In 1932, de Valera and his party Fianna Fáil came to power in the Irish Free State. Almost immediately, the new government ceased the payment of land annuities to Britain.[166] This suspension of payments was a breach of the financial agreements arrived at by the British and Irish governments in 1923 and 1926.[167] The British response was to impose duties on a number of Irish commodities – most notably agricultural products. The Irish government responded by imposing restrictions on imports of British coal, cement, sugar, iron and steel and machinery.[168] Writing in 1932, Charles Glynn noted that

> in 1928 the Irish Flour Millers went before the Tariff Commission and applied for a protection of about five or six per cent duty to be put on imported flour, they refused, the result is that practically every flour mill except ourselves is now owned, managed or financed by Englishmen … it has been a great struggle.[169]

The Tariff Commission was the subject of continued frustration for the Irish milling industry from the mid-1920s to the 1930s. It occupied a vast amount of correspondence between Glynn and his fellow millers. Additional information about the Commission was gleaned from Glynn's close friendship with McInerney,

the company in 1924 were £12,977. Insurance policy, Royal Insurance Company Limited to M. Glynn & Sons, 14 Oct. 1924; Glynn archive, box 12 (1920–30). **163** An example of the coal suppliers who Glynn contacted in the UK are as follows: Wigan Coal & Iron Company; Thrutchley & Co. Limited, Liverpool; and Read, Sherratt & Co. Limited of Liverpool. The Irish coal suppliers included Wallace Brothers Limited, and Thomas Heiton & Company Limited, both of Dublin; series of letters; Glynn archive, box 12 (1920–30). **164** M. Glynn & Sons to Kilrush Urban District Council, series of letters 1917–19; Glynn archive, box 11 (1910–20). **165** M.J. Murphy, town clerk to Messrs M. Glynn & Sons, 10 Feb. 1919; Glynn archive, box 11 (1910–20). **166** Cormac Ó Grada, *A rocky road: the Irish economy since the 1920s* (Manchester, 1997), pp 5–6. **167** Kevin O'Rourke, 'Burn everything British but their coal: the Anglo-Irish Economic War of the 1930s', *Journal of Economic History*, 51:2 (June 1991), pp 357–66. **168** J. Peter Neary and Cormac Ó Gráda, 'Protection, economic war and structural change: the 1930s in Ireland', *Irish Historical Studies*, 27:107 (May 1991), p. 250. **169** Charles E. Glynn to James McInerney, Springfield, IL, 26 Feb. 1932; Glynn archive, box 13 (1930–40).

21. A flyer for turf.

the accountant in the Board of Works who supplied information about the private plans of the Tariff Commission to impose an extra tax on the flour-milling industry.[170]

The Anglo-Irish Economic War of the 1930s had a major impact on the Glynns, in respect of locating a viable fuel source with which to operate their mills, maintaining their steady output and retaining their employees. However, it was clear that Charles E. Glynn supported the economic policies of de Valera and his government. In 1935, he wrote to de Valera:

> Since you have come to office, we have given practical support to your policy, this season we purchased 1,270 tons of Irish grain … we have exhausted 1,567 tons of turf to the great advantage of poor farmers in the district … although being the largest coal importers in the county we imported no British coal between 1932 and 1935 and as one of the largest distributers of sugar, we sold no foreign sugar when Irish sugar was available.[171]

Glynn was clearly underlining the contribution of his firm to the protection of the Irish economy and of his support for de Valera's economic policy of protectionism. The use of turf as a fuel source had featured widely in west Clare for generations and much of it was exported down river to Limerick. However, in the harsh economic reality of 1930s Ireland, the turf industry became a vital commodity in the safeguarding of the economy of west Clare. In August 1934, Glynn wrote to the secretary of the Turf Development Board and stated that '[A]t present we are burning forty tons per week … for which we paid cash for each load at 7d per cwt.'[172] Josephine Glynn provided the following account of turf being burned in the mill:

> When the national coal strike was on in 1926, my father needed coal for the mill and he couldn't get the coal and he started buying turf and it was brought in and when the coal strike was over, he was sick of those English [who would not give him the coal] and the mill used turf ever since. It would have been a bit more expensive and awkward but it helped the local farmers too.[173]

When the Anglo-Irish Economic War concluded in 1938, the Glynns almost immediately reconstructed their meal (animal feed) mill. It was installed by Henry Simon Ltd of Manchester, who described the Glynn enterprise: 'The mill is now driven by a steam engine which was installed in 1915 … an interesting and unusual

170 McInerney, obituary, *Limerick Leader*, 3 June 1931. 171 Charles E. Glynn to President de Valera, 27 Apr. 1935; Glynn archive, box 13 (1930–40). 172 Charles E. Glynn to the Turf Development Board, 15 Aug. 1934; Glynn archive, box 13 (1930–40). The Turf Development Board was established in 1933 and was replaced by Bord na Móna in 1946. 173 Interview with Josephine Glynn of Kilrush, Co. Clare (24 Apr. 2014).

point is that owing to lack of alternative fuel the boilers are fired entirely on turf.'[174] Josephine Glynn recalls the mill being rebuilt: 'Our mill was rebuilt preceding the war in 1937 or 1938 and moved down [to its present location]. We also had a building at the back of one of those stores that went on fire.'[175] A draft press release compiled to coincide with the opening of their new premises in 1938 noted that '[T]he mills purchased 8,700 loads of turf – about 4,000 tons – and it is estimated that each load represented a day's work for a man.'[176] It added that '[T]he full investment of this new mill is in the region of £50,000 and it carries stocks of flour, mill stuffs and grain to the value of £20,000.'[177] The *Irish Press* published its annual review of the Irish milling industry in 1935 and concluded that government regulation aided the industry.[178]

DETERMINED PERSEVERANCE WINS OUT

A prosperity rooted in local engagement had characterized the Glynn enterprise since its establishment in 1811, and Charles Glynn was determined to promote Kilrush as the finest and most useful harbour in the west of Ireland. In 1931, along with Clare County Council, he mounted a campaign to have Kilrush port designated an official stop for ocean liners and sea planes and suggested that '[T]he cost of a good service to this natural port would be trifling and no big government grant would be necessary.'[179] This was not the Glynns' first attempt to develop Kilrush harbour into a more extensive base for shipping. Thirty years earlier, Charles' brother Henry Richard Glynn had invited Pirrie, the chairman and proprietor of the Belfast-based shipbuilders Harland & Wolff, to establish a branch in Kilrush. Glynn had been supported by Kilrush Town Council, which welcomed a deputation to the town in 1899.[180] However, on that occasion, despite the *Freeman's Journal* reporting that 'Hector S. Vandeleur, the lord of the soil … had agreed to assist the council in its endeavour, the project did not materialise.'[181] Interestingly, local tradition lays the blame firmly on Vandeleur, as they claimed that he did not relish the possibility of being 'shown up by Pirrie', who was far wealthier and who had risen to the peerage. A decade later, in 1910 Henry Richard Glynn revisited the possibility and casually raised the idea with Pirrie's agent, Johnston, of whether there was 'any chance of getting Lord Pirrie to establish a branch at Kilrush … [W]e have the finest river in the United Kingdom with a

174 Henry Simon Ltd, occasional letter to clients at home and abroad, issue 184 (1948); Glynn archive, box 14 (1940–50). **175** Interview with Josephine Glynn of Kilrush, Co. Clare (24 Apr. 2014). **176** Draft press release, full date unknown, *c.*1938, stamped M. Glynn & Sons; Glynn archive (undated). **177** Ibid. **178** *Irish Press*, annual review of the milling industry, 11 Dec. 1935. **179** Pamphlet, 'Kilrush as a port of call: Scattery Roads as a seaplane base', reproduced by Glynn from an article that first appeared in the *Irish Times*, 1 Jan. 1931. **180** Henry Richard Glynn to William Pirrie, series of letters and telegrams, Sept. to Nov. 1899; Glynn archive, box 9 (1890–1900). **181** *Freeman's Journal*, 9 Nov. 1899.

railway to the water's edge.'[182] Again, the project did not come to fruition, but there is no documentary evidence available to explain why.

The memory of the Glynns as good employers is still clear in early twenty-first-century Kilrush, and their decent treatment of their workers was recalled by a former employee, Pat Brazil, who remarked that the Glynns were 'well ahead of their time … a forward looking employer and great for Kilrush and west Clare'.[183] These sentiments were echoed in a remarkable series of letters written by a west Clare emigrant to the United States, James McInerney, in 1932. McInerney had left Kilrush with his family in 1863, when he was 16. He recalled with great fondness: '[M]y father used to carry the money from the grain stores in Ballylongford, Co. Kerry to Carrigaholt, Co. Clare as there were no banks in those days and Mr Glynn used to meet him with his white coat and his dog named Spot.'[184] He also recalled 'the day that we were leaving Kilrush for the United States … [Y]our mother [Jane Lane-Joynt] she surely was a lady … she made her way to me and kissed me goodbye and a long farewell.'[185]

The business success of the Glynn family continued into the twentieth century, briefly interrupted by their defeat at the hands of Vandeleur over the foreshore rights at Kilrush Creek. However, the Glynns treated this as a temporary setback and aside from having to prove his financial solvency to his peers, Glynn did not sustain any long-term damage to either his reputation or his business. Glynn's dispute with Vandeleur was based on what he considered sound economic sense, and this pragmatism was still in evidence once more cordial relations with Vandeleur resumed within two years. This pragmatism and flexibility was even more obvious in the Glynn family's attitude to politics, as evident in their taking the popular side in the Land War while at the same time keeping clear of direct entanglement. They maintained a similar balance in their attitude to recruitment during the First World War, when they acted as enthusiastic and effective recruiters, probably for principled reasons but also because they also stood to gain by the requirements of the war-time economy. The prioritization of economic expediency over political involvement comes across again in the omission from their papers, both private and business, of major political events of the day.

By the early twentieth century, the family may have been less certain of their position than they had been in the nineteenth century. The sudden death of Henry Glynn in 1916 marked the end of a generation and a world, with an even greater break in 1920–2 when the changing political system meant that the assured place that the family had fought for determinedly was no longer clear. Indeed, Henry's demise in 1916 was the only major catastrophe to befall the family in that most contentious of years. The events of the 1916 Rebellion warranted only a passing

182 Henry Richard Glynn to Isaac Johnston, 11 Feb. 1910; Glynn archive, box 11 (1910–20). 183 Pat Brazil, email correspondence, 19 May 2014. Pat was the second generation of his family employed by Glynns and multi-generational employment was a common practice of the Glynns. 184 James McInerney to Mitchel Glynn (whom he did not realize was dead), 10 Feb. 1932; Glynn archive, box 13 (1930–40). 185 Ibid.

mention in the family's papers, being viewed primarily as a hindrance to commercial enterprise. During April 1916, M. Glynn & Sons were far more concerned with the cost and availability of wheat than any political agitation that was occurring in Dublin. The Limerick-based miller James Goodbody wrote to Henry Glynn:

> I hope you will be able to let us know soon whether you agree to exchange your Inverlyon [a ship] purchase for [illegible]: another sailor of the Pacific, belonging to Barretts, has been sunk off the coast so these wheats will probably be scarce in Ireland 'til they can be replaced. Maize is firmly advancing. I can offer you 200 tons on spot for 13/2/6 for reply today.[186]

From April to December 1916, concerns about supply, distribution and the soaring cost of carrying on their business characterized the correspondence of the Glynn flour-milling firm. Almost frantic daily enquiries about the cost of wheat and maize were exchanged between millers from Kilrush, Cork, Kerry and Limerick. A note from the Cork-based J.W. Green & Co. noted that '[W]heat advanced steadily until yesterday, when the Commission reduced prices to their wheats by 1/- per quarter. This however, still leaves quotations on a level higher than Millers can yet afford to pay.'[187]

From 1921 onwards, a new uncertainty, mixed with the old confidence, permeates the family papers. The Civil War affected them economically, yet while they could not recoup their losses they maintained their habit of communicating with 'the top', though this now had to take the form of letters to de Valera about non-political matters. The recognition of the family's and firm's contributions to the state was no longer assured: it was a long way from the viceregal approval for their war effort evident in the photo still hanging in the family's house to the polite but reserved responses to their letters to various administrations after independence. On the other hand, whatever the sense of displacement they experienced, their priority was not (and never had been) politics, and after independence, as before, they continued to prioritise business and the promotion of local industry and employment.[188]

186 James Goodbody to Henry Richard Glynn, 17 Apr. 1916; Glynn archive, box 11 (1910–20). **187** J.W. Green to M. Glynn & Sons, 3 Nov. 1916; Glynn archive, box 11 (1910–20). **188** W. Redmond, House of Commons, to Henry Glynn, acknowledgment of donation of £10 to the Irish Volunteer Fund, 6 Aug. 1914; Glynn archive, box 11 (1910–20); Charles E. Glynn to Senator T.V. Honan, copy of letter for a donation of ten guineas to the trustees of Fianna Fáil, 7 June 1938; Glynn archive, box 13 (1930–40).

CHAPTER SIX

Legacy and the new state

GEOGRAPHY LAY AT THE HEART of the Glynn family's rise to prominence in the life of west Clare. Kilrush's position on the Shannon was developed to become a thriving centre for the export of locally sourced provisions including flour, oats, bacon, turf and a host of other commodities. Geographical location and individual enterprise went together, and the location Kilrush on the navigable estuary of the river Shannon was exploited to its full potential by a group of ambitious and prosperous individuals who established themselves as wealthy provincial merchants and traders by the early years of the nineteenth century. These individuals comprised not only locals such as Glynn but also traders from beyond the county, most notably from Limerick city. Individuals from minor landed families also seemed to have made their initial fortunes from trade on the river. There was always trade on the river; however, Kilrush initially lacked the basic facilities to enable it to develop into a thriving port. This was resolved by the construction of Cappa pier in 1764, the only substantial pier that serviced Kilrush and west Clare. It was extended in 1829 and again between 1835 and 1839, which was reflective of its importance to the local economy. The construction of smaller piers and quays along the estuary further illustrated the development of trade links between the rural and the urban. However, the rise of Kilrush cannot be separated from the interest shown in it by the landed Ascendancy. Kilrush town was the property of the Vandeleur family. They too originally had been merchants, and had purchased lands in the late seventeenth century and developed a vast west Clare estate comprising of approximately 20,000 acres. Though not a typical estate town, Kilrush owed much of its development to investment by the Vandeleurs, who began its expansion in the late eighteenth-century.

The encouragement of entrepreneurs by Vandeleur led to the formation of a business relationship with James Paterson, a former gun-boat lieutenant who had resigned his commission to take up trading in the oats business. Paterson realized the potential that was offered by steamship communication and he established profitable trade links between Kilrush and Limerick city. Together, Ascendancy patronage and the emergence of a tourist industry accounted for the early growth of Kilrush. In tandem with Paterson's development of the oats trade in Kilrush, Vandeleur began an ambitious development of the town that resulted in the construction of several municipal buildings including a court house and a town hall, the addition of new streets and roadways and in the 1850s, gas lighting. Vandeleur and Paterson, though not equals in class and status, did share common traits as both had served in the military (Vandeleur being a colonel in the Clare militia) and both were Protestants. Their business relationship seemed to fit, and within a few years, the union of landlord and merchant created a prosperous business which provided the impetus for other merchants to establish businesses in the town. In 1837, Lewis in particular commented on the expansion of Kilrush and noted the increase in houses in the town,[1] while a decade later, the description of Kilrush in *Slater's Directory* noted 'an annually improving town and an excellent harbour'.[2] The development of Kilrush was broadly similar to the rise of other Irish towns in the nineteenth century.[3] Most Irish towns cultivated a staple industry of some kind. Westport in Co. Mayo developed a linen trade, while Ennistymon in Co. Clare established a thriving firkin-making industry. By the 1840s, Kilrush possessed a booming oat-export business and its success led to Vandeleur developing Kilrush Creek, which complemented the facilities at Kilrush pier. Mutually beneficial investment from the landed gentry and merchant class, after some decades of delay, led to the establishment of a railway connection to the town – in the 1890s. However, even with the advent of the railway the importance of the river did not decline and it continued to be the main artery for the distribution and transport of passengers and produce.

It was in this thriving local economy that the Glynn family first established themselves as enterprising merchants. The earliest known member of the Glynn family to conduct business in Kilrush was William Glynn, a mason, active during the development of the town from *c.*1780–1830. His skills must have brought him some considerable profit and thus enabled him to purchase land in a prominent location in Kilrush, in Market Square. In 1811, William's uncle Bartholomew Glynn began trading as a corn merchant. From the outset, Bartholomew Glynn appeared to emulate Paterson's business model. Glynn displayed an entrepreneurial confidence – and this was to become the defining characteristic of the Glynn enterprise into the future. Within thirty years, he had accumulated enough profit from his corn mill to purchase large granaries, a comfortable house and property throughout the town. Coupled with the Glynns' industrious spirit and willingness to diversify was the family's unbroken intergenerational management of the family business, which saw it thrive on innovation and measured risk.

Marriage as an avenue to advancement was part of the successful merchant's strategy, acquiring doweried wives for the sons of the family, and giving daughters the opportunity to improve their status through strategic unions with the sons of well-connected merchants and professionals. The 1859 union of Michael Glynn and Jane Lane-Joynt was such a marriage. It secured Glynn's rise in status and introduced him to the Limerick merchant scene, which facilitated the continued expansion of his enterprise. Astute businessman that he was, Glynn benefitted

1 Lewis, *A topographical tour of Clare*. 2 *Slater's Directory*, 1846. 3 Simms and Andrews (eds), *Irish country towns*; Simms and Andrews (eds), *More Irish country towns*.

from his brother-in-law's prominent social position and was introduced to well-connected landed proprietors and businessmen. Further advancement was offered by access to an elite education, which was available to the second generation of the Glynn family. Such an education allowed for the introduction of the sons of provincial merchants into genteel society. But an elite education did not tempt the Glynn family into the cul-de-sac of gentrification: nearly all the Glynn sons returned to Kilrush to run the family business, while at the same time utilizing the school-made friendships as a basis for further business relationships – and further advantageous marriage alliances. The resulting extended familial networks were the mainstay of the Glynn business and as such allowed for its steady and continued expansion at a time when numerous mercantile businesses were built on the network of kinship support. Commercial and social respectability went hand in hand with mercantile success, and by the end of the nineteenth century, the Glynn family were being presented at court and invited to state balls, and enjoying leisure pursuits more usually associated with the landed class.

This book raises the issue of using concepts of class in tracing the fortunes of a provincial family business. A 'one-fits-all' class-centred term to describe the Glynn family remains elusive, and the complications were compounded by the family's use of different terms to describe themselves. It appears that by the time the second generation of the Glynn family inherited the business, they were solidly middle class. If one considers the barometers associated with that class – wealth, land, property, birth, status, occupation or a combination thereof – the Glynns fit comfortably.[4] However, as this book has shown, something of a 'glass ceiling' continued to exist in relation to status accompanying the acquisition of wealth, contemporary sources such as trade directories not placing merchants in the category of 'gentleman' despite their large fortunes. Indeed, Glynn was not listed within this category until after his elevation in 1874 to the local judiciary. Michael Glynn was a hard-working member of an upwardly mobile class, who had emerged quietly in the early to middle years of the nineteenth century.

Gentrification could, as the career of James Paterson shows, bring increased status but also put an end to enterprise. Paterson was assimilated into the landed gentry and began to display traits more closely associated with that class. He built a large house in the centre of Kilrush, surrounded by cultivated grounds, vast orchards and a private chapel. His daughter's marriage into a well-connected wealthy Limerick-based family of gentrified merchants confirmed Paterson's own transition from merchant to gentleman. Without an heir, the business Paterson had built up over forty years was subsumed into his son-in-law's estate and ceased to exist. This is where the Glynn family business differed. Continued involvement in their business and an insight into local conditions and concerns go a long way to explaining the Glynn success story. In 2015, John Glynn suggested that the family

4 Jim Smyth, 'The men of property: politics and the languages of class in the 1790s' in Fintan Lane (ed.), *Politics, society and the middle class in modern Ireland* (Dublin, 2010), p. 7.

business survived because it was entrepreneurial and diversified during difficult social and economic conditions.[5] He attributed the success of the family business to being able to identify and provide farmers and consumers with what they required in terms of transport solutions, flour, wool, coal and animal feed. This Kilrush-centeredness was one of the secrets to success: Paterson had always been an outsider and was courted by Vandeleur, also an outsider (in class if not in the geographical sense), whereas Glynn was from west Clare, married locally and made Kilrush the centre of his enterprise.

If the longevity of the Glynn family's business in Kilrush is what set them apart from Paterson, their attitude to work and business management was even more important in explaining their success. The Glynns remained firmly involved in the day-to-day operation of the family business. Henry Glynn's diaries, in particular, whether shaped by his mother Jane's influence, or by his Jesuit education, or by his own personality, highlight his strong work ethic and attention to detail. The diaries, which cover the period 1880 to 1910, record his daily activities from morning to night:

> Be up at 6am, dressed at 6.20, breakfast at 6.25, prayers at 6.30, books til 6.35, flour mill at 6.40, meal mill at 6.45, factory at 6.50, grinding machinery at 6.55, engine and lower store at 7.05, brewery shed at 7.10, 7.15, coal, 7.20 'write out what I ought to do today', 7.45, wheat account, 7.50, think about John C. Mahony's offer …[6]

Ambition, hard work and a 'hands-on' approach to the running of the family business were all characteristics of the Glynn enterprise in each generation. Henry Glynn's ability to network within milling circles through diligence combined with the ability to forge relationships with the leading businessmen of the time attests to his standing as an astute businessman and ascending member of the rising Irish middle class. However, it must be stressed again that none of this would have had the same local impact without the family's unquestionable attachment to their home town, the family remaining firmly in Kilrush both in terms of their residence and the location of their business headquarters.

Administrative networks, whether in the local or county judiciary, as member of poor law boards, or on town councils, enabled the Irish merchant class to continue its rise while at the same time allowing them to exercise considerable influence in the running of local affairs. This was evidenced by Michael Glynn's support for the establishment of town commissioners for Kilrush. The control achieved by merchants and entrepreneurs in local government from the late 1880s onwards provided further evidence of the consolidation of the power of that class at the expense of the landed gentry, who were not represented. While Vandeleur

5 Email correspondence between the author and John Glynn, 5 Dec. 2015. 6 Henry Glynn, diary entry, 30 Oct. 1889; Glynn archive, box 8 (1880–90).

supported the setting up of Kilrush Town Commissioners, he did not sit on the council, which was comprised of local merchants, shopkeepers, farmers and professionals, appearing instead to prefer occupying a position on the Kilrush Board of Guardians.[7] The traditional hegemony of the landed class was being undermined both formally and informally by the political and economic changes in the later nineteenth century and families such as the Vandeleurs must have been acutely aware that landlordism was in decline. The Vandeleur family were in decline from the 1850s onwards, both in terms of their material fortunes and their local reputation, whereas the Glynn family were on the rise, reaching the zenith of their success between the 1860s and the foundation of the new state.

Kilrush and the Glynn enterprise provide a window into tensions between the rising local merchant and the established landed proprietor. Their relationship was distant in the early years of Glynn's enterprise. However, as the century progressed, the Glynns appeared on local committees patronized by Vandeleur, especially those relating to agriculture, like the West Clare Agricultural Society. This inclusion of individuals like the Glynns as volunteers on local committees and ultimately as colleagues on the hitherto gentry-exclusive magistracy highlighted the emergence of a 'new world'. However, the fragile relationship between merchant and landed gentry was not to last and in the 1890s Glynn (and later Kilrush Urban Council) and Vandeleur became embroiled in their bitter and protracted court case. The actions of Vandeleur, who seemed to have a 'foot in the past', were deemed to be 'negligent … and deplorable' by the town council.[8]

Success in business required caution in relation to politics, and it is difficult to ascertain precisely where the Glynn family saw themselves in terms of a political identity. The elite education that granted them access to an 'old-boys' network', their extensive business contacts throughout the United Kingdom and their relationships with key members of the British administration suggest that up to 1920 the family possessed a dual political identity – definitely conscious of their Irishness (or, perhaps more especially of their Clare-ness) while at the same time proud of their citizenship within the United Kingdom. In addition, membership of exclusive gentlemen's clubs in London helped to blur the lines in respect of their political attitudes. Perhaps Josephine Glynn best summed it up when she described her aunt Rose Ryan (née Glynn) as 'slightly British' – an assessment echoed by Kilrush resident James O'Brien, who described the Glynn family as 'sort of English until the 1960s'.[9] Following their elevation to the local and county lieutenancy, the next logical step would have been recognition on the king's birthday honours list (knighthood), but the emergence of the new state prevented this from happening. Surprisingly, some of the major political events of the time are never directly mentioned in the family's archive. For example, they conducted business in Belfast, but the signing of the Ulster Covenant in 1912 was not

7 Sheedy, *The Clare elections*, pp 771–87. 8 Statement of Kilrush Town Council, 16 Mar. 1891; Glynn archive, box 9 (1890–1900). 9 James O'Brien, Kilrush, Co. Clare, interviewed (24 Oct. 2011).

mentioned. Similarly, the 1916 Rebellion was mentioned in passing as a 'hindrance to business', which is telling in and of itself. However, when their ability to carry out business was interrupted by the events of the Civil War, that conflict was described in minute detail in their correspondence.

The Glynn family in their political attitudes were reflective of the eminently flexible middle class, but there is evidence to suggest that the family never came fully to terms with their sidelining under the Free State government. In the late 1930s, Charles E. Glynn wrote to de Valera and suggested that he employ the services of an eye surgeon, Doctor Adolf Paglenstieker of Wiesbaden, Switzerland, with whose expertise the Glynn family were acquainted.[10] De Valera graciously refused and subsequently declined to accept an invitation to lunch in their home when he was in Kilrush in 1938.[11] This must have been a reminder of their much-diminished status as local leaders and captains of industry within the new state. Under the previous administration, the merchant class had risen to visible prominence, and families such as the Glynns often entertained senior government officials in their homes. Although the position and influence of the provincial merchant class in their respective towns remained for the most part unchanged, their status beyond their towns and counties appears to have plateaued, and they never quite regained the direct and high-level access to government they had once possessed.

While the Glynn men occupied the role of 'provider', the Glynn women, far from only occupying a private and comfortable existence, carved out a niche for themselves as industrious and resourceful individuals within the family home, in the business, and beyond – in the sphere of charity. Philanthropic endeavours such as the National Council of the Blind are synonymous with the Glynn women in west Clare. Just as the Glynn men courted the landed gentry in pursuit of their commercial interests the Glynn women courted ladies of the genteel class to support their charitable endeavours – and this practice seems to have continued into the twentieth century, unlike the male socio-commercial relationships, which seem to have foundered in the new state. In a sense, the women's continuing involvement in good causes suggests that charitable endeavours transcended class in the twentieth century. Class was no barrier to fundraising, and anyway, the activities of the Glynn women (especially Eileen Glynn) suggest that they were more practical than the men in their attitude to class distinctions, and while they were involved in charitable work managed to avoid a patronizing attitude towards those they helped. The Glynn women, even though they were deemed to occupy the role of homemaker, conducted their own 'micro-businesses' – family, accounting, management of staff, overseeing of house improvements, involvement in charitable endeavours. The Glynn women generally outlived the men: Michael predeceased Jane; Charles died many years before Eileen; Mitchel (40), George

10 Charles E. Glynn to Miss O'Connell, 21 Mar. 1936; Glynn archive, box 13 (1930–40). 11 K. O'Connell, personal secretary to de Valera, to Charles E. Glynn, 10 May 1938; Glynn archive, box 13 (1930–40).

(33) and Henry (51) – all unmarried – died young; and William died before his wife May. The Glynn women quietly assumed the role of 'regents of the family businesses' until their sons came of age, and they still continued to exercise a role thereafter.

Although access to an elite education introduced the Glynn sons and daughters to individuals from their own class, it also firmly placed them in a setting where they had the opportunity to form lifelong friendships that served as the basis for future business relationships, and also presented the prospect of securing marriage alliances that strategically enhanced the family business. However, it was the entrepreneurial spirit, seemingly inherent in the Glynn family, that lay behind its members' emergence as de facto leaders in Kilrush in the nineteenth century. This leadership role was not a strict hegemony and hinged on the family's practice of reinvesting in the town, introducing new industry – such as the woollen factory in the 1870s – that offered direct employment to large numbers. Moreover, it was the provision of indirect employment – the purchase of turf – that underpinned their reputation as the largest employers of labour in the county. Although the Glynn family operated business concerns in many locations throughout Clare, Kerry and Limerick, it was their decision to locate their main business in Kilrush – and not to move it to a larger town or city – that proved the determining factor in their intergenerational success. Coupled with the extended family's involvement in the social and cultural affairs of the town, the Glynn business was a Kilrush-centred operation synonymous with trade and enterprise in Kilrush and west Clare for over two hundred years. However, the Glynn's role in the economic development of Kilrush and west Clare would not have been possible were it not for the position of the town on the Shannon estuary. That factor alone facilitated the growth of the Glynn enterprise, connecting it with the myriad of piers, quays and harbours that peppered the estuary, thereby locating the provincial firmly in the broader economic and social context.

Glynn family tree

HUSBAND **BARTHOLOMEW GLYNN**

Born	*c.*1774–5
Died	23 Aug. 1855, Kilrush
Buried	Kilrush Churchyard
Husband's father	Glynn
Husband's mother	Crowe

WIFE **BIDDY McINERNEY**

CHILDREN

F **MARY GLYNN**
Born *c.*1812–13
Died 9 Mar. 1835
Buried Kilrush Churchyard
Spouse Andrew Kelly
Married 16 Feb. 1830, Kilrush

M **JOHN GLYNN**
Born *c.*1815–16
Died 1876
Spouse Ellen Scanlan
Married 18 Feb. 1849

M **MICHAEL GLYNN**
Born 1819
Died 17 May 1889, Kilrush
Buried Old Shanakyle, Kilrush
Spouse Jane Lane-Joynt
Married 28 Apr. 1859, St Michael's (C. of I.), Limerick

F **CATHERINE GLYNN**
Born *c.*1821–2
Died 13 Nov. 1888, Market Square, Kilrush
Buried Kilrush Churchyard
Spouse Andrew Madigan
Married 12 Feb. 1843, Kilrush

F **ANNE GLYNN**
Born *c.*1824–5
Died 20 Apr. 1893, Frances Street, Kilrush
Buried Kilrush Churchyard
Spouse John Culligan
Married 11 Feb. 1855, Kilrush

F **MARGARET GLYNN**
Chris'd 21 Feb. 1829, Kilrush
Died Before 13 Dec. 1834

F **JANE GLYNN**
Chris'd 12 Oct. 1830, Kilrush
Died 4 Sep. 1847, Kilrush
Buried Kilrush Churchyard

F **BRIDGET GLYNN**
Born *c.*1833–4
Died 22 Feb. 1864
Buried Kilrush Churchyard
Spouse James Morrissey
Married 2 Oct. 1861, Kilrush

F **MARGARET GLYNN**
Chris'd 13 Dec. 1834, Kilrush

F **MARY GLYNN**
Chris'd 11 Sept. 1836, Kilrush

HUSBAND	**MICHAEL GLYNN**	
	Born	1819
	Died	17 May 1889, Kilrush
	Buried	Old Shanakyle, Kilrush
	Married	28 Apr. 1859, St. Michael's (C. of I.), Limerick
	Husband's father	Bartholomew Glynn
	Husband's mother	Biddy McInerney
WIFE	**JANE LANE-JOYNT**	
	Born	*c.*13 Oct. 1833, Limerick
	Chris'd	13 Oct. 1833, St John's (C. of I.), Limerick
	Died	11 Dec. 1909, Kilrush
	Buried	13 Dec. 1909, Old Shanakyle, Kilrush
	Wife's father	William Persse Joynt
	Wife's mother	Arabella Lane

CHILDREN

M MICHAEL (MITCHEL) GLYNN
Born 27 Jan. 1860
Chris'd 28 Jan. 1860, Kilrush
Died 26 May 1900, Meath Hospital, Dublin
Buried Old Shanakyle, Kilrush

F JANE LANE GLYNN
Born 29 June 1861, Kilrush
Chris'd 3 July 1861, Kilrush
Died 4 July 1861

M WILLIAM JOYNT GLYNN
Born 21 Sept. 1863, Kilrush
Chris'd 22 Sept. 1863, Kilrush
Died 1 Sept. 1932, Pella House, Kilrush
Buried Old Shanakyle, Kilrush
Spouse Mary Teresa Hilliard
Married 24 Oct. 1895, Clare

M HENRY RICHARD PATRICK GLYNN
Born 15 Mar. 1865, Frances Street, Kilrush
Chris'd 17 Mar. 1865, Kilrush
Died 18 Nov. 1916, Kilrush House, Kilrush
Buried Old Shanakyle, Kilrush

F ARABELLA LANE JOYNT GLYNN
Born 21 Nov. 1866, Frances Street, Kilrush
Chris'd 20 Nov. 1866, Kilrush
Died 6 Apr. 1936
Buried Mount Jerome Cemetery, Dublin
Spouse Herbert Montgomery Wright
Married 24 Apr. 1889, St Anne's (C. of I.), Dublin

F (JANE) ALICE GLYNN
Born 11 Jan. 1869, Kilrush
Chris'd 12 Jan. 1869, Kilrush
Spouse William J. de Courcy
Married 15 Sept. 1891, Kilrush

F FLORENCE ELIZABETH GLYNN
Born 24 Aug. 1870, Clare
Chris'd 27 Aug. 1870, Kilrush
Died 26 Dec. 1940
Buried Old Shanakyle, Kilrush

M WALTER GLYNN
Born 1 May 1872
Chris'd 3 May 1872, Kilrush
Died 19 Oct. 1874

M GEORGE EDWARD GLYNN
Born 12 Aug. 1873, Clare
Chris'd 19 Aug. 1873, Kilrush
Died 26 Sept. 1906, Leadmore House, Kilrush
Buried Old Shanakyle, Kilrush

M ROBERT GLYNN
Born 30 May 1875, Merchant's Quay House, Kilrush
Chris'd 3 June 1875, Kilrush
Died 26 June 1875

M CHARLES EDMUND GLYNN
Born 5 June 1877, Kilrush
Chris'd 7 June 1877, Kilrush
Died 11 Sept. 1941, Kilrush House, Kilrush
Buried 13 Sept. 1941, Old Shanakyle, Kilrush
Spouse Eileen Mary Josephine Dorgan
Married 24 Apr. 1918, Dublin

F ROSE ANNA GLYNN
Born 1 Sept. 1878, Frances Street, Kilrush
Chris'd 3 Sept. 1878, Kilrush
Died *c.*1950
Spouse John Charles ('Jack') Ryan
Married 14 Feb. 1901, Clare

HUSBAND **WILLIAM JOYNT GLYNN**

Born	21 Sept. 1863, Kilrush
Chris'd	22 Sept. 1863, Kilrush
Died	1 Sept. 1932, Pella House, Kilrush
Buried	Old Shanakyle, Kilrush
Married	24 Oct. 1895, Clare
Husband's father	Michael Glynn
Husband's mother	Jane Lane-Joynt

WIFE **MARY TERESA HILLIARD**

Born	11 Feb. 1874, Clare
Chris'd	19 Feb. 1874, Kilrush
Died	14 Apr. 1963
Buried	Old Shanakyle, Kilrush

CHILDREN

M **WILLIAM HILLIARD GLYNN**

Born	6 June 1897, Clare
Chris'd	10 June 1897, Kilrush
Died	5 July 1972, Hertfordshire, England
Buried	11 July 1972
Spouse	Catherine Sara Cullen
Married	31 Jan. 1934

M **PATRICK GLYNN**

Born	17 Mar. 1899
Died	17 Mar. 1899
Buried	Old Shanakyle, Kilrush

M **(MICHAEL) DESMOND GLYNN**

Born	9 June 1902, Pella House, Kilrush
Died	10 Mar. 1975, Pella House, Kilrush
Spouse	Mary Kathleen McMahon
Married	2 Sept. 1930, Dublin

F **(ELIZABETH) ENID GLYNN**

Born	22 Aug. 1903, Clare
Died	2 June 1946, Frances Street, Kilrush
Buried	4 June 1946, New Shanakyle, Kilrush
Spouse	Dr Richard J. Counihan
Married	20 Jan 1926, Kilrush

F **(MARY) JEANETTE GLYNN**

Born	14 Apr. 1905, Pella House, Kilrush
Died	3 Sept. 1978
Buried	New Shanakyle, Kilrush
Spouse	Dr Richard J. Counihan
Married	12 Dec. 1947, Clare

M **GEORGE CHARLES GLYNN**

Born	7 June 1907, Pella House, Kilrush
Died	30 Nov. 1988, Carrigoran, Clare
Spouse	Claire M.J. Culligan
Married	19 Dec. 1933, Clare

M **HENRY GLYNN**

Born	8 Mar. 1909
Died	19 Mar. 1909
Buried	Old Shanakyle, Kilrush

M **NORMAN GERARD GLYNN**

Born	9 Apr. 1910, Clare
Died	10 Aug. 1991
Spouse	Eve Bett
Married	28 Nov. 1937

HUSBAND **CHARLES EDMUND GLYNN**

Born	5 June 1877, Kilrush
Chris'd	7 June 1877, Kilrush
Died	11 Sept. 1941, Kilrush House, Kilrush
Buried	13 Sept. 1941, Old Shanakyle, Kilrush
Married	24 Apr. 1918, Dublin
Husband's father	Michael Glynn
Husband's mother	Jane Lane-Joynt

WIFE **EILEEN MARY JOSEPHINE DORGAN**

Born	26 Apr. 1896, Cork
Died	7 Apr. 1978
Buried	Old Shanakyle, Kilrush
Wife's father	Jeremiah Dorgan
Wife's mother	Josephine Mary Nash

CHILDREN

M **HENRY GEORGE FRANCIS PATRICK GLYNN**

Born	8 Mar. 1919, Cork
Died	24 Nov. 2000, Kilrush Community Hospital
Buried	27 Nov. 2000, All Saints, Shanakyle, Kilrush
Spouse	Gwendoline Martha Roantree
Married	22 Nov. 1944, St Michael's, Dún Laoghaire, Dublin

M **CHARLES DORGAN GLYNN**

Born	18 Dec. 1920
Died	17 Mar. 2004
Spouse	Joan M. Murphy
Married	4 Apr. 1956, St Joseph's, Terenure, Dublin

F **EILEEN ROSE GLYNN**

Born	15 Apr. 1924, 18 St Patrick's Place, Cork
Spouse	Heinz Röhr
Married	8 Aug. 1951, St Senan's, Kilrush

F **JOSEPHINE MARY GLYNN**

Born	22 Dec. 1928

Bibliography

ARCHIVES AND MANUSCRIPTS

Ampleforth Abbey and College, school registers, 1920–1.
Clare County Archive, Vandeleur Estate Papers.
Clongowes Wood College, Kildare, school ledger and lists, 1814–1932.
Glynn Family Archive, boxes 1–13 (1811–1940).
Haddo Estate, Estate Office, Mains of Haddo, Tarves, Ellon, Aberdeenshire, correspondence 1910.
Library of the Reform Club of London, membership records and entry rules, 1900–5 (uncatalogued).
Loreto Convent, Wexford, extracts provided by Noreen Goggin.
National Archives of Ireland, Business Records Survey (1977), Glynn & Shannon Steamship Company Collection CL4/33/–CL4/38.
National Archives of the United Kingdom, Kew, Trevelyan Papers, Mann to Routh, 14 Dec. 1847, T64/369B (1) – extract provided by Angus Campbell.
National Library of Ireland, manuscript, leases and assignment of plot of ground adjoining market house in Kilrush, Co. Clare: principal parties Frances Russell of Limerick, William Glynn and Thomas Studdert; 1827–32, D. 26,736–8.
National Library of Ireland, manuscript, Will of William Glynn of Kilrush, Co. Clare, 1 Dec. 1831, D.26, 739.
Sisters of Mercy, Baggot Street, Dublin, central archive.
University College Cork, student register, 1914–15.

INTERVIEWS AND EMAIL CORRESPONDENCE[1]

Brazil, Pat, Kilrush, Co. Clare, email correspondence (19 May 2015).
Campbell, Angus, Kilrush, Co. Clare, email correspondence (11 Aug. 2014).
Glynn, Bryan, Kilrush, Co. Clare, email correspondence, 12 Dec. 2011, 10 Jan. 2012, 12 Mar. 2012, 28 Dec. 2012, 14 July 2013, 31 July 2013, 17 Oct. 2013, 12 May 2015.
Glynn, Charlie, Kilrush, Co. Clare, email correspondence, 8 Dec. 2010, 12 Mar. 2012, 29 Aug. 2013, 29 June 2015.
Glynn, Jane, Kilrush, Co. Clare, email correspondence, 10 Aug. 2014, 23 Aug. 2014, 29 Jan. 2015.
Glynn, John, Kilrush, Co. Clare, email correspondence, 12 Dec. 2011, 10 Jan. 2012, 12 Mar. 2012, 28 Dec. 2012, 14 July 2013, 31 July 2013, 17 Oct. 2013, 12 May 2015.
Glynn, Josephine, Kilrush, Co. Clare, interviewed 10 May 2013, 10 Aug. 2014, 19 Mar. 2014.
Glynn, Michael, Boston, MA, interviewed on 2 Dec. 2014.
Honan, Kay, Kilrush, Co. Clare, interviewed on 23 Nov. 2012.

1 Sound recordings archived in Mary Immaculate College, Library.

Lidane, Mick, Kilrush, Co. Clare, interviewed on 10 Apr. 2013.
O'Brien, James, Kilrush, Co. Clare, interviewed on 24 Oct. 2011.
O'Brien, Sean, Kilrush, Co. Clare, interviewed on 19 Feb. 2012.
Phoenix, Éamon, email correspondence, 2 May 2014, 15 Mar. 2015.
Scully, Thomas, Kilrush, Co. Clare, interviewed on 8 Apr. 2015.
Wirzburger-Glynn, Deirdre, email correspondence, 8 May 2012, 24 May 2015, 5 June 2015, 8 June 2015.

GOVERNMENT REPORTS

Clare election: Minutes of evidence taken before the select committee on the Clare election petition, with the proceedings of the committee (1860).
Landowners in Ireland: Return of owners of land of one acre and upwards in the several counties of cities and counties of towns in Ireland (Dublin, 1876).
Royal commission appointed to inquire into the manner in which railway communications can be most advantageously promoted in Ireland, [145] 449, vol. 35.
Second report of the commissioners appointed to consider and recommend a general system of railways for Ireland, H.C. 1838 [145] 449, vol. 35.

NEWSPAPERS AND PERIODICALS

Aberdeen People's Journal
Belfast Newsletter
Clare Advertiser
Clare Champion
Clare Freeman
Clare Journal and Ennis Advertiser
Clonmel Herald
Cork Examiner
Dublin Evening Mail
Dublin Evening Packet and Correspondent
Dublin Evening Post
Dublin Mercantile Advertiser and Weekly Price Current
Dublin Observer
Dublin Weekly Register
Freeman's Journal
Hartlepool Mail
Irish Independent
Irish Life
Irish Press
Irish Society
Irish Times
Irish World and American Industrial Liberator
Kilrush Herald and Kilkee Gazette
Kilrush Magazine and Monthly Journal Express
Limerick and Clare Examiner
Limerick Chronicle
Limerick Leader
Limerick Reporter and Tipperary Vindicator
Limerick Standard
London Gazette
Munster News
Nation
Nenagh Guardian
Penny Despatch and Irish Weekly Newspaper
Public Ledger and Daily Advertiser
Saturday Record
Saunders's Newsletter
Scotsman
Sheffield Daily Telegraph
Sheffield Independent
South Wales Daily News
Sunday Post
The Times
Tipperary Vindicator and Limerick Reporter
Tralee Chronicle and Killarney Echo
Tuam Herald
Waterford Mail
Waterford News
Yorkshire Post and Leeds Intelligencer

DIRECTORIES AND SURVEYS

Ashe's Limerick City Trade Directory (Limerick, 1892)
Bassett's Directory of Clare (Limerick, 1875)
Bassett's Directory of Clare (Limerick, 1880)
Burke's Irish family records (Britain, 1976).
Griffith's Valuation, 1855
Guy's Directory of Munster (Cork, 1893)
Lucas' Trade Directory (Dublin, 1788)
Mason's Parochial Survey (Dublin, 1814, 1816, 1819)
Parliamentary Gazetteer of Ireland (Glasgow, 1845)
Pigot's Directory of Clare (Dublin, 1824)
Slater's Directory of Ireland (Dublin, 1846, 1856, 1870, 1881, 1894)
Thom's Official Directory of the United Kingdom and Ireland (Dublin, 1909)
Thom's Official Directory of the United Kingdom and Ireland (Dublin, 1913)

OTHER PRINTED SOURCES

Balchin, A.T., 'The justice of the peace and county government in the East Riding of Yorkshire, 1782–1836' (PhD, University of Hull, 1990).
Bartlett, T., *Ireland: a history* (Cambridge, 2010).
Beeton, I., *Mrs Beeton's book of household management* (London, 1868).
Bielenberg, A., *Cork's industrial revolution, 1780–1880: development or decline?* (Cork, 1991).
—, 'Entrepreneurship, power and public opinion in Ireland: the career of William Martin Murphy', *Chronicon* (1998), pp 1–35.
— (ed.), *Irish flour milling: a history, 600–200* (Dublin, 2003).
—, 'The industrial elite in Ireland' in Fintan Lane (ed.), *Politics, society and the middle class in modern Ireland* (Dublin, 2010).
—, *Ireland and the industrial revolution: the impact of the industrial revolution on Irish industry, 1801–1922* (England, 2009).
Binns, J., *Miseries and beauties of Ireland* (London, 1837).
—, 'Miseries and beauties of Clare, 1835' in Brian Ó Dálaigh (ed.), *The strangers gaze: travels in County Clare, 1534–1950* (Ennis, 1998).
Black, R.D.C., 'William James Pirrie' in Conor Cruise O'Brien (ed.), *The shaping of modern Ireland* (London, 1960), pp 174–84.
Blundell, J., *Rules and constitutions of the Society of Religious Brothers* (Dublin, 1832).
Bonsall, P., *The Irish RMs: the resident magistrates in the British administration in Ireland* (Dublin, 1997).
Bourke, M., *The O'Rahilly* (Tralee, 1967).
Bradbury, J., *Celebrated citizens of Belfast* (Belfast, 2002).
Breen, R., 'Dowry payments and the Irish case', *Comparative Studies in Society and History*, 26:2 (1984), pp 280–96.
Broderick, D., *The first toll-roads: Ireland's turnpike roads, 1729–1858* (Cork, 2002).
Buck, J., 'The role of *Ne Temere* in the decline of an Irish custom regarding the religious affiliation of the children of mixed marriages', *Australian Journal of Irish Studies*, 11 (2011), pp 28–43.
Callan, P., 'Recruiting for the British army in Ireland during the First World War', *Irish Sword*, 17:66 (1987), pp 42–56.

Callery, F., *History of the National Council for the Blind of Ireland* (forthcoming).
Campbell, F., 'The social dynamics of nationalist politics in the West of Ireland, 1898–1918', *Past & Present*, 182 (Feb. 2004), pp 175–209.
Christian Brothers, *Souvenir of the golden jubilee of the Christian Brothers, Kilrush, 1874–1924* (Ennis, 1924), pp 41–3.
Clare County Library, 'List of freeholders: County of Clare, 1821', clarelibrary.ie/eolas/coclare/genealogy/freeholders_1821/list_of_freeholders_1821.htm, accessed 15 May 2011.
Clark, S., 'The social composition of the Land League', *Irish Historical Studies*, 17:68 (Sept. 1971), pp 447–69.
Clarke, F., 'O'Brien (Arnold-Forster), Florence Mary' in *Dictionary of Irish biography*, dib.cambridge.org/viewReadPage.do?articleId=a6468&searchClicked=clicked&searchBy=&browsesearch=yes, accessed 15 July 2014.
Clear, C., *Nuns in nineteenth-century Ireland* (Dublin, 1988).
—, *Women of the house: women's household work in Ireland, 1922–1961* (Dublin, 2000).
Coldrey, B., 'The social classes attending Christian Brothers Schools in the nineteenth century', *British Journal for Educational Studies*, 38:1 (1990), pp 63–79.
Colli, A., *The history of family business, 1850–2000* (Cambridge, 2003).
Committee for the Organisation of Recruiting in Ireland, *The astonishing record of Ireland's armies: why we should be proud of them* (Dublin, 1915).
Committee of the County Club, Limerick, *The County Club, Limerick: a short history of a hundred years of club life* (Limerick, 1913).
Coolahan, J., *Irish education: history and structure* (Dublin, 2012).
Corcoran, T., *The Clongowes Record, 1814–1932* (Dublin, 1932).
Costello, P., *Clongowes Wood: a history of Clongowes Wood College, 1814–1989* (Dublin, 1989).
Courtis, A., 'Becoming elite: exclusion, excellence and collective identity in Ireland's top fee-paying schools' in Jon Abbink and Tijo Salverda (eds), *The anthropology of elites: power, culture and the complexities of distinction* (United States, 2013), pp 163–85.
Crossman, V., *Local government in nineteenth-century Ireland* (Belfast, 1994).
Dann, J., 'The representation of British sports in late nineteenth and early twentieth century elite Irish school publications', *Media History*, 17:2 (2011), pp 133–46.
Davidoff, L. and C. Hall, *Family fortunes: men and women of the English middle class, 1780–1850* (London, 1997).
Department of Recruiting, 'Attitude of the Department of Recruiting towards the raising of recruits' (Dublin, 1916).
Dickson, D., 'City, seasons and society' in John Crowley, Robert Devoy, Denis Linehan & Patrick O'Flanagan (eds), *Atlas of Cork city* (Cork, 2005), pp 127–34.
—, Justyna Pyz and Christopher Shepard (eds), *Irish classrooms and British empire: imperial contexts in the origins of modern education* (Dublin, 2012).
Donnelly J.S. Jnr, *Captain Rock: the Irish agrarian rebellion of 1821–1824* (Cork, 2009).
Dooley, T.P., *Irishmen or English soldiers? The times and world of a southern Catholic Irish man (1876–1916) enlisting in the British army during the First World War* (Liverpool, 1995).
Dooley, T., *The decline of the big house in Ireland: a study of Irish landed families, 1860–1960* (Dublin, 2001).
Dudley, R., *The Irish Lottery, 1780–1801* (Dublin, 2005).
Dutton, H., *Statistical survey of the county of Clare* (Dublin, 1808).
Falconer, A., 'Ecumenism in Ireland', *Bürgerkieg und Religion*, 10:1 (1997), pp 74–88.
Fernihough, A., C. Ó Gráda and B.M. Walsh, 'Mixed marriages in Ireland a century ago', UCD Centre for Economic Research, Working Paper Series (2014), pp 1–47.

Fitt, F.M., 'Some plain statements about the South Clare Railway Company Limited made by F.M. Fitt solicitor …' (1884).

Fitzpatrick, D., *Politics and Irish life, 1913–1921: provincial experiences of war and revolution* (Dublin, 1977).

—, *The two Irelands, 1912–1939* (Oxford, 1998).

Foreman-Peck, J., E. Boccaletti and T. Nicholas (eds), 'Entrepreneurs and business performance in nineteenth century France', *European Review of Economic History*, 2 (Cambridge, 1998), pp 235–62.

Gleeson, P., *St Senan's Roman Catholic church Kilrush: 150 years, 1839–1989* (Kilrush, 1989).

Glynn, C.E., *List of Kilrush men who served with colours during the Great War, 1914–1918* (Waterford, 1919).

Gregory, A., 'Ireland and Britain' in John Horne (ed.), *A companion to World War One* (Oxford, 2012), pp 403–18.

Griffin, B., 'Irish cycling clubs, 1869–1901' in Jennifer Kelly and R.V. Comerford (eds), *Associational culture in Ireland and abroad* (Dublin, 2010), pp 105–27.

Griffith, L.M., 'Social mobility and the middling sort: Dublin merchants, 1760–1800' (PhD, Trinity College Dublin, 2009).

Grogan, D., *The Glynns: a west Clare business family* (Kilrush, 1989).

Hall, C., *White, male and middle class* (New York, 1992).

Hargreaves, J.A., 'Playing like gentlemen while behaving like ladies: contradictory features of the formative years of women's sport', *British Journal of Sports History*, 2:2 (1985), pp 40–52.

Hearn, M., *Below stairs: domestic service remembered in Dublin and beyond, 1880–1922* (Dublin, 1993).

Hogg, W., *The millers and mills of Ireland of about 1850* (Dublin, 2002).

—, *Millers and the mills of Ireland, 1700–1900* (Kildare, 2000).

Horne, J. (ed.), *Our war: Ireland and the Great War* (Dublin, 2008).

Huggins, M.J., 'More sinful pleasures? Leisure, respectability and the male middle classes in Victorian England', *Journal of Social History*, 33:3 (2000), pp 585–600.

Humphry, M., 'The possible royal descent of Dr Michael Rynne', humphrysfamilytree.com/OMara/rynne.html#royal.descent, accessed 23 Apr. 2015.

Jefferson, H., *Viscount Pirrie of Belfast* (Belfast, 1948).

Jeffery, K., *Ireland and the Great War* (Cambridge, 2000).

Jones, G., 'The introduction and establishment of roller milling in Ireland, 1875–1925' in Andy Bielenberg (ed.), *Irish flour milling: a history, 600–2000* (Dublin, 2003), pp 104–31.

Johnson, A., 'Middle-class culture and civic identity in mid-nineteenth century Belfast' (PhD, Queen's University Belfast, 2010).

Kehoe, S.J., 'Accessing empire: Irish surgeons and the Royal Navy, 1840–1880', *Social History of Medicine*, 26 (2013), pp 204–22.

Kelly, J. and R.V. Comerford (eds), *Associational culture in Ireland and abroad* (Dublin, 2010).

Knott, M., *Two months at Kilkee: a watering place in the County Clare, near the mouth of the Shannon, with an account of a voyage down that river from Limerick to Kilrush, and sketches of objects of interest in the neighbourhood, which will serve as a guide to the coast scenery* (Dublin, 1836).

Lansberg, I., *Succeeding generations: realizing the dream of families in business* (Boston, 1995).

Lee, J., *The modernisation of Irish society, 1848–1918* (Dublin, 1973).

Lee, J., 'The provision of capital for early Irish railways 1830–53', *Historical Studies*, 16:61 (Mar. 1968), pp 33–63.

Leigh, S., *Leigh's new pocket road-book of Ireland* (London, 1835).

Lewis, S., *A topographical dictionary of Ireland* (London, 1837).

Lloyd, J., *A short tour; or, an impartial and accurate description of the county of Clare with some particular and historical observations* (Ennis, 1780).

Long, P., 'Pirrie, William James' in *Dictionary of Irish biography*, dib.cambridge.org.libraryproxy.mic.ul.ie/viewReadPage.do?articleId=a7357&searchClicked=clicked&quickadvsearch=yes, accessed 11 Mar. 2011.

Luddy, M., *Prostitution and Irish society, 1800–1940* (Cambridge, 2007).

—, *Women and philanthropy in nineteenth-century Ireland* (Cambridge, 1995).

—, *Women in Ireland, 1800–1918: a documentary history* (Cork, 1995).

Manners, J., *Notes of an Irish tour* (Edinburgh, 1881).

McDermid, J., *The schooling of girls in Britain and Ireland, 1800–1900* (New York, 2012).

McDowell, R.B., 'The Irish courts of law, 1801–1914', *Irish Historical Studies*, 10:40 (1957), pp 363–71.

McGrath, J., 'An urban community: St Mary's Parish, Limerick and the social role of sporting and musical clubs, 1885–1905' in Jennifer Kelly and R.V. Comerford (eds), *Associational culture in Ireland and abroad* (Dublin, 2010), pp 127–41.

McMahon, R., 'The court of petty sessions and society in pre-Famine Galway' in Raymond Gilespie (ed.), *The remaking of modern Ireland, 1750–1950: Beckett Prize essays in Irish History* (Dublin, 2004), pp 101–37.

McNamara, S., 'Making the middle-class mind: middle-class culture in Limerick, 1830–1840' (PhD, Mary Immaculate College, University of Limerick, 2010).

Medjuck, S., 'The social consequences of economic cycles on nineteenth-century households and family life: the case of Moncton, New Brunswick, 1851–1871', *Social Indicators Research*, 18:3 (1986), pp 233–61.

Menton, W.A., *The Clongowes Wood centenary chronicle* (Clane, 1997).

Milne, G.J., *Trade and traders in mid-Victorian Liverpool: mercantile business and the making of a world port* (Liverpool, 2000).

Milne-Smith, A., 'Clubland: masculinity, status, and community in the Gentlemen's Clubs of London, *c.*1880–1914' (PhD, University of Toronto, 2006).

Moloney, T., 'The impact of World War One on Limerick' (MA, Mary Immaculate College, University of Limerick, 2003).

Moss, M. and J.R. Hume, *Shipbuilders to the world: 125 years of Harland & Wolff, Belfast, 1861–1986* (Belfast, 1986).

Murphy, I., 'The Kilrush-Kilkee railway and the reclamation of Poulnasherry Bay', *The Other Clare*, 6 (1982), pp 16–19.

—, *Before the Famine struck: life in west Clare, 1834–1845* (Dublin, 1996).

Murphy, J., *Abject loyalty: nationalism and monarchy in the reign of Queen Victoria* (Cork, 2001).

Neary, J.P. and Cormac Ó Gráda, 'Protection, economic war and structural change: the 1930s in Ireland', *Irish Historical Studies*, 27:107 (May 1991), p. 250.

Nenadic, S., 'The small family firm in Victorian Britain,' *Business History* (1993), pp 86–114.

Norman, E.R., *The Catholic church and Ireland in the age of rebellion, 1859–1873* (London, 1965).

O'Brien, C.C. (ed.), *The shaping of modern Ireland* (London, 1960).

O'Brien, K., *Without my cloak* (London, 1936).

O'Brien, P., 'Provincial recruiting in the First World War: the Glynn's of Kilrush Co. Clare', *Military Heritage Trust of Ireland* (July 2013).

Ó'Cleirigh, N., 'Lady Aberdeen and the Irish connection', *Dublin Historical Record*, 39:1 (Dec. 1985), pp 28–32.

Ó Confhaola, P., 'The naval forces of the Irish State, 1922–1977' (PhD, National University of Ireland, Maynooth, 2009).

O'Connor, A., '"Influences affecting girls", secondary education in Ireland, 1860–1910', *Archivium Hibernicum*, 41 (1986), pp 83–98.
O'Connor, J., *Hostage to fortune* (Dublin, 1983).
Ó Dálaigh, B. (ed.) *The strangers gaze: travels in County Clare, 1534–1911* (Ennis, 1998).
Ó Dálaigh, B., 'Milling on the Fergus', *The Other Clare*, 28 (2014), pp 41–9.
O'Dea, D., 'What it says in the papers or a hundred years ago on this day' in Noel Mulqueen (ed.), *Kilrush CBS centenary souvenir, 1874–1974* (Kilrush, 1974), pp 107–10.
O'Hagan, J., 'The Irish Catholic University question', *Irish Monthly*, 26:297 (Mar. 1898), pp 113–22.
Ó hÓgartaigh, M., 'A quiet revolution: women and second-level education in Ireland, 1878–1930', *New Hibernia Review*, 13 (2009), pp 36–51.
O'Neill, C., 'Rule Etonia: Educating the Irish catholic elite 1850–1900' (PhD, Trinity College Dublin, 2010).
—, (ed.), *Irish elites in the nineteenth century* (Dublin, 2012).
—, 'Education, imperial careers and the Irish Catholic elite in the nineteenth century' in David Dickson, Justyna Pyz and Christopher Shepard (eds), *Irish classrooms and British empire: imperial contexts in the origins of modern education* (Dublin, 2012), pp 98–110.
—, 'Power, wealth and Catholic identity in Ireland, 1850–1900' in O. Rafferty (ed.), *Irish Catholic identities* (Manchester, 2013).
O'Rourke, K., 'Burn everything British but their coal: the Anglo-Irish economic war of the 1930s', *Journal of Economic History*, 51:2 (June 1991), pp 357–66.
Pašeta, S., 'Trinity College Dublin, and the education of Irish Catholics, 1873–1908', *Studia Hibernica*, 30 (1998/9), pp 7–20.
—, *Before the revolution: nationalism, social change and Ireland's Catholic elite, 1879–1922* (Cork, 1999).
Pearson, R. and D. Richardson (eds), 'Business networking in the Industrial Revolution', *Economic History Review*, 54:4 (2001), pp 657–79.
Pembroke-Fetridge, W., *The American Travellers' Guides: handbooks for travellers in Europe and the east, being a guide through Great Britain and Ireland, France, Belgium, Holland, Germany, Austria, Italy, Egypt, Syria, Turkey, Greece, Switzerland, Tyrol, Denmark, Norway, Sweden, Russia, Spain and Portugal* (London, 1881).
Pennay, B., 'Meagher, John (1836–1920)' in *Australian dictionary of biography*, adb.anu.edu.au/biography/meagher-john-7545, accessed 15 May 2012.
Perkins, J., *Women and marriage in nineteenth-century England* (London, 1989).
Potter, M., 'The rise and fall of local democracy', *History Ireland*, 19 (Mar.–Apr. 2011), pp 40–3.
—, 'The Shannon estuary group' in Ciaran O'Neill (ed.), *Irish elites in the nineteenth century* (Dublin, 2013).
—, *Amazing lace: a history of the Limerick lace industry* (Limerick, 2014).
Power, J., Education in Clare: Clare County Library, clarelibrary.ie/eolas/coclare/history/teachers/kilrush.htm, accessed 19 Sept. 2012.
—, *Clare and the Great War* (Dublin, 2015).
Proceedings of the Catholic Association in Dublin, 13 May to 11 February 1823 (London, 1825).
Prochaska, F.K., 'Charity bazaars in nineteenth-century England', *Journal of British Studies*, 16:2 (1977), pp 62–84.
Puirséil, N., 'War, work and labour' in J. Horne (ed.), *Our war: Ireland and the Great War* (Dublin, 2008), pp 183–94.
Raymond, R.J., 'Pawnbrokers and pawnbroking in Dublin, 1830–1870', *Dublin Historical Record*, 32:1 (1978), pp 15–26.

Robins, J., *Champagne and silver buckles: the viceregal court at Dublin Castle, 1700–1922* (Dublin, 2001).

Rose, M.B., 'Beyond Buddenbrooks: the family firm and the management of succession in nineteenth-century Britain' in Jonathan Brown (ed.), *Entrepreneurship, networks, and modern business* (Manchester, 1993), pp 127–43.

Rothery, M., 'The wealth of the English landed gentry, 1870–1935' in *Agricultural History Review*, 55:2 (2007), pp 251–68.

Royal Bank of Scotland, 'National Bank Ltd', heritagearchives.rbs.com/companies/list/the-national-bank-ltd.html, accessed 12 Jan. 2015.

Royal Western Yacht Club of Ireland, 'Confirmed membership and yachts, 1827–37', westernyachtclub.com/cms/index.php?page=club-history, accessed 1 Mar. 2015.

Scanlan, S., 'Passenger services on the Lower Shannon', Clare County Library, clarelibrary.ie/eolas/coclare/history/kilrush_notes_1760_1960/passenger_services.htm, accessed 7 Mar. 2013.

Sheedy, K., *The horse in County Clare* (Dublin, 2001).

—, *The Clare elections* (Dublin, 1993).

Silverman, M., 'Custom, courts, and class formation: constructing the hegemonic process through the petty sessions of a south-eastern Irish parish, 1828–1884', *American Ethnologist*, 27:2 (May 2000), pp 400–30.

—, and P.H. Gulliver, '"Common sense" and "governmentality": local government in south-eastern Ireland, 1850–1922', *Journal of Royal Anthropological Institute*, 12 (Mar. 2006), pp 109–27.

Simms, A. and J.H. Andrews (eds), *Irish country towns* (Cork, 1994).

—, *More Irish country towns* (Dublin, 1995).

Smyth, Jim, 'The men of property: politics and the languages of class in the 1790s' in Fintan Lane (ed.), *Politics, society and the middle class in modern Ireland* (Dublin, 2010), pp 7–21.

Solar, P.M., 'Shipping and economic development in nineteenth-century Ireland', *Economic History Review*, 59:4 (2006), pp 717–42.

Somerville-Woodward, R., 'The Ossianic Society, 1853–1863', Department of Modern Irish History, University College Dublin, ucd.ie/pages/99/articles/somewood.html, accessed 16 June 2015.

Song, B.K., 'Landed interest, local government, and the labour market in England, 1750–1850', *Economic History Review*, 51:3 (Aug. 1998), pp 465–88.

Staunton, M., 'Kilrush and the Munster Fusiliers: the experience of an Irish town in the First World War', *The Old Limerick Journal*, 30 (1993), pp 35–8.

—, 'Kilrush, County Clare and the Royal Munster Fusiliers', *Irish Sword*, 16:65 (1986), pp 268–72.

Taylor, G. and A. Skinner, *Maps of the roads of Clare* (2nd ed., Dublin, 1783).

Transactions of the Ossianic Society for the year 1856, 9 (Dublin, 1856).

Trinity College Dublin, 'Admission records, 1847–1876', digitalcollections.tcd.ie/home/index.php?DRIS_ID=MUN-V-23-6_001&utm_expid=68026435-1.utkesif9QkKGoMll18G2NQ.0, accessed 10 June 2015.

Wakefield, E., *An account of Ireland, statistical and political: in two volumes, volume one* (London, 1812).

Walsh, B., *Roman Catholic nuns in England and Wales, 1800–1937: a social history* (Dublin 2002).

Webb, A., *A compendium of Irish biography* (Dublin, 1878).

Weir, H., *Houses of Clare* (Clare, 1984).

Wilcox, M., 'The development of retailing in Ireland, 1900–2010' in Edmund O'Callaghan and Don O'Riordan (eds), *Retailing in Ireland* (Dublin, 2012).

Wilson, R.G., *Gentlemen merchants: the merchant community in Leeds, 1700–1830* (Manchester, 1971).
Williams, C.W., *Observations on the inland navigation of Ireland and the want of employment for its population with a description of the river Shannon* (Liverpool, 1833).
Zangerl, C.H.E., 'The social composition of the county magistracy in England and Wales, 1831–1887', *Journal of British Studies*, 11:1 (Nov. 1971), pp 113–25.

Index